Praise for *Crack the Funding Code*™

"Judy Robinett nails it with *Crack the Funding Code!* Her decades of experience and knowledge show brilliantly in this guide to startup funding. But more than just funding—she provides sound advice beyond funding. Her 'Nine Numbers' are the map to attracting, acquiring, engaging, and ultimately satisfying investors. Read this, have everyone on your team read it, follow the advice, and you will succeed. Wisdom like this is priceless."

—**COLIN MCCLIVE,**
director, U.S. insurance industry, Microsoft

"Judy is one of the most connected people that I know. She has taken the art of making valuable connections to the next level—whether that be in support of the entrepreneurs who she works with or the nonprofits that she endorses. Part of her magic is that she treats every relationship like it's the most important one—always making sure that the introductions that she makes have the potential to be mutually beneficial."

—**CINDY PADNOS,**
founder and managing partner, Illuminate Ventures

"Judy's experience and expertise make her one of the most important advisors to entrepreneurs, investors, and executives in the global knowledge economy. For anyone interested in building, growing, or leading a great company, this book is an incredibly valuable resource and 'no-nonsense' guide for protecting a startup from self-sabotage."

—**DAVID DESHARNAIS,**
senior VP and general manager, American Express

"Judy seems to know everyone, but more importantly is genuinely helpful to others and has created a massive network of people who can fund great opportunities."

—**WILL BUNKER,**
founding partner, GrowthX

"You had a great idea, assembled a remarkable team, and have worked like dogs to make your dreams happen. You have everything you need, except the funding to turn your hard work into the results you crave. That is where Judy Robinett comes in. She has a long track record of bringing big funding dollars to deserving startups. You created the spark—let Judy help you set it ablaze."

—**LEO HOPF,**
author of *Rethink, Reinvent, Reposition: 12 Strategies to Make Over Your Business*

"Judy's skill and energy are amazing! She effectively connects with companies that need funding, introduces them to the professionals who can help them groom their business for funding, and then introduces them to the investors most likely to provide the funding."

—REGINALD HUGHES,
CFO and business plan writer

"Judy Robinett is an individual who truly embodies the concept of adding value, always, wherever she goes. Any book, show, or presentation by Judy—I'm there, and I've never been disappointed. Even the launch party for Judy's first book was not about 'Judy,' but brought in thought leaders from far and wide for a star-based panel, which she joined. When it comes to authentic thought leadership, Judy is one of the best."

—CHERYL SNAPP CONNER,
founder and CEO, SnappConner PR

"I have known Judy for several years and found her to be very effective at helping businesses understand the startup fundraising landscape, how to raise capital, and how to position their businesses to scale."

—PAUL GROSSINGER,
cofounder, Gaingels Syndicate

"Investors choose to fund founders they trust, like, and know. Nobody is better than Judy Robinett at giving people a step-by-step, proven process to get people to trust, like, and know you. No matter what your industry is, Judy's principles of cracking the funding code will get you funded fast."

—JOHN LIVESAY,
author and podcast host, *The Successful Pitch*

"Judy Robinett is a force to be reckoned with. She has amazing energy and is a people connector everywhere she goes. In the world of rapidly evolving business models and accelerated innovation, the most likely disruptor to an existing business is increasingly not the traditional competitor, but one that blindsides its competition. Judy recognizes the importance of funding ideas and companies in this ever-changing environment and provides actionable steps for individuals to secure funding. The future is waiting for new ideas, new companies, and new competitors. Judy has helped so many already write their destiny, and this book will help even more people. Well worth the read!"

—RACHEL MUSHAHWAR,
tech industry executive

"As an entrepreneur, Judy Robinett does the hard work of turning ideas into businesses. First she tells us to describe why our idea, our dream, is worthy. Then she guides us to the funding that will make our dream come true. In *Crack the Funding Code*, Judy shares funding tips and lessons. She inspires us to persevere and turn potential losses into victories."

—L.J. RITTENHOUSE,
candor expert and author of *Investing Between the Lines*

"Robinett knows better than most the true power that lies in connecting. Throughout her extensive and impressive career, she's networked her way to become the 'woman with the platinum Rolodex' and, with her new book, *Crack the Funding Code*, she gives excited entrepreneurs and innovators her years of experience wrapped in a road map to raising capital for their ideas and new business ventures. And with the wealth of private funds available globally to these individuals, her direction and insights could not be more important for today's business success."

—JOHN RUHLIN,
author of *Giftology*, founder and CEO of the Ruhlin Group

CRACK
THE
FUNDING
CODE™

CRACK THE FUNDING CODE™

How **Investors Think** and What They **Need** to **Hear** to Fund Your Startup

JUDY ROBINETT

HarperCollins
Leadership

AN IMPRINT OF HarperCollins

Published by HarperCollins Leadership, an imprint of HarperCollins.

Book design by Elyse Strongin, Neuwirth & Associates.

ISBN 978-0-8144-3984-5 (eBook)

Library of Congress Control Number: 2018960960

ISBN 978-0-8144-3983-8

Printed in the United States of America
18 19 20 21 22 LSC 10 9 8 7 6 5 4 3 2 1

To all the entrepreneurs who wish to make the world better:

Bless you! Above all, persist in good times and bad.

Everything you need is out there. Go after it.

CONTENTS

FOREWORD

By Kevin Harrington
"As Seen on TV" Pioneer, Investor, Original "Shark"
on *Shark Tank*

I put my career into three buckets. First, I've been an "As Seen on TV" pioneer and product guy for thirty-five years. I invest in products, create "As Seen on TV" infomercials and digital marketing funnels, and build brands through the power of television. I still do about twenty-five trade shows a year—I'm speaking, I'm taking booths, I'm talking with people who are there to pitch their ideas. It's an outlet for me to connect with thousands of entrepreneurs in the world of products.

Second, I'm a business influencer. I speak at about one hundred entrepreneurial events a year globally, where thousands of people show up looking for advice and help to take their ideas, products, and businesses to the market. I've also got a million-plus businesspeople that follow my blog and social media—that's a pretty powerful network. And some of those are funding people. We have an angel investors' network following us, and we also have venture capitalists, investment bankers, and product owners. So to be able to utilize my influencer network is exciting and powerful for me, because I never know what the next kind of new thing is going to be, but there's generally an opportunity to get in on the ground floor.

My third bucket is as an investor. I have about twenty-five different companies and investments; I sit on boards; I'm an advisor and a mentor. At any given time, I'm following all of the deals I'm involved with, including six or seven public companies, a few startups, and other more mature companies that I have equity in.

As part of all three buckets, entrepreneurs are pitching me constantly. I figure that over the past thirty-five years I've taken over fifty thousand pitches, which is a couple thousand a year. I once took ninety-six five-minute pitches in one day! That experience is one of the reasons I ended up on *Shark Tank*. In 2008 I met with Mark Burnett, and he explained how the show would work: Entrepreneurs would come out, and five "Sharks" (investors) would be sitting there. Each person would get three minutes to pitch, and the Sharks would have to decide right away whether they were going to invest.

I told Mark, "Guess what? I've been doing that for twenty-five years at every trade show I go to. People line up, maybe one hundred of them at a time, and I give them five minutes each to pitch me their idea." I did a screen test, and a week later they called and said, "You are the first Shark we are green lighting." That's why I'm called the "original" Shark. I was on the show from 2009 to 2011, and those episodes are still running in syndication all over the world.

When entrepreneurs pitch me, at a conference or trade show or even on *Shark Tank*, a lot of them come in with the attitude of, "I've got this great thing, and you're going to want to invest in it and give me $1 million for a 6 percent return on your investment." But they never make the effort to understand the mentality of me as the investor, and what I want to see in a deal. When I invest my money, if I put up $1 million, I don't want $1.1 million back—I want to get back $10 million, because I'm taking all the risk. Of course, I'm being facetious: Any investor would ultimately be happy to put up $1 million and get $2 million back. But the model of venture is risk/reward, and if entrepreneurs are asking people to invest in a startup, those investors are counting on getting a lot more money back at the end of the deal.

Out of all those fifty thousand pitches I've heard over the past thirty-plus years, I've funded about eight hundred deals, around 1 to 2 percent of the pitches I've taken, and that's a typical percentage for most angel or venture capital (VC) investors. But there are different funding levels, of course. I didn't write each of those eight hundred entrepreneurs checks for $1 million; we might have only funded a $10,000 test to determine whether the idea is worthwhile. You see, in my business you need to know how to fail fast and fail cheap. You can lose $100,000 five times in a row if your next deal does $20 million. But if your business model fails four out of five times, then you can't be too happy with just getting double your money back.

Here's what I mean: out of the 800 deals that we funded, we only made money on 150 of them. But those 150 deals generated *$5 billion* in sales.

Now, the ten to one business model is my business model; but every venture capitalist, angel investor, or friend or family member you ask for money will have their own investment desires and wishes—their "sweet spots," as I call them. And you need to adjust your pitch to an investor based on what their sweet spots are. I once raised $20 million for a company, and we met with ninety-seven individual investors one-on-one, in their office, my office, a coffee shop, their home, wherever. And each and every one of those investors had a different sweet spot of what they might be looking for. One person wanted healthy profit margins, another wanted intellectual property protection, and so on.

You might say, "Who wouldn't want healthy profit margins?" Well, when Mark Zuckerberg was raising money for Facebook, he couldn't show profits or even sales, but what he did have was a pathway to customer acquisition. At the time a million people were subscribed to Facebook, and venture capitalist Peter Thiel told Mark, "I'll give you $5 million if you can show me how you're going to get ten million subscribers." Mark did, and Peter got 10 percent of Facebook for his $5 million investment. Smart man—in 2012 he cashed out his stake in Facebook for $1 billion.

For me, when it comes to the products I invest in, my "sweet spot" is straightforward: Show me a problem, and then convince me that nobody else is solving it the way you are. I also look for some kind of "magical transformation" that will be visual, powerful, and change lives along the way. Tony Little was a former bodybuilder and fitness expert when he came to me with a product called the Ab Isolator. For a lot of people, the first place where they want to reduce fat is their abs. Tony told me, "Most people don't like to do sit-ups, but the Ab Isolator assists them in doing sit-ups. This product makes your abs thin very quickly, in two to three months." He also showed me dozens of product users who had trimmed their abs, lost weight, and looked great. A product that solves a problem in a unique fashion and creates magical transformation—I was in. We did $350 million in sales with the Ab Isolator. And since that first product, Tony and I have done almost $1 billion in sales.

I believe this is the greatest time ever for anyone to become an entrepreneur, because the world has changed. People used to work thirty years for a company and then get a gold watch when they retired. Now most CEOs last around three and a half years in their jobs—they have to perform or they're out. We're now in the gig economy, where people work for themselves or on contract, so they don't have to work nine to five. What that means is no one has to quit a job to start a company. Entrepreneurs can keep their full-time job until their "side business" revenues replace their full-time income. And with digital marketing's ability to target specific customer niches, people can be shipping products all around the world with something they do part-time.

Here's an example of how you can create a million-dollar business using digital marketing. A year or so ago I was speaking at an event in Boca Raton, Florida, and two young guys came up to me and said, "We own the patent for a nightlight for your toilet bowl." And I thought, "Who cares? You walk into the bathroom, you're ten feet from the toilet, and it lights up. What do I need that for?" But there *are* people who are excited about a toilet bowl nightlight. Mothers need it for their kids who wet the bed because they're afraid to get up in the dark, but now they want to get up and see what color the toilet bowl is. Seniors need it, so they don't have to turn on the lights when they get up in the middle of the night to pee. So we created twelve different digital funnels to reach specific niches, and we've sold millions of the GlowBowl™ Toilet Night Light without ever putting the product on TV.

Here's my point: when I asked these guys how long they'd had the idea for this product, they said, "Three or four years." I said, "Why did you wait so long?" They answered, "Oh, we didn't have any money, we needed the patent, we were both working . . ." and on and on. They lost three or four years of potential profit to excuses—and I lost three or four years of potential profits as their investor. Whatever your idea, whatever your business, *now is the time to act on your idea.* Today people with money are looking for places to invest, and there's more money than there are good deals. But you've got to know where the money is and how to present your ideas successfully. And a lot of entrepreneurs don't know how to package their presentations in a way that will appeal to the investors they need.

Thirty years ago my infomercial product company was at $50 million in sales with a $5 million profit, but I needed money for inventory to grow the business. With those numbers I thought getting a $2 million line of credit would be no problem. But I went to bank after bank and was turned down every time. I couldn't get money anywhere. I thought, *What am I doing wrong?*

Then I ran into a retired bank president at a chamber of commerce meeting in Philadelphia. He looked at my presentation and said, "You know how to sell products on TV, but you don't know how to raise money. I'm the guy that you'd be pitching, and I know how to pitch to the guys like me." So he showed me how to talk to the investors, joined my team, and raised $3 million in ninety days. It was the same company, but the difference was suiting the packaging and the pitch to investors' needs.

That is why I think *Crack the Funding Code* is an important book for entrepreneurs looking to be funded. Judy Robinett is the real deal, a no-nonsense kind of person who is offering you access to "insider" secrets to raising capital. I can honestly say I don't know many people as well connected as Judy is in the marketplace. She opens up her "platinum Rolodex™" and makes amazing things happen. *Crack the Funding Code* is filled with wisdom drawn from both sides of the table. It will show you how to create the right pitch, get to the right people, and package your offer the right way, so you can land your own million-dollar deal—no matter which "Sharks" you are pitching.

ACKNOWLEDGMENTS

This book would not have been possible without Dee Burgess, and the never-ending help and support she gave me during the writing, editing, and publishing process.

Many thanks to the brothers I never had, Ivan Dimov and Sergey Sholom, who are the best business partners any person could have wished for, and who have supported my efforts in so many ways.

Thank you to Jared Burgess, who pitched in and helped with references; Mike Young, director, and Tanner McClune, Northern USU SBDC region, who edited the artwork. Between them, they did pretty much anything that was needed to get this book into the hands of the publisher.

Thank you to Victoria St. George of Just Write, who, despite pushing it to the wire, knocked it out of the park again.

Thanks to my agent, Wendy Keller, who encouraged me to take up the challenge again, and thanks to Tim Burgard, my editor at Harper Collins, for all of his patience and support in this endeavor.

For everyone who helped, supported and contributed to this book: Thank you all for all you did to make this book happen. Thank you Kevin Harrington, Annette Lavoie, John Livesay, Richard Swart, Colin McClive, Alex Migitko, Cheryl Snapp Conner, Cindy Padnos, Cole Smith, Dave Berkus, David Desharnais, David Meister, Dominic Giancona, Jeff Harvey, Kay Koplovitz, Leo Hopf, Marcia Nelson, Marilyn Magett, Matthew Sullivan, Paul Grossinger, Paul Martens, Ramphis Castro, Reginald Hughes, Sean Sheppard, Will Bunker, Loretta McCarthy, and Andrew Goldner. Your wisdom and business acumen will help a lot of worthy entrepreneurs to get the funding they need to build great businesses.

CRACK
THE
FUNDING
CODE™

INTRODUCTION

For more than thirty years I've helped entrepreneurs find needed capital by connecting them with venture capitalists, angel investors, family offices, and other funding sources, and then guiding them through the dealmaking and due diligence process. I'm good at this because I've been on both sides of the table. As a CEO of public and private companies, I know what it's like to pitch to investors. As managing director of Golden Seeds Angel Network and a member of the advisory boards of Illuminate Ventures (an early-stage VC firm), Pereg Ventures VC, Springboard Enterprises (a network supporting female tech entrepreneurs), and Women Innovate Mobile (an accelerator also dedicated to female business owners in tech), I've probably seen as many pitches from entrepreneurs as the industry titans on *Shark Tank*. The startup deals I've brokered range from $50,000 to $15 million, and many of them have made sizeable profits for the investors and entrepreneurs alike.

In 2015 I partnered with Dee Burgess (first controller at Skullcandy and a guru of operations) and John Livesay ("The Pitch Whisperer™" and founder of *The Successful Pitch* podcast) to create a course that would help entrepreneurs develop their fundraising expertise, so they could find the money to grow their companies. We love helping founders develop a great pitch while getting them in front of the right investors, and we were proud to watch as these men and women received multiple offers of investment capital.

Cole Smith was one such entrepreneur. He came to us with no pitch deck and no connections, but a great business idea: a mobile platform that would instantly inform first responders and parents when there was an emergency at school, as well as providing a color-coded floor plan of where the problem was occurring. John worked with Cole on his pitch, focusing on how this app could help save lives in schools and give parents and teachers the peace of mind of having a security and communications plan in place.

As you'll see in Chapter 6, the business founder and team are key elements of a successful pitch, so John encouraged Cole to explain how his overseas military security background made him the ideal person to lead the business. We worked with Cole to make sure his financial projections and executive summary (Chapter 7) were based on logic and reasonable numbers. Then Cole edited his slide deck and practiced his pitch (Chapter 8) until he was completely confident with his presentation.

At the same time, I was opening up my "platinum Rolodex" to find the right investors for Cole's business. When he was ready, I introduced him to an angel investor who then invited him to pitch to the Salt Lake City (SLC) Angels investing group. He was given only ten minutes of pitch time and then ten minutes of Q&A. (Entrepreneurs need to be ready to adjust their pitch length to whatever amount of time the potential investor allots them.) John and I prepared Cole to explain his concept in the allotted time, and then worked with him to be ready to answer any questions investors would be likely to ask.

The goal of almost every pitch isn't a commitment to invest. It's more like a first date, where the parties are deciding if there is enough interest to warrant a second date. Well, Cole got the second date! He was asked to come back and pitch to a larger group of angel investors, again for ten minutes but with a thirty-minute Q&A session. The investors told Cole that his deck and presentation were in the top 5 percent of any they had ever seen.

But that was just Cole's first win. Based on his success in Salt Lake City, I was able to get him in to present to the New York Angels (a large and prominent angel investor group). They were impressed that he already had an offer of funding, and they began to court him with their connections to the FBI that could help him scale up fast.

One of the questions the New York Angel investors asked Cole was who would be funding his next round. This is where most founders fail. However, I had introduced Cole to Claudia Iannazo, who sits on the board of Pereg Ventures, an early-stage venture capital firm. Claudia said that her husband had connections to JetBlue Airways, and she would be interested in taking Cole's platform to airports once he needed series A venture capital funding in a year or so. Both angel groups were happy that Cole already had a relationship with a venture capitalist, even though he would not need venture capital until he hit certain milestones that he planned to reach with their investment.

Cole was offered $1 million from a family office. He turned it down. Then the New York Angels offered $700,000. He turned them down too. He finally accepted two rounds of angel funding ($100,000 and $175,000 respectively). John and I worked with him during his due diligence process. We also connected him to the Los Angeles School District and UCLA hospital for potential new clients. Today Cole's company, Tresit Group, is providing security software solutions for airports, businesses, schools, government offices, and hospitals.

Through the years I've noticed that many entrepreneurs wait until outside money is critical to keep the doors open before they actively pursue investors. I believe this is a mistake, because the process of fundraising brings two significant benefits. First, it forces entrepreneurs to think strategically about every aspect of their business: to examine their concepts, customers, sales, marketing, financials, processes, and execution to ensure that the fundamentals are sound.

Second, bringing in outside investors also brings access to their extensive networks of other industry and financial professionals with expertise the entrepreneurs may lack. As I wrote in my first book, *How to Be a Power Connector* (McGraw-Hill Education, 2014), the quality of our networks helps determine our success. That's why the wealth of connections that outside investors and advisors bring with them is often more valuable than the dollar amount of their contributions.

Unfortunately, for many entrepreneurs the world of corporate investment is difficult to understand, much less navigate. As a result, Cole's success is not that common. For every company that is funded, there are thousands of other, equally great startups that never get the money they need to get off the ground or to keep going. Even in an environment where angels, VCs, and family offices are looking for great businesses in which to invest, they still fund only 1 to 4 percent of the deals they see in a given year—not because the entrepreneurs' ideas aren't solid, but because those entrepreneurs simply don't know where to look for funding, or how to present their businesses in the best way.

Entrepreneurs can overcome those daunting odds by understanding the funding process from the inside out. You must get inside the mindset of your "customers"—i.e., the people who will give you the funding you need to get your business up and running, or to keep you going until you are profitable. Then you must package your business to make it easy for funders to say *yes*. I wrote this book to give any business owner or startup founder the guidance they need to (1) secure the funding they desire, so they can (2) grow their businesses effectively and (3) either sell the company or take the company public, thus (4) producing sizeable returns for themselves and their investors.

Dianne Feinstein once said, "You have to learn the rules of the game. And then you have to play better than anyone else." That's true of anyone looking to grow a business using OPM (other people's money). There are rules to the funding game that you must learn and follow. *Crack the Funding Code* lays out, in clear terms, exactly what entrepreneurs must know and do to find and secure the outside investment that can help them succeed. It shows them where to look, where the money is "hidden," and how to present themselves and their businesses in such a way that investors are eager to say *yes*. It walks you through the fundraising process, from initial offer to final close, so you can avoid any hidden pitfalls and end up with the best possible deal.

You'll not only be learning from me: In these pages many of my friends and colleagues have contributed their own wisdom about getting funded.

You'll hear advice from prominent entrepreneurs, angel investors, venture capitalists, and founders of accelerators and incubators, as well as specialists in crowdfunding, initial coin offerings (ICOs) or securities token offerings (STOs), and peer-to-peer (P2P) online lending. What's more, in the appendices you'll discover tools, checklists, and samples you can use to structure your own business plans, pitches, and deals.

Crack the Funding Code is meant as an introduction and guide to raising capital for your business, based upon the current U.S. fundraising landscape. That said, new capital sources (some more risky than others) are opening up all the time. Some will stand the test of time and provide entrepreneurs with money over the upcoming decades; others will vanish as quickly as the startups they fund. Regardless of the business capital source you're seeking, the fundamental principles described in this book will continue to be valuable for entrepreneurs who want to turn their ideas for a business into reality and need money to help them do so. These principles include having a sound business idea, a solid team, a provable plan for profitability, a clear exit strategy, and a network of people who know, like, and trust you. Then you must have a clear funding roadmap that will take you from your first meeting with an investor through every aspect of due diligence and closing the deal.

Just as it takes time and effort to build a business, it will take time and effort to create a great offer and then present it to the right investors. Will you get funded immediately? Probably not. It's inevitable that you will face a lot of rejection as you pitch your "great idea." But by following the guidance in this book and heeding the advice and examples offered throughout, I believe that you can find and approach the right investors with greater confidence and a far higher chance at success. You'll find yourself in the right room, in front of the right people, ready to deliver the right information in the right way. And once you crack the funding code, exponential growth and profit can be your reward.

CRACKING THE CODE OF ENTREPRENEURIAL SUCCESS

Getting in front of investors takes several steps in preparation before you can expect to find and reach the right investors, meet with these investors, and close any funding.[1]

—CHANCE BARNETT, general partner, Decentra Capital

1

THE FUNDING MINDSET
How to Think Like an Investor

> Learn to raise capital by any means. That's your primary job as an entrepreneur.
>
> **—RICHARD BRANSON**

magine that it's 1491 and you're Christopher Columbus, looking for your next profitable venture. You notice that all the trade routes from Europe to the lucrative markets in India and China are long and perilous. You believe that if you sail west across the Atlantic Ocean you can find a new, shorter trade route to the Far East—but you need money to build and equip the ships for your voyage. You approach the king of Portugal and then the merchants of Genoa and Venice, but they all turn you down. Finally, you get an audience with Queen Isabella of Spain. You'd been building relationships within the Spanish court since 1485, but this is your last chance to raise the money you need. You walk in and make your pitch for Spain to finance your great venture.

What do you imagine Queen Isabella is thinking as she listens to your proposal? "Let me see if I understand: This guy wants me to give him a lot of money to build three ships to reach the East by sailing west, which, according to every expert, can't be done. Smart people in Portugal, Genoa, and Venice have already turned him down flat. Why should I be crazy enough to give him money?"

Of course, Queen Isabella was crazy enough, and the Spanish court gave Columbus the modern equivalent of $14,000 to build his ships. Columbus sailed west, "discovered" the New World, and (for good or ill) created the foundation for the great Spanish empire. And because of Columbus's voyages, during the sixteenth century Spain laid claim to much of North and South America and became a dominant world power.

By the way, it also extracted the equivalent of $1.5 trillion in gold and silver from its American colonies. Not a bad return on a $14,000 investment.

Columbus's story is a metaphor for what entrepreneurs are doing every day: inventing new or better products or services that solve problems, and then starting businesses to turn those ideas or inventions into reality. The Global Entrepreneurship Monitor estimates that approximately 100 million businesses worldwide—that's three businesses every second—are launched each year.[1] In 2017 in the United States alone, approximately 540,000 new businesses were started each month.[2]

But while some legendary enterprises began on a shoestring in a garage or basement, even the "leanest" startup needs capital to open its doors. According to a 2015 study by Intuit, 64 percent of U.S. entrepreneurs started their businesses with investments of less than $10,000.[3] That money either comes from the entrepreneur's personal savings (57 percent of the time) or a combination of personal funds plus investment by family and friends (82 percent of the time).[4]

However, starting a venture isn't the same as keeping it up and running. The Kauffman Firm Survey (which studies business activities of startup companies) estimates that, on average, it takes a minimum of $80,000 to operate a small business in its first year.[5] That's a lot more capital than most people can raise every year, either from personal assets or from friends and family. So like Columbus, at some point many entrepreneurs will need to find outside investment to finance operations.

The good news is that today, a lot of outside money is available to fund great businesses. Consider the following:

- The National Small Business Association reported that 75 percent of small businesses used some kind of financing in 2015–2016. Sources of these funds included loans, credit cards, venture capital, and crowdfunding.[6]

- In 2015 bank loans going to small businesses totaled approximately $600 billion.[7] That same year, businesses received $593 billion in funds from venture capital (VC) firms, angels, and finance companies other than banks.[8]

- In 2016 "angels" (individuals investing their own money in companies) funded 64,380 entrepreneurial ventures to the tune of $21.3 billion.[9]

- In 2017 VCs invested a total of $84 billion in 7,783 companies—the highest level of investment since the early 2000s.[10]

- In 2017 the number of direct investment deals funded by family offices (which manage investments for high-net worth individuals and families) was more than twice the number of deals funded by traditional VC firms.[11]

- Alternative finance lending (which includes crowdfunding and P2P online lending) is growing rapidly as a resource for businesses. In 2016, $8.8 billion in alternative business funding was raised in the U.S. by 143,344 businesses.[12] U.S.-based companies used equity-based crowdfunding to raise $569.5 million, while revenue/profit-sharing crowdfunding produced $28.5 million.[13]

- In 2017 companies worldwide raised $5.6 billion through initial coin offerings (ICOs), where investors used funds to purchase tokens or digital currency that could then be traded on online exchanges.[14]

In some ways, entrepreneurs are in what could be called a "golden age" of fundraising, with the advent of P2P online lending, equity and revenue/profit-sharing crowdfunding, tokenization, and blockchain-based digital currency adding to the healthy numbers for venture capital, family offices, and seed and early-stage angel investing. But while it seems as if the funding landscape is expanding dramatically, the same perennial three questions exist for anyone who needs capital for their business: (1) Where's the money? (2) How can I gain access to the people and institutions that have it? And (3) what will it take to persuade them to give/loan it to or invest it in my startup?

Unfortunately, entrepreneurs often lack the time, expertise, or knowledge to take on the complex task of finding the funding that can help them reach their goals. As a result, for every startup that becomes the next

Airbnb, Amazon, Lyft, or Warby Parker, thousands of other, equally great companies never get the money they need to get off the ground or to keep going. According to Fundable (a business crowdfunding platform), in 2014 less than 1 percent of startups received funding from angel investors, and 0.05 percent by VCs. Banks weren't much better sources of capital, providing funds for only 1.43 percent of startups.[15]

The problem with most startup businesses isn't their ideas, or even their businesses: it's that they don't know where to look or how to present their businesses in a way that "closes the sale" with investors. How can startups find the cash they need to open their doors and keep the business going until they turn a profit? It begins by *thinking like Isabella rather than Columbus.* Whether you're going to your community bank for a business loan, pitching a top venture capital or angel investment firm for millions of dollars in exchange for equity, or posting your product or startup idea on a crowdfunding or peer-to-peer (P2P) online lending site, in every situation someone will be evaluating your offer based upon one fundamental question: Will your business make them money? Entrepreneurs must do what they can to access the investors' mindset so they can meet their needs and convince them to invest.

Cindy Padnos is founder and managing partner of Illuminate Ventures, an early-stage VC, and she remembers when she was an entrepreneur seeking venture capital for her own startup. "A very experienced VC investor corrected me when I said that I was 'fundraising.' 'To be clear,' he said, '*I* raise funds for investment. *You* raise capital to build a company.' Fortunately, I remembered the sound advice I had received to focus on what was actually important and not to argue semantics. This perhaps overly picky investor ended up being incredibly helpful, making introductions that led to our first round of financing."[16]

One of the core tenets of business is to think like your customers and deliver what they want, rather than what you think they should want. The same principle is true when it comes to your investors. In the same way you conduct market research to help shape your product or service to meet your customers' needs, you must understand the type of investors you want to reach, and then shape your business proposition to meet those investors' needs.

The Three Things Entrepreneurs Need to Get Funded

As someone who has spent more than thirty years helping entrepreneurs find and connect with sources of capital, and then guiding them through the process of pitching and closing the deal to get them the money they need, I believe only three things separate entrepreneurs whose ideas and businesses get funded from those who don't: *information, access,* and *expertise.*

Information

Many startup entrepreneurs believe that their only funding options are (a) savings or personal credit, (b) friends and family, or (c) bank loans. But personal savings and credit can run dry long before the business is profitable, and friends and family can be relied upon for only so long (and for a finite amount of money). The next logical resource is a loan from the local bank— *if* you have the collateral necessary, and *if* your local bank is still around. (After the Great Recession of 2008–2009, many bank branches that provided loans to small businesses disappeared, and other, larger lending institutions have not picked up the slack.[17]) In 2015 a Federal Reserve survey reported that only 38 percent of startups that had been in business for less than five years were approved for loans.[18] And businesses that are able to secure loans are often subjected to strenuous terms and high collateral requirements that can restrain the growth of a struggling enterprise.

Entrepreneurs need *information* about a wider portfolio of funding sources, such as VCs, micro or seed-stage VCs, angel investors, super angels, angel syndicates, and family offices, to name a few. In addition, recent regulations have opened a new category of lending to entrepreneurs: crowdfunding for businesses, online angel/investor "matchmaking" sites like GUST, and P2P online platforms like Lending Club, Prosper, and Upstart. These sites bypass traditional lending institutions and allow accredited and non-accredited investors to invest directly in businesses. Many municipalities, states, and even large corporations also offer grants to startups (often in conjunction with training programs). Finally, accelerators and incubators provide guidance as well as financial support to help entrepreneurs turn their ideas into viable startups.

Different categories of investors are active at different stages of the funding cycle, and they have specific requirements and guidelines for the kinds of businesses they sponsor. Entrepreneurs need to understand the differences between investors while being able to deliver the universal basics of a solid business plan, a great pitch, and a deal that works for all parties. We will discuss categories of investors, and when in your business development it is best to approach them, in Part II.

Access

The good news is that people with money are always looking for companies with potential for great deals and great returns. Angel investors and VCs need to have a series of deals in various stages of development. When one deal matures and the business either goes public, is sold, or the investors receive a return on investment in some other way, this frees up capital to invest in the next great business. It's paramount that these investment firms have quality "deal flow"—that is, new deals in the pipeline. If your startup has potential, you are solving a problem for investors who need to put their money in great businesses.

But to access these investors and investment firms, you either need to know these people yourself, or find someone who knows them to introduce you. *The number one way investors find deals is through referrals from people they know, like, and trust.* According to Case Western Reserve University business professor Scott Shane, most early-stage investors won't even look at a potential investment unless someone they know and trust brought them the deal.[19] Therefore, unless you already know who these investors are, or better yet, you know someone who knows who they are, you're unlikely to get a chance to tell them about your business.

When it comes to someone trusting you with their money, your personal connections are some of the most valuable currency you can have. You need to build a quality network of business connections, and then use them to reach the investors you need.

Let me give you an example that I wrote about in my first book, *How to Be a Power Connector.* My good friend Dr. Annette Lavoie had invented a permanent contraceptive device for women, but she spent eight years trying to obtain the funding to get it to market. I had already put Annette in touch with several of my investor connections and helped her develop a funding strategy. Then one day I was invited to a breakfast in Salt Lake City, Utah, where Geena Davis and Gloria Steinem were in attendance. I quickly called Annette and asked her to come over to talk about her device. Gloria Steinem offered to introduce Annette to someone at the company that manufactured the "next day" pill to see if they would be interested in investing. In short order, Annette used the funding from investors and the company to go into production. Not long after, she sold her device to the corporation and her investors received a 300 percent return on their investment. The combination of a great product, a great founder, a solid business plan, and access to the right people in the right industry allowed Annette and her investors to succeed.

Nowadays it may be easier than ever to find the names and contact information of pretty much anyone you want to reach, but knowing who you need to reach and then finding a way to get a warm rather than cold introduction can make the difference between getting a chance to pitch your idea and being stuck in the back of the line.

Expertise

A 2009 U.S. Bank study revealed the challenges many businesses have with cash flow and described two important causes of business failure: 73 percent of entrepreneurs stated they had been overly optimistic about achievable sales, money required, and what needed to be done to be successful, and 70 percent said they had failed to recognize (or they had ignored) what they didn't do well, and they had not sought help from those who were experts in those areas.[20] In other words, almost three-quarters of entrepreneurs whose businesses failed believed it was because they lacked the necessary *expertise*.

Many entrepreneurs have a great idea for a product or service, but they aren't great at the business side of their businesses. However, when entrepreneurs seek outside investment they are *forced* to think strategically about every aspect of their enterprise. They must examine concept, customer, sales, marketing, financials, processes, and execution to ensure that the fundamentals are sound. They also have to "sell" their business well enough for investors to want to say *yes*. Therefore, in the fundraising process most entrepreneurs become better businesspeople. They understand more about their market, their customers, and the "nuts and bolts" of their business systems. They become experts in their businesses rather than simply being someone with a great idea or product but no plan for long-term profitability.

There is a second advantage that comes from seeking outside investment. Outside investors not only provide access to greater capital than entrepreneurs can raise on their own, but they also bring access to extensive networks of industry and financial professionals with expertise entrepreneurs may lack. As part of many financing deals, investors ask for representation either on the business's board of directors or advisory board. (In fact, having an advisory board already in place can be a positive sign for investors that you are smart enough to recognize that you don't know it all and are willing to accept advice and direction from others.)

"Entrepreneurs have limited time, knowledge, and resources. Therefore, they need to focus on what matters most to them and what they need to do better than their competitors," writes Punit Arora, assistant professor of strategy and entrepreneurship at the Colin Powell School of Civic and Global Leadership, City University of New York. "But the rest still needs to get done."[21] Advisors and industry experts can provide a wider business expertise and viewpoint so that entrepreneurs can focus on whatever makes them truly unique.

Entrepreneurs who are smart enough to take advantage of the mentoring and advice of industry experts and investors have a much higher success rate. For example, the overall survival rate for most tech startup companies is approximately 20 percent. However, the survival rate for early-stage firms that complete the mentoring programs offered by tech incubators (such as DreamIt Ventures and 500 Startups) is as high as 80 percent.[22] When entrepreneurs receive outside investment, they also may receive advice, experience, and perspectives that will be far more valuable than any amount of investment dollars.

Ramphis Castro is the cofounder of ScienceVest, a VC fund for hard-tech and life science companies, and Impact Science Angels, an angel group focused on companies that can positively impact more than one million lives. After building two tech companies, he decided that he wanted to help founders avoid the pitfalls he went through. "I help founders avoid the mistakes myself and others have made so they can focus on making their unique brand of mistakes," he says. "I get to deep dive with founders on their hardest problems on a wide range of different areas, but without all the actual weight of being the founder. If the company survives and thrives, hopefully we all make a bit of money to go and help other founders."[23]

Even with information, access, and expertise, however, getting investors to open their wallets and put money into your company is a challenge. No matter how great your business idea, how profitable your projections, or how solid your business plan, the odds of getting funding are not in your favor, simply because the number of deals that produce any ROI for most investors is dismally small. Research by Harvard Business School senior lecturer Shikhar Ghosh showed that 30 to 40 percent of startups funded by investors ended by liquidating all their assets, and another 25 to 30 percent fail completely. According to Ghosh, "if a startup failure is defined as not delivering the projected return on investment, then 95 percent of VC companies are failures."[24]

With statistics like that, it's no wonder that so few deals can get funded. A typical VC firm will review proposals from approximately twelve hundred companies, hold face-to-face meetings with representatives of five hundred of those companies, proceed to due diligence with fifty of those five hundred, and finally make investments in only ten of those fifty. And out of those ten, only *one* may provide a return on investment.[25] Can you see the challenge investors face when evaluating your business?

The harsh reality is this: Investors have a million reasons to turn you down. Not enough collateral. Not a large enough market. Not a good enough product. The business plan isn't complete, or the projections are too optimistic. The pitch is weak. The venture isn't in their area of specialization. The proposal comes in "cold"—that is, without a recommendation from someone they know. The team, or the founder, or the timeline is wrong. The investors are low on liquid capital and need to wait for one of their other deals to bear fruit. They think your product or service needs more development. The deal terms aren't favorable enough. There's not enough upside. You already have too many investors. They're in a rush to catch a plane and don't have time to evaluate your deal. It's Friday. It's Monday. And on and on. . . . That's why it is so vital for entrepreneurs to do everything they can to position themselves and their businesses in the best way possible: to provide the *information*, plan, and story that will intrigue and impress investors, to use whatever *access* they can find within their networks to gain warm introductions to key decisionmakers, and to develop the *expertise* needed to go through the funding process successfully.

How to Crack the Funding Code and Turn Your Business into a "High-Potential" Startup

Investors identify a high-potential entrepreneur by looking for two characteristics: (1) the entrepreneur understands the investors' objectives, and (2) the entrepreneur builds their startup with the exit strategy in mind. When entrepreneurs understand how investors think, they can position themselves and their businesses to attract those investors. Making it easy for investors to say *yes* is an essential skill for every entrepreneur. I call it "cracking the funding code." It's like having the combination to a safe with all the funding you need inside of it: To open the safe, you must hit all the numbers of the combination exactly. One digit off and you won't get the cash.

I realize that some entrepreneurs may believe that they don't need (or can't find) corporate investors. But the principles covered in this book can help those who are seeking funds from *any* source—friends and family, banks, grants, foundations, accelerators, incubators, and yes, VCs, angel investors, and family offices—to create a clear, irresistible offer that demonstrates the value of their business and outlines compelling reasons for investment.

Here are the nine "numbers" you need to crack the funding code. Each of these is described in detail in this book.

1. An understanding of what goes on inside investors' heads: what keeps them up at night, what makes them worry, what objectives they consider critical. You must think of investors as a different kind of "customer," so you can meet their needs and make a "sale"—i.e., get them to invest. When entrepreneurs understand how investors think, they can position themselves and their businesses attractively.

2. Seeking the right funding from the right sources based upon your industry, location, and stage of development. Investors often specialize in particular industries (tech, for example), or invest mostly in a certain geographical area (this makes it easier for investors to do their due diligence and provide advice). Other investors may not be interested in putting money into mature companies, and many VCs won't look at your business until it has a track record. You need to match your funding requests to the proper funding resources.

3. A great founder and a great team who are passionate about the business. Have you heard the expression, "Bet the jockey, not the horse"? Investors will evaluate the business founders first, then the team, and then the business. They're looking for founders with a clear vision for the company, people who can share their vision with enough energy and enthusiasm that others will want to join the team. Startups are all-consuming endeavors, and they require every bit of an entrepreneur's passion and energy to survive, much less succeed. Investors want to be sure you have the drive to make your business profitable in the short- and long-term.

4. A solid business plan/executive summary with realistic (not optimistic) projections for profitability. Your two-page business plan/executive summary should describe everything about the customer (who will buy the business's product or service, how much will they pay, how will they access the product, and who will facilitate that sale) and all of the important aspects of the business execution (what is needed to get the product or service to market, who will help, and how much money is required). It must show how your business will avoid potential roadblocks and chart a clear path to profitability, even in changing markets. It will include financial projections, how much money you are looking for, and a quantification of investors' potential return.

5. A compelling pitch that tells the story of the company and lays out why someone should invest. When you pitch your business to investors, you are "selling" yourself and the opportunity—and if you can't sell to them, they will worry about how you can sell to customers. Your story must be so memorable that you will stand out from the thousands of other

pitches these investors have heard. It must have a value proposition that it is consistent, concise, and compelling. Your pitch must include a dynamic pitch deck and executive summary that distills the most complex concepts so investors not only can understand your business but also are intrigued and want to know more.

6. The ability to answer any questions from investors about potential risks. The six kinds of risk that concern investors most are product risk, market risk, management risk, execution risk, financial risk, and competitive risk. You must be ready with strategies and suggestions to mitigate these risks and eliminate any possible roadblocks to funding.

7. A clean deal that works for both you and your investors. This starts with a specific request for the amount of investment needed and a clear description of what the business will give in exchange for that investment. Remember, investors are going to be comparing your investment with other opportunities in the marketplace. The cleaner your deal is, the better your opportunity looks.

8. Strategies for the deal's legal process and due diligence. You must know what are dealbreakers for you and your company, and be ready to negotiate on items that your investors consider dealbreakers. You also must be clear about what you consider non-negotiable, and be willing to walk away from the deal if necessary.

9. A clear exit strategy showing how and when the entrepreneurs, their teams, and the investors will realize a (significant) return.

Notice that nowhere on this list are "a great product or service," "a demonstrable need or problem," or "an established customer base." All of those things are important and will make your fundraising easier, but some of the most successful businesses of the last hundred years started with one or none of those elements. Who knew that ride-sharing services like Uber or Lyft would replace taxicabs? Or Facebook, Instagram, Twitter, or Pinterest would become part of our daily lives? The most successful entrepreneurs often had what seemed to be the craziest ideas, but they also had passion, understood the minds of their investors, had great business plans, and were able to explain in clear and compelling terms exactly what their businesses were going to accomplish. And eventually all of these businesses produced significant returns for their founders and investors.

With these nine elements in place, investors will see your business as a "high-potential" startup, one they will be eager to fund. And when you walk into a pitch meeting or contact a potential source of funding, you will be able to do so with the confidence that you will beat the odds and be the one-in-ten (or less) business deal that this particular VC/angel/family office/foundation/incubator/P2P will want to do.

Even with the best business and pitch in the world, will you still get rejected? Yes. But as every entrepreneur knows, persistence is the secret to success. Remember: Even though Columbus had never captained an expedition and had been turned down by multiple investors, Isabella gave him the money. With the right offer, the right pitch, and the right plan, you will find the right deal.

2

THE 3 Cs THAT INVESTORS SEEK— AND THE DEALBREAKERS THAT WILL MAKE THEM RUN

[At] its heart, a startup investment is an investment in the entrepreneur. [1]

—DAVID HORNIK, August Capital

Y ou'd think that investors would consider the quality of the business before the character of the entrepreneur. But time and time again when you talk with angels or VCs, you hear the expression, "Bet the jockey, not the horse"—meaning, the entrepreneur or founder of the startup is more important in the funding decision than the business itself.

This evaluation is not simply based upon the founder's past experience. Granted, serial entrepreneurs with proven track records are far more likely to be funded than first-timers (60 percent versus 45 percent), and they also receive funding earlier (on average at twenty-one months in business, versus thirty-seven months for a first-time founder). [2] But when it comes to evaluating a startup for financing, investors consider the temperament of the entrepreneur (and the entrepreneur's team) as much if not more than the startup's product or service. As *The American Angel* 2017 report says, "First and foremost, angels invest in people. The quality of the founding team in terms of both experience and personal characteristics are most critical to angel investors." [3]

The bottom line is this: The initial bet that they're taking is really about you. *Investors must know you, like you, and trust you before they will fund you.*

In Chapter 5 you'll learn more about developing a strategic network that will allow you to get "warm" introductions to potential funders, which will help with your being known, liked, and trusted. However, once you've gotten the introduction, it's up to you to present yourself and your business in such a way that an investor will want to give you money. As serial entrepreneur turned VC investor Mark Suster writes in his blog, *Both Sides of the Table*, "Fundraising is a sales process. The investor is a customer and they have money to spend but only for a limited number of companies. They are buying trust in you that you will build a large business that will be valuable."[4]

I believe entrepreneurs must demonstrate three essential qualities to win investors over: *character*, *confidence,* and *coachability*. Then founders must be sure to avoid any red flags or dealbreakers that might get in the way.

Character

In my first book, *How to Be a Power Connector*, I wrote about the importance of character in choosing people to be part of your network: "When it comes to choosing the people for your own strategic relationships, you need to select them first and foremost on the basis of who they are instead of what they have accomplished."[5] Well, character is doubly important when it comes to persuading investors to trust you with their capital.

It shouldn't be surprising that from your first email contact, to your first meeting, pitch, second meeting, term sheet, due diligence, mentoring, until the final exit, investors are going to be evaluating your character. After all, every investment in a first-time startup is a leap into the unknown, and the earlier the stage of investment the bigger the leap. If this is the founder's first startup, investors are taking a big leap indeed, so the evaluation of the founder's character becomes even more critical. Simply starting a business puts tremendous stress on founders as well as their teams, and fundraising adds an additional layer of herculean effort that falls squarely on the shoulders of the founders. In such circumstances, character—which includes qualities like commitment, grit, and persistence—is often the only thing that will pull entrepreneurs through.

"No one, no matter how much money they have, will part with it without being very sure that it is used very intelligently by great, capable, trustworthy experts," writes Emlyn Scott, founder and managing director of Capital Pitch, an Australian collective of founders and investors. "An investor needs to know that you are a trustworthy and imminently capable group of founders, capable of following through on commitments and delivering positive investment returns."[6]

Character is also critical because many funders are looking to create long-term relationships with founders and their companies. As you'll see when we talk about coachability, angel and VC investors typically plan to invest not just capital but also valuable time, sharing their expertise, connections, and guidance along the company's path to profitability. So they need to feel that they will enjoy their relationship with the startup team. "The first 'blink' evaluation [investors] make is about *you* and only when they've subconsciously decided whether they find you smart, likable, credible, a good leader, inspirational, competitive and all of the other subconscious attributes they'll look for do they begin to truly think about whether your business idea has legs," writes Mark Suster.[7]

Investors will be looking to answer these questions about you:

- *Are you competent?* "Can you do this?" is the question that nearly every financial backer will ask. You need to demonstrate that you know your business, your product, and your market inside and out. Be ready to answer any and all questions thoroughly and with certainty. (But don't be afraid to say you don't know either—see below.) Demonstrating competence is easier if you have been part of or perhaps founded an earlier startup. If you're a first-time startup founder without a track record, your personal work history and credit history can help show professional and financial competence. What was your job performance like at your last position? If you worked at a previous startup, were you a leader within the team? Did your team or department have a track record of meeting or exceeding performance targets or revenue goals? How is your personal financial track record? Considering that you will be responsible for spending the investors' money, they will want to know that you handle credit and debt responsibly.

- *Are you totally committed to your startup? How hard do you work?* While you can *start* a company while working another job, by the point you are talking with investors they're going to expect that you're 1,000 percent dedicated to your startup's success. And that usually means working long hours with no downtime. I once heard an investor say that true commitment was having a bunkbed over your desk. What's your level of commitment?

- *Are you honest? Do you tell the truth?* When asking for funding, entrepreneurs may be tempted to "fudge" numbers to look better to investors. But smart angels and VCs will always ask questions to discover the truth. Any lies on your part will inevitably backfire. As Howard H. Stevenson, Sarofim-Rock Baker Foundation professor emeritus of Harvard Business School and known as the "lion of entrepreneurship," once said, the first time you hear anything dishonest out of a founder's mouth, you should run, not walk.[8]

- *Are you trustworthy? Do you keep your word?* According to research into decisions made by angel investors, when they believe an entrepreneur can be relied upon to keep their word, angels are more likely to provide funding.[9] "I once gave a term sheet to an entrepreneur because he delivered on a number of assertions he'd made about his business at a meeting three months earlier," writes David Hornik. "There's nothing better than an entrepreneur who delivers the goods."[10]

- *Are you the kind of person we would want to be around and will be happy to introduce to our networks?* As investors evaluate your business, they will be evaluating you as a potential business associate. Most investors plan to spend time with you, offering advice and guidance. So they want to know, are you someone they will enjoy interacting with over the next three to five years (the typical timeframe for a company to either be sold or for the investor to exit)? Even more important, are you the kind of person investors will feel comfortable introducing to their connections? In business, every time you introduce someone to the people in your network, you are putting your own reputation on the line. Will investors feel that you will represent them well?

Remember, any investor—whether it's a friend or family member, bank, nonprofit, angel investor, venture capital firm, family office, or a "crowd" you reach via a crowdfunding campaign—has many different investment opportunities. Even if your startup represents the potential for spectacular returns, if investors don't feel your character is trustworthy, then they won't invest.

Confidence

John Livesay is better than anyone I've ever seen at helping entrepreneurs craft compelling pitches that inspire angels and VCs to invest, and he often speaks about the importance of confidence for any startup founder. "If you don't believe that your idea is going to work with consumers, if you don't have the confidence to attract the right members to your team, and if you don't have confidence that investors are putting their money in a place that is going to give them a strong return on investment, then you will not get a yes," he says.

Entrepreneurs also need confidence in themselves, their ideas, and their teams so they can make it through the challenges that inevitably show up. Indeed, at times confidence is the *only* thing that will get an entrepreneur to the goal. Dominic Giancona is a U.S. Navy veteran who had the idea for Shaker Sleeves™ (recyclable, disposable shaker cup inserts designed to keep shaker cups clean) when he was still in the service. He raised the initial $20,000 for his business from four of his shipmates, none of whom had a lot of money to invest. "I thought at the time it was all due to the idea. In retrospect, I know the people who took a chance on Shaker Sleeves were convinced more by the confidence I had in myself and what I felt I could do with this idea than anything else," he says.

If you find your confidence waning for any reason, try an exercise that John Livesay recommends, called "stacking your moments of certainty." Think of moments from your past when you felt confident—times where you could say, "That was a moment where I knew I nailed it," as in the following examples:

- You studied for a test in school, knew you were prepared, and when you finished the test you thought, "I did really well."
- You went on a job interview and walked out saying, "I am going to get another interview, or maybe they're just going to make me an offer."
- You went out for a sports team and aced the tryout.

- You walked into a prospective customer's office certain that you'd get the sale—and you did.

Write down three to five of those moments, and next to each write the feeling that went with it: "fantastic," "exhilarating," "happy," "totally confident," and so on. Once you have your list, reread it regularly. As you "stack" all of those moments and feelings together, your confidence level will go up, and that will show in your demeanor. Your nonverbal communication (what you say with your face and body) is the first thing that people notice about you. Psychological studies indicate that it can take as little as *one-tenth of a second* to form an unconscious evaluation of the trustworthiness of someone you meet.[11]

This exercise is akin to the success visualization techniques used by many professional athletes prior to a game or match. As an entrepreneur, you need to be at the top of your game, too. Before your next meeting, presentation, or pitch, try focusing on these successful events from your past. Remember, as a startup founder you will need to get used to hearing *no* from investors, clients, bankers, even family and friends, so you need to be able to generate self-confidence no matter what.

At the same time you must not appear overconfident—or worse, arrogant—to investors. Being overconfident can prevent you from being able to hear valid advice or objections from the very people who may be able to help you make your company better. Make sure that your confidence is backed up with facts and figures, not just dreams and unfounded assumptions, and be confident enough to accept the valuable coaching that many investors are eager to give.

Coachability

How well do you listen? How well do you learn? I can't tell you how many pitch events I've judged where we couldn't get the entrepreneur to shut up and listen to us. We knew instantly that they were never going to get funded because they weren't receptive to input or feedback, and therefore they were unlikely to be receptive to mentoring or coaching.

The importance of coachability to angel investors in particular cannot be overstated. Angels love to mentor. They regard their contributions of knowledge and connections as being equal to, if not more important than, their capital. So they want to work with entrepreneurs who are willing to listen and learn. A 2014 academic study based upon data from the Tech Coast Angels (an early-stage angel investment group with more than three hundred members) showed that perceived receptivity to coaching and mentorship increased investors' interest in proceeding to due diligence with a startup.[12] "Research has found that investors do believe their involvement and advice (e.g., as a board member or a mentor) will help the company grow and ultimately lead to greater ROI," study authors write. "[A]ngel investors want to feel their time is well spent, and . . . that the advice they offer the entrepreneur is taken into action. Therefore, angel investors want to invest in an entrepreneur who is open to their mentorship and to taking on a role as a protégé in a mentor-protégé relationship with the investor."[13]

GrowthX is an early-stage venture capital firm that believes in the value of coachability in any successful startup team. "Our first core value is people first. A core part of our investment thesis is to look for great product founders who have what we call a 'GrowthX mindset,' which is to be a learn-it-all, not a know-it-all," says one of the company founders, Andrew Goldner.[14]

"We focus on helping founders who recognize that they don't know what they don't know about market development, and they acknowledge that our help is more important than our money," adds cofounder Sean Sheppard. "We always wanted to help. That's our passion, we're founders and entrepreneurs ourselves. We love getting in there and digging in and working alongside them."[15]

Investors understand that receptivity to outside feedback is an essential quality because it indicates the entrepreneur's adaptability, and the willingness to learn from their mistakes and change their assumptions, even their business model if needed. Ron Conway, an active early-stage angel investor in companies like Google and PayPal, puts it this way: "Coachability enables a willingness to be open to make the necessary and often numerous course corrections and morphing that startups require."[16] And considering that more than 73 percent of startups end up having to pivot to a different market in which to sell their products or services, the ability to take in quality feedback and make changes quickly are critical skills that will help investors to recoup their investments and founders to have successful exits.[17]

Red Flags and Dealbreakers for Investors

Even with character, confidence, and coachability, investors still need to feel that you and your startup are a strong bet. In fact, they're usually looking for reasons *not* to invest in your deal. I call such reasons red flags and dealbreakers: the things that keep investors up at night and make them worry. And many of these dealbreakers are not about your startup, but about *you*.

There are seven categories of red flags or dealbreakers that can show up anytime during the investment process. You must avoid them at all costs.

1. *Being dishonest.* Lying about any aspect of your business or yourself sows doubt about your honesty in the minds of investors. If there's no moral code, most investors feel that their money is history. So never, ever fudge your numbers, hide information, exaggerate past business successes, fail to mention past failures, or hold back important data. Most investors are pretty smart and will verify your claims before giving you their money. If you don't know something, say you don't know. Just be honest and you will save yourself a lot of time and trouble.

2. *Saying that you have no competition.* This one makes investors chuckle, because it would mean there's nobody to buy your product or service! Even if you have the most innovative product or service in the world, you are either disrupting a current business model, or you are creating a new market that will quickly fill with competitors. Being clear about your competition shows that you have done your research and are realistic about your market rather than being idealistic or naïve.

3. *Saying that you only need 1 percent of market share.* This shows that you don't understand sales or your customer acquisition cost. Investors want your sales plan to be built from the bottom up. They want you to know how many phone calls you are going to have to make per sale, what's going to be your close rate, what's your sales cycle, and so on. Don't talk market share: Instead, prove to your investors how many customers you

need, how much you will spend to get them, and how long it will take you to get to that number.

4. *Failing to meet your commitments.* Marcia Nelson is managing director of Alberleen Family Office Solutions, which works to connect family offices with what Alberleen believes are quality investments. When asked what might kill a potential investment deal for her clients, she says, "[The startup's] management taking too long to get us requested information—while it may not kill a deal, it will certainly make us cautious."[18] Investors want to know that you take your commitments to them seriously, and you are prepared to meet their requests in a timely manner.

5. *Being desperate.* Most investors know that startups don't have a lot of money—that's why founders are pitching them. But coming across as desperate or pushing too hard will not inspire confidence. Investors may worry that you won't be able to manage the money you're asking for. Even if you're down to your last dollar, you need to inspire confidence in yourself and your business.

6. *Being arrogant or defensive.* There's a difference between the self-confidence of "My startup is going to crush the competition" and the arrogance of "You are stupid if you don't see how great I am or how successful my business will be." As Mark Suster says, that arrogant "chip on your shoulder" attitude can alienate investors quickly. So, too, can being defensive when investors ask questions of founders. As you'll see in Chapter 8, during a pitch it's a *good* sign when investors ask questions. But if you regard questions as attacks on you or your business and come across as defensive or evasive, you're unlikely to get funded. The same is true if your investors ask questions after they've put money into your company. Remember, most investors want to help your company succeed, so approach their questions as opportunities for clarifying your systems and goals or as suggestions that will help your business be better.

7. *Not being willing to listen to input.* Emlyn Scott observes, "Angel investors don't usually like entrepreneurs who act like they need no help and have all the answers. A healthier, more productive attitude is for entrepreneurs to own their weaknesses and actively seek advice."[19]

When you're pitching, or in other conversations with investors, it may be tempting to interrupt their questions and deliver what you think they want to know without really understanding the issues they want to raise. However, this can send a message to investors that you're not open to input or feedback from them or anyone else. And considering that angel investors consider their coaching and mentoring even *more* valuable than their money, failure to take input is a serious red flag indeed.

Your job as a founder is to make it easy for investors to say *yes* to both you and your startup. You do this by exhibiting the kind of character, confidence, and coachability they want, and by eliminating any possible deal-breakers or red flags from you and your pitch. However, you too should watch for red flags and dealbreakers in potential investors. Your investors will be part of your business from the moment they put in their money, but you too are making an "investment" of sorts in the angel or VC. So while investors are vetting you, do the same for them. Make sure that your partnership will be a great deal for all parties concerned.

II

HOW TO FIND THE RIGHT INVESTORS

Just as it takes a quality idea and pitch to find success, it also requires a quality investor.[1]

—MURRAY NEWLANDS, entrepreneur, investor, founder of Due

3

WHO'S GOT THE MONEY?

Where to Look (Including Some Places You've Never Heard of)

Ask any entrepreneur about his or her greatest challenge, and the conversation will likely turn to capital. Finance is the lifeblood of every company, but for new firms, capital is especially critical.[1]

—JASON WIENS and JORDAN BELL-MASTERSON

Every business needs capital to open its doors and to keep them open until it reaches profitability. According to the U.S. Small Business Administration, more than half of startups use personal funds first, and then they reach out to friends and family. Typical initial startup funding ranges anywhere from zero, to less than $5,000, and up to $25,000.[2] "Cash not only allows startups to live and grow, a war chest is also almost always a competitive advantage in all ways that matter: hiring key staff, public relations, marketing, and sales," says Geoff Ralston of Y Combinator. "[However, the] amount of money needed to take a startup to profitability is usually well beyond the ability of founders and their friends and family to finance. Thus, most startups will almost certainly want to raise money."[3]

While banks would seem to be the first place to turn, there are other sources of funding that are willing to take a chance on your startup. Investors are constantly looking for places to put their money. They know that even though startups can be a risky choice (two-thirds of early-stage investments fail to return the full investment amount), the ROI for early-stage venture capital for the businesses that succeed has averaged 21.5 percent annually over a thirty-year time period.[4] That beats the average S&P 500 returns over the same period of 11.69 percent per year.[5]

To connect with investors and get funding for your startup, you must learn where the money is and who has it. We'll start with the places where most entrepreneurs get their first money: themselves, friends and family, and conventional lending institutions. Then we'll cover grants; accelerators and incubators; angel investors; venture capital firms; and corporate venture capital. Finally, you'll learn about family offices (a source of funding that few people know about), and you'll learn about some new and exciting ways to raise money via crowdfunding and ICOs (initial coin offerings) or STOs (securities token offerings). Depending on the stage of your company and your funding needs, you can use a combination of these sources of capital to get your business up and running.

You, Friends and Family, and Customers

Most founders have invested their time, energy, and effort in getting their businesses off the ground. Well, investors are looking to see if you've invested your own capital as part of that effort. Even if you can't put in a lot of money, any amount indicates your commitment to making this business a success. It also will be a great selling point when you approach friends and family— usually the next step in a startup's funding journey. According to statistics collected by Fundable (a crowdfunding platform), as of 2013 close to 38 percent of all startups got some funding from friends and family.[6]

Now, you may be fortunate enough to have a few rich relatives (with whom you're on good terms) who will lend you the money and think nothing of it. Or you may be more like Dominic Giancona, who wasn't able to raise capital from his family at first, so he went to his shipmates, one by one, until he found four who were willing to invest $5,000 each in his Shaker Sleeves startup. Whether it's easy or hard to raise money from friends and family, keep these three things in mind.

- Turning friends and family into investors can complicate your relationships with them. So before you talk with anyone, think about what will happen if your startup fails. Can your friends and family afford to lose all of the money they give you? How will you feel if they do? Make sure everyone understands the risk in this investment and that they can afford to take the hit. If not, go elsewhere for the money.

- Jamie Pennington, cofounder and co-CEO of SeeItFit.com recommends that instead of asking for money, ask for help.[7] Even friends and family who don't have enough capital themselves may introduce you to someone who becomes your investor.

- Even if it's just a small loan from a parent or college friend to get the business started, ask an attorney to draw up a written agreement that outlines the investment amount, the terms, and whether the investor receives debt or equity. If it's debt, include the interest rate, repayment terms, and the length of the loan period. If it's equity, make clear how many shares or what percentage of the company they are purchasing, and when you will issue those shares.

Getting money from friends and family may signal later investors that you are willing to go to whatever lengths necessary to get your business up and running. On the other hand, when you go outside of friends and family to look for funding, you will tap into a network of investors that may provide you with leads for future rounds. It might be a reason to turn to seed-stage investors quickly.

Some of the best sources for startup funding are early-adopting customers. They provide your business with proof of concept to future investors as well as the cash you need to operate today. If necessary, think of offering early adopters incentives to purchase your product or service before its release. You can use deep discounts, extra services, multiple months of subscription for free, rewards for introducing you to other customers, and so on. As you'll see later in this chapter, offering incentives for customers who buy prior to the release of your product or service is used successfully in crowdfunding.

Commercial Loans

The next source of funding that most startups turn to is a commercial lending institution. According to the Kauffman Foundation, approximately

40 percent of startup capital comes from bank lending.[8] Banks provide loans, which means you are taking on debt that must be repaid with interest according to terms dictated by the bank. There will be a maturity date on the loan when the principal and interest must be repaid. On the plus side, assuming that you are able to make the payments, you do not have to give any equity away. You can keep a greater share of the value of the business. On the minus side, banks usually require some kind of collateral (personal or business assets) to loan you money.

Since many startups have no collateral nor any revenues to prove viability, it can be difficult to secure loans. To make it easier, consider this:

- Approach smaller community banks rather than big institutions. Local banks are more likely to take the time to learn about you and your business and to take a risk on you based on their belief in your ability to repay the loan even if you are prerevenue.

- Develop a relationship with your bank before you approach it for funding. A strong relationship with multiple touch points (a checking account, a personal car loan or mortgage, for example) makes it easier to access the credit you need.

- Banks will need certain documentation: a written business plan, cash flow statements (if you have them), a list of business or personal assets (again, if you have any), and so on.

- The fact that you will be responsible for monthly payments to the bank no matter how well or poorly your startup is doing can be a significant drag on a young company. Take that into account and only borrow the amount of capital you need.

Another banklike option is an investment source associated with the U.S. Small Business Administration (SBA). Small Business Investment Companies (SBICs) are privately owned entities that use money provided by the SBA as well as their own capital to invest directly in small businesses. Investments can be in the form of either debt or equity. While many SBICs will invest mostly in more mature businesses that already have some cash flow (and not all industries are eligible for funding), each

SBIC has its own guidelines. Investments can range from $250,000 to $10 million with a term of around three years, and you will need a written business plan to apply. Research SBICs in your area to see which ones are actively investing in your type of business.[9]

Grants and State/Local Accelerators

While there is no such thing as "free" money, you sometimes can find grant programs and state and local accelerators that provide funding to startups. In addition to grants, some government-run programs also offer low interest loans that do not have to be paid back. There are grants for startups run by entrepreneurs who fit into specific categories (women, veterans, and minorities, for example), and a wide range of grants available through federal, state, and even local communities. A handful of companies like Intuit, FedEx, and Walmart also offer grants or prizes, often through pitch competitions.[10]

Grants and state and local accelerators will usually require you to fulfill certain eligibility requirements, and there is often a lengthy and cumbersome application and vetting process and a lot of competition for the few spots available. However, winning a grant or a place in an accelerator can be a powerful signal to future investors about your startup's viability.

Incubators and Investor-Run Accelerators

Even more than money, early-stage startups often need mentoring and access to resources and expertise to help them get past their initial stumbling blocks. That's the rationale behind investor-run incubators and accelerators: They are organizations dedicated to helping startups succeed. As of 2016 there were more than 7,000 business incubators and accelerators internationally, many of them nonprofit and focused on community economic development.[11]

Incubators are designed for early-stage startups—those that have an innovative idea but need help with a business model, regulatory compliance, or reaching the marketplace. As a result, businesses in incubators may be mentored for longer periods of time.[12] Incubators can serve a wide diversity of business types, from tech to design to manufacturing to food. They often are regionally focused, with a goal of growing businesses in a particular area. Other incubators receive their funding from universities or local economic development organizations.[13] With both incubators and accelerators there is a rigorous application process, and few startups are accepted. It's been shown that companies that go through incubators have much higher survival rates and grow faster than other startups.[14]

A unique program similar to an incubator is Goldman Sachs 10,000 Small Businesses. Its attendees (all small-business owners at different stages of development) are given a range of tools and training to help them grow their businesses, including access to a variety of lenders. One of the primary focuses of the Goldman Sachs program is innovation, and businesses are encouraged to develop and launch new products or services. Program participants spend around a hundred hours in class and an equal amount of time working on their development plans outside of class. Most small businesses that enroll increase their revenues, secure capital in higher numbers, and learn better how to innovate.

Accelerators tend to focus primarily on technology companies and are designed for businesses that are well past the idea stage (although a few will accept idea-stage startups). Accelerator programs usually last only a few months and the goal is to make the startup more "investor-worthy." Founders accepted by accelerators may need to relocate to the program's city for the duration of the program. Startups enrolled in accelerators may receive funds in the range of $10,000 to $150,000 in return for a small equity stake in the business. Accelerator programs often culminate in "demo days," where founders pitch their companies to VCs. Because of these connections with angels and VC investors, graduating from an accelerator can provide greater access to future funding. Investors feel that startups that have graduated from accelerator programs have been "vetted," so to speak, so they present better opportunities for return.

Kay Koplovitz is the chairman (and one of the founders) of Springboard Enterprises, a nonprofit dedicated to helping women build successful, high-growth technology-oriented companies. Since its founding in 1999, more than seven hundred women have benefited from Springboard's accelerator programs, where they received coaching and investor introductions that allowed them to raise $8.6 billion in capital.[15] Spring-board also has partnerships in Israel and Australia and runs programs in those countries.

Kay Koplovitz describes the criteria that Springboard seeks when they accept an entrepreneur into its programs: "In Springboard's world, the entrepreneur is key. She has to have a clear vision, a very large market potential, demonstrated execution skills, an A team even if only a few people, and she must demonstrate agility. This last point is really very important. If we are going to pour years of human capital into her success, we want to know she can learn and adapt quickly. No business plan for a startup company is ever really right: It will be tweaked or completely pivoted along the way. Therefore, it is very important that the entrepreneur is inquisitive, reaches out for advice, and knows when and how to adapt."[16]

Now we move into several of the primary sources of startup equity financing: angel investors and venture capitalists. While VCs and angels fund a small number of startups proportionately, together they wield significant influence due to the connections, business acumen, resources, and expert guidance they can offer.

Angel Investors

Angels are wealthy individuals who invest in promising startups, usually in exchange for equity or sometimes for a combination of debt and equity (see Chapter 4). The primary difference between angels and VCs is that angels use their own money, while VCs invest other people's money (with occasionally some of their own capital thrown in). Angel investors fund 90 percent of high-potential deals and sixty times as many startups as venture capital firms.[17]

Angel investors can range in age from their early twenties to their late eighties; they are more ethnically and gender diverse than VCs; and they can be found in communities and states across the U.S. Angels can invest on their own, or through one of more than three hundred angel groups located throughout the U.S. They also may choose to come together and form syndicates, pooling their resources and sometimes letting one or two of their members take the lead in vetting investments.

Angels' contributions to business are significant: The Angel Capital Association estimates that angels invest up to $24 billion per year in more than 64,000 startups in the U.S.[18] The median check size angel investors wrote in 2017 was around $35,000, although amounts vary greatly depending on the angel. The average rate of return sought by angels is a nine times multiple within a five-year timeframe.

Dave Berkus, one of the first early-stage angel investors (and still actively investing), says that there are five things of value angel investors can offer startups:

1. *money* (only one of the five)
2. *context*—angels can assess if entrepreneurs' ideas are right for this time and place, or way ahead or behind the industry
3. *process*—angels have taken products to market multiple times, so they can save entrepreneurs money by streamlining their processes
4. *relationships* with producers, suppliers, funders, and other contacts—angels can reach people the entrepreneur could never get to
5. *time*—especially the time it takes to develop or manufacture the product in the critical early stages[19]

What's most important for angel investors is quality deal flow. They get most of their deals through referrals from the top bankers, lawyers, and accountants. They also are friendly with the top incubator managers because these people see a lot of deals and can say, "Out of all these people coming through our incubator, these three have a winning business module: you can make money with them." Because angels are investing for themselves and don't have to consult with anyone else, their decisionmaking process is faster (meaning, you can get funded faster).

Angels also can target their investing choices based not just on financial return but also upon causes or categories of people they wish to support. There are angels that fund green startups; others that specialize in social impact investing; still others that seek to fund startups in their local communities, far away from the investment capital "hubs" of California, New York, or Boston. One example of a "targeted" angel investor is Gaingels, an early-stage investment syndicate that does both angel and VC-led deals. As Paul Grossinger, a Gaingels' managing member, describes their focus, "David Beatty and I wanted to drive social change through business, and there was a clear gap we saw in the marketplace: No one was explicitly investing in early stage and growing companies with LGBT leadership."[20] Gaingels funds startups that have at least one LGBT founder, C-level executive, or board member.

Another angel network that focuses on women is Golden Seeds. (I am a former managing director of the organization.) Golden Seeds was founded in 2005 to help women entrepreneurs in their search for investment capital. Since that time, more than 150 women-led early-stage companies have received over $100 million in funding from seven hundred investors (women and men). Golden Seeds has chapters in twenty-two states and provides active support and mentoring for its startups. It also has relationships with VC firms to help these startups when they are ready to go to the next funding level.

Angels operate in communities across the world, and many of them are more interested in funding local businesses so they can actively mentor founders. To find angel investors that are a good match for your company regionally as well as by funding stage and interest, you can consult Angel List and GUST, which represents eight hundred angel groups globally and acts as a "matchmaker" between entrepreneurs and investors. You also can search for LinkedIn Groups related to angel investing and early-stage venture capital for leads.

Angels sit on panels and give speeches in the hopes that you will find them, so shift your thinking to understand that when you bring a great startup to an angel's attention, you're solving a problem, because they're always looking for good deals.

Venture Capital Firms and Corporate Venture Capital

There are over five hundred VC firms in the U.S. (less than half than were active before the 2008 recession) and only forty are considered top tier. Venture capitalists (VCs) and private equity (PE) groups invest other people's money (OPM), from sources such as private foundations, pension plans, retirement funds, insurance companies, endowments, university capital funds, and so on—institutional investors who have large sums of money. There also are a few limited partners, or LPs, who are ultra high net worth or high net worth individuals investing their own money through a VC firm.

VCs usually invest in companies in exchange for equity, not debt. While some VCs may invest in early-stage startups, it's more common for them to come in for later rounds simply because they can write bigger checks (for millions, instead of the thousands that angels usually invest). So the companies they fund tend to have experienced teams and viable products with proven sales. Because there are greater sums at stake, VCs focus on building companies with a firm eye on realizing a high multiple on their investment, either by the company being acquired or by going public via an IPO. It's also considered typical for VCs to ask for greater control of the company through board seats or provisions to replace founders with more professional management. On the plus side, venture-backed companies tend to grow faster, be more innovative, and have more sales and faster time to market. They also are more likely to go public and do better after the IPO.[21]

Within a VC firm different people have different roles. There are general partners (GPs), who actively manage the fund; limited partners (LPs), who are passive investors; and associates or analysts, who work with partners to find and vet deals for the partner to review. When you pitch a VC firm, you may be speaking first with an associate and talking directly with the partner only in later meetings. The good news is that associates *want* to find great companies for the partners, so they are often happy to hear your pitch. When partners come in, however, they will tend to bring a more realistic approach to vetting your company before investing. Eventually multiple partners at the fund will be involved in the decision to fund your company.

Partners have different specialization areas—sometimes within a vertical (consumer products, for example) or within a particular market (B2B). And because of the large amounts of capital they bring to the table, partners usually want to be actively involved in the companies they fund—taking board seats, for example—which limits their capacity to take on too many startups at once. Therefore, your job is to do your research on the VCs you will be pitching, and then get the partners so excited about your company that they will believe it will be worth not just their money but also their time. We'll talk more about the process of pitching a VC in Part III.

GrowthX is a VC firm that seeks out promising tech startups outside of the usual regions and then spends significant amounts of time training founders and their teams on the best way to bring their products to market. "The majority of these tech startups fail because they don't know how to make money—they only know how to raise it," says Sean Sheppard, founding partner. "Our focus has been on not developing products and raising money, like it is for most entrepreneurs and those that help them. Ours is focused on developing *markets* and *making* money."[22]

Nowadays the lines between angel investors and VCs are blurring somewhat, with the advent of so-called "super angels" or "micro VCs" that invest smaller amounts earlier in a startup's development. And some VCs will fund early-stage companies that show significant promise. There are several VC databases (VentureXpert, Dow Jones VentureSource, and Crunchbase, for example) that list active venture capital firms, and the National Venture Capital Association (NVCA) releases quarterly data on VC deals.

Many large companies, such as Google and Intel, have VC departments that focus on identifying and investing in startups. Also known as Corporate Venture Capital (CVCs), these investors are looking for innovation that will help their companies to grow, complementary products and services to their own offerings, and ways to shortcut product development and take advantage of new market opportunities. According to the Kauffman Foundation, corporate VC investment can offer startups access to corporate facilities and skilled R&D personnel, and greater manufacturing and regulatory know-how.[23] It's also more likely that the corporate VC may become the acquirer of the company down the road. However, the tradeoff for startups is the risk of the corporation simply adapting the new technology for its own purposes without acquiring the startup. Therefore, if you are considering working with a CVC, make sure to put safeguards in place to protect your IP, patents, or any other proprietary information.

Family Offices

Family offices are sources of funding that few startups know about, yet they represent vast pools of wealth seeking investment return. Family offices manage the assets and investments of high net worth individuals and families. As of 2016 there were more than three thousand family offices worldwide, managing a total of $4 trillion in assets.[24]

Family office money comes from two sources: inheritance from past generations, and wealth accumulated by current and former entrepreneurs. The focus of family offices is often primarily wealth preservation rather than growth, but today some younger entrepreneurs and inheritors are looking for growth as well.

Family offices typically have executive directors and possibly chief investment officers to oversee the family's capital. Historically, family offices have put the majority of their capital into hedge funds, real estate, and private equity via VC funds. However, as some family offices look to grow wealth instead of simply preserving it, they are becoming more open to investing in startups directly. In particular, when a family office's wealth has come from an entrepreneur's own businesses rather than an inheritance, there is often an interest in finding startups to mentor as well as fund.[25]

Family offices often take a longer-term approach to their investments: They are less interested in a three- to five-year exit than in realizing higher returns by building the company they are funding over time. However, because family offices typically invest on a deal-by-deal basis, there also can be more of a desire for active oversight of company operations via a seat on the board. Marcia Nelson has worked with family offices and their advisors for more than twenty years. She advises that if you are interested in approaching a family office for funding, make sure that you have a long-term business plan that demonstrates a commitment to providing lasting value for investors.[26]

While there are directories of family offices available, the deals these investors will consider are almost always sourced through their networks of investment bankers, other business executives, and colleagues of founders of previous deals. If you are interested in family office funding, see if you can connect to the executive director or chief investment officer through your network.

Crowdfunding

Crowdfunding of products and nonprofits has been around for at least a decade. However, in the last few years two new crowdfunding trends have directly affected startups looking for funding. First was the advent of peer-to-peer (P2P) online lending platforms, which put people and companies needing money together with those who are willing to lend it. Then in 2016, the JOBS Act—Title III (Regulation Crowdfunding) and Title IV (Regulation A+)—went into effect. For the first time in the U.S., companies were able to use online crowdfunding as a means to sell equity in their business to accredited investors. Companies can raise up to $1 million this way, but they must comply with SEC requirements to file financial and disclosure documents. In a little over two years, over $100 million in capital commitments had been raised in the U.S. through equity crowdfunding.[27] This is clearly an important new opportunity for startups to bypass traditional funding sources and to go straight to the "crowd" for their capital.

My friend and colleague Richard Swart, Ph.D., will cover crowdfunding in detail. Richard is the former director of Research Program for Innovation in Entrepreneurial and Social Finance at the University of California, Berkeley and coauthor of *Crowdfunding: The Corporate Era* (London, UK: Elliott & Thompson, 2015).

Richard Swart, Ph.D.: Crowdfunding: A Roadmap for Entrepreneurs

Crowdfunding—the use of online platforms to gather small amounts of money from a large and distributed network of individuals—has become a multibillion-dollar industry since its inception less than a decade ago.

As of 2017 more than $19.2 billion has been raised globally via crowdfunding. Startups, nonprofits, individuals, even large multinational corporations have utilized crowdfunding to underwrite the development of products and services, support artistic endeavors, and finance a variety of new ventures.

Crowdfunding is part integrated marketing campaign, part early-stage capital formation, part branding, and part sales. Just as the digital revolution has democratized the creation of knowledge, services, and products, crowdfunding has opened up traditional approaches to early-stage capital in an unprecedented way. Today equity crowdfunding investment opportunities are available in over eighty nations. Crowdfunding allows savvy entrepreneurs to maintain finer control over their companies, set terms with investors (rather than allowing the investor to set terms), and provide non-dilutive capital. Founders can overcome the obstacles posed by traditional funding sources, including reduced seed-stage funding, slow decisionmaking cycles of traditional funders, and the inability or unwillingness of many VCs to fund risky or newly established entities.

There are three main categories of crowdfunding: (1) donation and rewards, (2) "presale" crowdfunding, and (3) debt and equity crowdfunding.

In many ways *donation* crowdfunding is identical to the donation drives that charities and nonprofits have long used to raise funds. If you've seen a GoFundMe campaign to raise money for someone's medical bills or to help fund a school trip, you know this format. The donation model then evolved into *rewards* crowdfunding, where project backers or donors receive rewards tied to their level of contribution. There is a moral obligation to provide the promised reward, but no contractual obligations are established. (However, some state attorneys general have filed fraud charges against entrepreneurs who did not deliver promised products.)

A variation of rewards crowdfunding is the *"presale" model*, in which an entrepreneur offers a product before its manufacture through a presale campaign. The entrepreneur tests the market—"If I build it, will you buy it?"—without having to commit the usual up-front marketing, production, and distribution costs. Some of the most successful presale campaigns solicited not only capital but also feedback from contributors, which was then incorporated into product design and marketing. Campaigns like the "Pebble Smartwatch" essentially funded the process of taking a prototype into production. Entrepreneurs running successful presale campaigns gain access to non-diluted capital—actual revenue from sales before initiating production. They also gain a stronger hand when negotiating with investors, while investors lower their risks by making investments in products that have been validated by customers.

Equity and *debt crowdfunding* are distinct from the donation, rewards, and presale models in that entities are legally allowed to issue shares or debt instruments. Participants have the opportunity to profit from their investments rather than simply providing financial support for the project, organization, or firm seeking funding. Allowed by law in over eighty nations, the *equity crowdfunding* model involves the sale of a securities instrument (stock) in a company through a regulated, online platform. For early-stage ventures, equity crowdfunding is the equivalent of moving the "friends and family" round of financing online and including not just friends and family but also "followers and fans." It can also be a substitute or complement to angel investing.

For entrepreneurs and small enterprises, equity crowdfunding lowers the barriers required to offer shares in their companies and thereby enhances their access to capital. Raising funds online increases the pool of investors, speeds the funding lifecycle, and creates shared repositories of information that can be accessed at any time by investors or entrepreneurs. And since about 9 percent of crowdfunding backers end up being accredited investors, while their initial checks may be small, there's a real possibility to foster a relationship that can lead to larger, more strategic investments.

If an organization decides to utilize equity crowdfunding to raise capital, it should be understood that equity shares in crowdfunded companies must be considered illiquid assets that cannot be traded on active markets. Pay careful attention to the regulations of the country in which you launch your campaign. Regulations vary substantially across the world but generally require a process of background and financial checks before an investment offer can be distributed. Startups should conduct a process, legal, and accounting review of the crowdfunding model being considered before they launch.

In *debt-based crowdfunding*, individuals loan money to other individuals (peer-to-peer, or P2P) or to small businesses (peer-to-business, or P2B).

The debt platforms screen the applicants, underwrite the loans, assign an interest rate, and then essentially create an auction market where individuals are able to see available opportunities and lend parts of the total loan amount to the individuals or businesses. As of 2016, P2P loan volume in the U.S. was $35.4 billion.[28]

The P2P business provides a valuable channel for many startups to receive non-dilutive capital. Ventures that once required a VC backer may now be able to use crowdfunding and social networks to raise similar amounts of capital in a more fair, transparent, and entrepreneur-driven way.

Here are four keys to running a successful crowdfunding campaign.

1. *Focus on tangible, outcome-focused projects.* Crowdfunding must begin with a clear mission or passion that can be socially shared and is sufficiently concrete for others to understand. Running a series of crowdfunding events that support a broader growth plan is more effective than running a single, generalized fundraising campaign.

2. *Stay in touch with your "crowd" and convey passion, not lofty goals.* Backers often are motivated by being part of a community; the tangible reward or the ultimate outcome is less motivating than the experience of feeling like part of a crowdfunding campaign and being able to back the passion of an entrepreneur.

3. *Prepare for radical transparency.* Entrepreneurs must operate in a highly transparent manner, revealing their motivations and reasons for seeking funding. Granted, there are some risks inherent in public disclosure of technology, which starts the clock on the process of patent applications. Some firms also express concern that the degree of required disclosures may expose too much of their business plan and technology to potential competitors before they have the resources to compete effectively.

4. *Build credibility with the crowd via social media.* While building credibility with a large and engaged base of followers, friends, fans, and advocates is critical to crowdfunding success, there are specific restrictions on what can be shared on social-media platforms when a company is doing an equity crowdfunding raise under Regulation Crowdfunding of the JOBS Act of 2012. Essentially, the startup can only talk about

the fact that it is seeking investments and then direct traffic to its offering page on one of the approved platforms. The company cannot discuss terms of the offering, including the amount being raised, the share price, or any other detail of the security offering.

Crowdfunding has disrupted traditional early-stage investment and will likely continue to do so in profound and unexpected ways. By leapfrogging traditional models of investing and aggregating potential investors, crowdfunding has proven able to create multinational networks of backers that efficiently and transparently channel millions or tens of millions of dollars into new ventures and projects.

Initial Coin Offerings (ICOs) and Securities Token Offerings (STOs)

Imagine that you are an investor looking to purchase an equity stake in a brand-new, attractive startup. But when you go online to contact the company, you discover that the only way to invest is to purchase the firm's own digital currency, or tokens, that will be sold via an initial coin offering (ICO) token offering, or STO. The company will use the sale proceeds for its funding, and you as an investor will receive tokens that represent your equity share. Unlike traditional startup funding, however, where your money is tied up until the company either is acquired or goes public, your tokens are liquid from the first moment of purchase. You can trade them on secondary markets for an agreed-upon price. If the company does well, the value of tokens will go up. If not, you still have the chance to sell at any time and redeem at least some of your investment.

STOs are like a cross between an IPO and crowdfunding, combined with blockchain technology. As Matthew Sullivan, founder and president of the blockchain-based real estate marketplace, Quantum RE, states, "The idea is to take an asset, and the token becomes a currency, or a representation of the value of the asset."[29] In many cases, the asset can be equity in the company itself. During the STO, tokens are sold to investors. Once the STO is complete, the tokens would be available for secondary market trading on regulated, blockchain-secured exchanges. Capital raised from the sale of tokens represented $5.9 billion in capital investment in the United States alone in 2017, and, according to its advocates, may outstrip venture capital investing totals worldwide as of 2018.[30]

Liquidity is one major advantage of tokenized investments. With typical VC or angel investment, the earliest point they can realistically expect to realize a return is five to ten years. But as Matthew Sullivan observed, with tokens, liquidity can be front-ended as opposed to being back-ended, and there is potential for a return within a much shorter timeframe—something almost any investor would be excited about.[31]

That said, STOs are still evolving as a capital strategy, and regulatory bodies in the United States and elsewhere are looking closely at the ramifications of how STOs are offered. In the United States, STOs are securities that need to be registered with the SEC or operate under a relevant exemption. Do you need to be an accredited investor to buy into an STO? If you are interested in exploring an STO for raising capital, consult a good securities attorney and CPA first.

Paul Martens advised Lendroid, a blockchain-based global lending and margin trading system. He is a passionate advocate for tokenized offerings and their power to disrupt and democratize the fundraising experience for entrepreneurs. Here's his story.

In 2015 I moved to San Francisco from Florida, wanting to launch my startup among the best and the brightest, to give my company a fighting chance. To make ends meet and stockpile a bit of cash for personal runway I worked at three companies over a period of three years: one post-IPO, one that had just finished their Series B, and a company which just received their seed capital. Simultaneously I was hunting for the best talent.

Running a software company is more than just a great founding team, however: it's also procuring world-class investors. While I was looking for a cofounder, an old friend pulled me part-time into his startup: Lendroid. At the time Lendroid was hardly a blip on the radar. It was slowly building up key technology partnerships. More important than that, I discovered quickly, it was creating grassroots momentum among potential investors.

While it's always been the task of an entrepreneur to build hype around a product, never in the history of tech could that hype directly and immediately transfer to financial support from the masses. The audience we wanted to reach wasn't VCs with limited technical knowledge; instead, we sought deeply technical individuals worldwide who were ready to put their money on the line.

It's clear that the fundraising rules for tech have changed drastically in a brief period of time. Blockchain didn't just decentralize how we want databases run, but it also decentralized how capital is raised as well. We were witnessing firsthand a sixty-year-old capital raise model disintegrate before our very eyes. At Lendroid we were thrilled when we got $6 million of non-VC investor support, but that quickly pushed past $50 million. And that fundraising came from anywhere but Silicon Valley.

Today I advise clients who've also realized that the tech and funding landscape has radically shifted. Young entrepreneurs now recognize that decentralized technology is a path to a more ethical and secure relationship with customer data. The modern tech entrepreneur with blockchain technology in their arsenal still plugs away at product and protocols, but this new tokenized funding strategy demands every idea be incredibly ambitious and be pitched internationally.

Gone are the days where the right thing to do was head to Silicon Valley and raise seed support from a handful of investors. The wise tech entrepreneur now has to solve problems of enormous magnitude with the help of thousands from around the world.[32]

I have been working closely with Sergey Sholom, who used crowdfunding to raise capital for GNation, an innovative gaming platform. Here is a little of his story.[33]

The project started in a truly dark time. We split ways with a partner we had worked with for almost ten years. Our recently released projects were not performing well enough to support their own existence. We had just two hopes remaining: a new game, and a third party mobile store platform. We had continuously spent more and more on building it, and the revenue from our previously released games was running out fast.

Then we accidentally met some people that were dealing with something new to us: cryptocurrencies and blockchain. For us as game developers, the concept of virtual money wasn't new, as well as the idea that such money can have a real value, but it was still so strange that I couldn't even find any starting point to evaluate using this to raise money for our company. In the end I had to rely on my gut feeling. That was scary.

In mid-2016, we were trying to find a business model that could be applicable. We added all the possible value we could: our names, games, the store platform, and everything else, but it still wasn't working. On the one hand no investor from the classical world would give us a dime, and I could understand it—at that moment ICOs were completely unexplored. We'd put a lot of effort into finding some natural way to grow our new venture, but nothing was working out and we were running out of money.

In the end, we accepted the idea of crowdfunding. It took us four months to prepare for it: understanding the strategy, presenting it to the people, doing the roadshows. It was hard, and so was the crowdfunding period itself (which lasted for a month but I believe took several years of life from everyone in our team). Raising funds from crowdfunding brought a great responsibility for all of us. We needed to define a lot of new products and new strategies as well in this quickly changing world. But we didn't have a right to give up. We could only keep working, evolving our ideas and products.

That was exactly the moment GNation was born: when we realized that something we are creating is so big it cannot be named in some casual way. We were not any more in the "mobile store" business. We were creating a new way for the whole gaming industry to operate with real people. Our goal was to redefine everything that existed before, start from scratch and give all the benefits to those who really deserve it: the gamers and game developers who make up more than 30 percent of the world's population. In our belief, GNation is going to become the largest force for good in this planet by uniting billions of people and providing them with all the abilities and tools to make this world a better place altogether. It's so enormous—absolutely inspiring and terrifying at the same moment. And it was our crowdsale, and the trust of thousands of people, that allowed us to reach this moment.

No matter how you raise capital or who you raise it from, the key is to understand your funding needs for the stage of your business, and then approach the right investor and the right investment form at the right time. That's the focus of our next chapter.

4

YOUR FUNDING ROADMAP

How to Find and Reach the People Who Can Help You

> Fundraising is a process that takes time and is rarely quick or painless. The earlier you start planning your process and developing relationships, the better off you will be.[1]
>
> **—CARLOS EDUARDO ESPINAL**

Few entrepreneurs enjoy fundraising. They started businesses to bring great ideas to market, and taking time away from that endeavor is tough, especially in the early stages of the company where it seems they have to do everything themselves. In addition, fundraising is not an activity designed to boost the ego. You're likely to get dozens of *no*'s before you hear one *yes*. "Fundraising. It definitely has a 'd' in it, as in *it's really not fun, raising*," writes VC and entrepreneur Mark Suster. "But it's critical for your business, for you as a leader, and people who excel at fundraising have an extreme advantage over those who do not."[2]

For the majority of startups, fundraising is necessary because they need more capital than founders can provide or than first revenues can support. So the goal should be to make fundraising as efficient and effective as possible. You can do this in four ways. First, you must get yourself ready by *knowing your numbers*—meaning your cash burn rate, capital structure, and capitalization table. Second, you'll need to *set your funding goals* based on where you are, where you want to be, what stage you consider your company to be in, the period of time you want investor funding to cover, and what milestones that funding will allow you to reach. You'll have to determine what you believe the company valuation is today and how much debt or equity you're willing to give in exchange for investor capital.

Third, you must *target the investors you wish to reach*, researching their needs to determine how you can position your startup to gain their interest and eventually their capital. Finally, you must understand the funding process—seed rounds, preseed rounds, early-stage rounds, series A, B, and so on—and *create a roadmap* that will help you maximize the time you spend in the actual fundraise itself.

As I said in Chapter 3, the best capital you can receive comes from customers paying for your product or service, as that revenue validates your business model. At the same time it doesn't dilute your share of the business, or put you under obligation to banks or investors. Therefore, the worst thing you can do is to let fundraising distract you from building your business. But in the same way you should create and follow a business plan to be more effective as an entrepreneur, you should build a plan to make your funding campaign more efficient and effective.

Step 1: Know Your Numbers

Every entrepreneur who faces the sharks on *Shark Tank* has heard the commandment, "Know your numbers." Before you can ask an investor for funding, you need to be completely clear as to the amount of money you need to take your product from idea to demo (in the case of preseed funding) or to keep your business growing until it is acquired or goes public (in the case of later rounds). That requires you to have a clear picture of where you are today, before any additional funding. You must know (1) your current *cash burn rate*, and (2) your startup's *capital structure*, which lays out the equity and debt you have used to build and run the business so far. You also should have (3) a *capitalization table*, or *cap table*, so you can see everyone who currently owns the equity in your startup.

Your cash burn rate is the amount of money you "burn" through each month to run the business. Knowing how much you spend on a monthly basis today will allow you to figure out how much more you will need to hire a key employee, or build your product, or fund a marketing campaign. That and other key milestones will form the basis of the calculation of your request for funding. Your cash burn rate also helps you figure out how much time you have left until you run out of money—an important metric that you (and investors) will use to determine the survivability of your company, and how much time an investor's money will be able to give you. Especially in the beginning, smart startup entrepreneurs do their best to keep their cash burn rate as low as they can.

The capital structure of your business essentially shows who you owe what (in the form of debt and equity), and the order in which each of those holders gets paid back in the event of a liquidation event, acquisition, or IPO. For example, loans to your business might be classified as senior (meaning, they are paid back first) or subordinated (paid after senior loans). Other forms of debt include *convertible notes*: loans that can be converted into equity at a certain point in the business's life, usually at the discretion of the convertible noteholder (often when the startup raises its first round of investor capital). Because a valuation does not need to be established or negotiated to issue a convertible note, it is often a fast way for founders to raise money. Like traditional debt, a convertible note has a principal amount and interest, which accrues over the term of the note and is added to the amount available to convert into equity. There often is a target valuation for the startup on a convertible note, and a cap on the amount that noteholders will pay for shares no matter when they convert the debt to equity.

Equity in a business represents the holders' ability to access portions of a company's future profits. It comes in two forms: common and preferred stock. A startup typically will issue common shares early, as a simple way to represent the value of the company to founders, employees, and early investors. Owners of common stock are the last to receive any profits from the company's activities.

Professional investors will usually insist on receiving *preferred* shares, which can be converted into common shares at a later point in the start-up's life. Preferred shares receive participation preference—meaning, in the event of a liquidation, acquisition, or IPO, preferred shares are paid off right behind debtholders, usually with an amount equal to or a multiple of the original investment. Other preferred share rights are negotiated as part of the investment deal. However, unlike common shares, preferred shares usually have no voting rights.

Because debt (including principal and interest) has to be paid off before equity, a debt-heavy capital structure is less attractive to investors. It may mean that a company receives less investor interest and harsher terms. It's also the reason that even seed-stage startups will tend to use equity to compensate founders, employees, and initial investors. After all, equity is essentially a promise that the shareholder will benefit from any profits or increase in the business's value—in the future. So in a way, it costs founders nothing to give valued team members and outside investors equity in the company. However ... every percentage of equity that you give away *dilutes*, or reduces, the percentages held by previous investors (including the founders). The number of shares a company issues is meaningless—it's only the percentages that count. And while adding new investors will dilute the founders' stock, if the infusion of capital will be used to grow the company it will increase the value of every share and thus benefit the founders in that way.

To see how the equity in your company has been allocated, you need to create a *capitalization table*, or *cap table*. Your capital structure and cap table are important because they tell you who owns pieces of your company and how much they own. It also will give you an idea of how much flexibility you have when giving shares of equity in exchange for an investor's capital. You should keep a detailed cap table as a way of tracking shareholder information, but for the purposes of investment rounds and assuming you are a seed-stage startup, you only need the following information:

- Number of common shares given to founders.

- Number of common shares given to any "friends and family" investors.

- Number of common shares (issued and unissued) allocated to the employee option pool. These stock options "sweeten the pot" for employees and also can be used to pay for services by attorneys or accountants in addition to (or in lieu of) cash.

- Any warrants that have been issued. Warrants are options for outside parties to purchase equity from the company at a certain price. You may give warrants to early investors in lieu of actual common shares.

Here's a sample premoney cap table—meaning, before any new investment capital has been raised.

Shareholder	Shares	Percent
Founder 1	500,000	41.6
Founder 2	450,000	37.5
Friend (investor)	50,000	4.2
Employee Option Pool: Issued	0	0
Employee Option Pool: Issued	200,000	16.7
Warrants	0	0
Total	1,200,000	100

Remember, the number of shares doesn't matter, only the percentages. You will use your current cap table in step 2, when you set your funding goals and run the numbers on how much capital to raise and how much equity you should give in return. You also will use the cap table to determine the current valuation of your company.

Step 2: Set Your Funding Goals

Armed with your cash burn rate, capital structure, and cap table, you're ready to establish specific goals as to (1) what you want to do next to make your business grow, (2) how long you think it will take you to do those things, and (3) how much money you will you need to keep going during that time. These funding goals are not based upon a particular dollar figure but driven by what you need to accomplish to reach the next stage of business growth. For example, are there key hires you need to make? Do you need to build a product prototype, or begin to manufacture? Is it time to bring in a marketing firm to run a campaign to reach more users, or to prove there is a significant market for your product or service?

Set your goals for the next twelve to eighteen months and put in timelines for the specific milestones you wish to reach, and then calculate how much money you will need (on top of your current monthly cash burn) to accomplish those milestones. Augment this number by at least 10 to

40 percent to cover unexpected costs as your company grows. This will be the starting number for your request for investor capital. It's better to ask for too much than too little: Not being able to reach a milestone because you ran out of cash makes you appear less than impressive to an investor. Asking for a specific amount that is clearly linked to the accomplishment of specific milestones will make you seem a more credible risk than simply asking for a round sum like $500,000 or $1 million. Investors will find it easier to judge your progress, and see it as an incentive to continue investing in your business. That said, especially in the seed stage it's important for you and your investors to allow for pivots and drastic changes to necessary milestones.

Using milestones as a gauge for the funding you need gives you the opportunity to suggest a range of investment rather than just one number. For example, imagine that you have a potential investor who asks you how much you would like to raise. You can reply with something along these lines: "This is what I need: [ideal number based on what you think will be key milestones], but this is what I can accomplish [one or two other meaningful milestones behind the big one] with this [smaller number] capital."[3] It's a powerful strategy to use when you are at seed stage, speaking with angel investors who might not want to cover the full amount you are asking for but who will be happy to give you enough to prove yourself and your business model. Indeed, it's good to create multiple funding plans based upon your ability to raise different amounts under different conditions. Investor Heidi Roizen calls this a *waterfall chart*: It's a spreadsheet showing what happens to your equity if you take X amount from Investor A in exchange for Y percent, or if Investor B gives you a convertible note that grants her XX preferred shares at a subsequent funding round.

With your funding requirements in hand, next you need to determine how much equity that money will buy. You do this by calculating the current premoney value of your startup. ("Premoney" means before you receive the investment capital.) As president of Junior Achievement Worldwide Asheesh Advani points out, valuation is more of an art than science, especially prior to any investing round. Your job as founder is to establish a starting point valuation so you can determine how much equity you will offer investors in exchange for their money.

Once you enter into any fundraising, however, the marketplace (i.e., investors) will set the valuation of your business. While we will discuss several business valuation methods in Chapter 10, Advani recommends that founders of any prerevenue, idea stage, or seed-stage startup compare the company to similar ones in its industry and region. There also are attorneys and CPAs who specialize in valuing businesses; it might be worthwhile to engage their services.[4]

Once you have an estimated valuation, you can use your cap table to calculate the premoney price per share and value of each equity shareholders' stake. Let's take the cap table you saw earlier and plug in a premoney valuation of $2.4 million.

Shareholder	Shares	Value	Percent
Founder 1	500,000	$1,000,000	41.6
Founder 2	450,000	$900,000	37.5
Friend (investor)	50,000	$100,000	4.2
Employee Option Pool: Issued	0	0	0
Employee Option Pool: Issued	200,000	$400,000	16.7
Warrants	0	0	0
Total	1,200,000	$2,400,000	100
Price per share: $2,400,000 / 1,200,000 = $2.00			

Finally, you need to compare the valuation to the amount you need to raise in order to reach the milestones you described earlier, and see if it is realistic based upon the amount of equity you would need to give up. With the above example, if the founders wanted to raise $1 million, with a premoney valuation of only $2.4 million they would have to give up almost half of the equity in the company—and that's too much. The goal is to give up no more than 10 to 30 percent dilution per round, to allow the founders, employees, and earlier investors to have something left after investors have taken their share.

On the other hand, you don't want too high a valuation either. An overly high early valuation can cause a startup to run the risk of a "down round"—a later round of funding with a valuation below the previous figure. (Investors want to see valuations go *up* between rounds, as this indicates the startup is finding its feet and starting to perform. Rising valuations make investors more likely to pour more capital into a company as it looks like a better risk.) Even though many founders like high valuations because it means they have to give less equity in exchange for an investor's money, a relatively accurate valuation will be better for the business in the long run.

Be sure that you know what percentages work for you when it comes to giving investors equity in your business. Walk in with an idea of what you believe would constitute a reasonable portion of equity, and if appropriate, be like the entrepreneurs in *Shark Tank*: Tell investors up front how much capital you are looking for and what percentage of your company you're willing to give in return. "I like entrepreneurs to make the first offer in equity," said Gina Danner, an investor with Women's Capital Connection. "They had the idea. I want to make sure the equity I'm taking keeps them engaged and thrilled to grow it."[5] Remember that in every subsequent funding round you may be called upon to give up a few more percentage points of the value of your company. You're doing the hard work of growing your startup—make sure you feel you will be rewarded for those efforts.

In a blog post on "How to Raise Money," Y Combinator founder Paul Graham wrote, "There are almost two distinct modes of fundraising: one in which founders who need money knock on doors seeking it, knowing that otherwise the company will die or at the very least people will have to be fired, and one in which founders who don't need money take some to grow faster than they could merely on their own revenues."[6] When you know your numbers and your funding goals are clear, you're ready to go out and find the investors you need.

Step 3: Target Your Ideal Investors

In Chapter 3 you learned about the different types of investors that are appropriate for different stages of fundraising. Now you're going to focus in on finding your ideal investors, based upon your company's history and stage of development.

Start by envisioning your "dream team" of investors. Yes, I know, you might not have done any research yet, so you don't know which angel, angel group, VC, family office, or investing platform is best for you. But you *can* put together a list of the qualities you want in these people. "Just like there's a specific audience for the unique product or service you're trying to launch, it's also true that there's a unique, target investor base for your company," observes startup entrepreneur Mike Belsito. "Before you begin pitching just anybody, sit down and outline the ideal investor types you want on your team."[7]

Think especially carefully about your first investors, as they will tend to have an outsized effect on your company simply because they are first. What do you want them to bring to your team? Market expertise? Customer insights? Connections? What are you missing that these investors could supply? Do you need greater financial acumen? Someone who can create systems for reaching and supporting customers? A "think outside the box" industry maven? A manufacturing or product development expert? A brand builder? A connector who can put you in touch with other people and investors to help you grow?

Then choose the category of investors that would be most suited to the stage of your company and the level of funding you will be seeking. Do you need to focus on angel investors first, and if so, should you reach out to angel groups? (When getting ready to approach angels for funding, make sure you create an online profile for your startup on sites like AngelList and GUST.) Should you start locally, especially if you are outside of the typical venture capital hubs of California, New York, and Boston?

Most investors tend to specialize in particular industries or regions, so do your research. Look at written material about them, their firm, any angel or VC groups they belong to, and so on. Check out archive editions of publications like *Venture Beat* and *PitchBook*, as well as the Angel Capital Association, and the National Venture Capital Association, to see what deals they have done. Talk with the entrepreneurs whom they have funded or other people the investor knows.

You should target anywhere from twenty to forty investors to research thoroughly. Here are a few of the questions you should ask about each investor you are targeting.

- What's their specialty as far as investing? What size deals do they seem to prefer? What's their average check size? How big is their fund, and is it fully subscribed or is there still some more room? If someone is used to closing $1 million deals and you come to them asking for $100,000 at the idea stage, they won't take you seriously. And if you need $1 million and approach a local angel whose biggest investment to date has been $35,000, that's not going to work either.

- What deals have they already done? Find out deal size, length of time, how many successful exits, and other deal characteristics they seem to prefer.

- How many investments do they make a year, and how many active deals are they involved with? This is a key question, as angels are investing their own funds, and the VC might currently be busy raising capital to start a new fund because the old one is fully committed. Do they have specific equity ownership targets that they like to propose?

- How well connected are they? Have they ever coinvested with anyone?

- Are they young and hungry and more likely to get you in on the ground floor of the latest funding trend? Or is this a seasoned investor who can mentor you and give you the benefit of forty years of business experience? What's their overall style of communication, and are you both a good fit for each other? Make sure to ask about the last company they backed, and why.

- What value can they bring to your startup in addition to money? "Professional investors usually bring 'smart money' to the table, defined as money that comes along with good advice and great relationships for corporate growth," writes the "dean" of early-stage angel investing, Dave Berkus.[8]

- What's the likelihood that they will be the first to say *yes* to your offer? The hardest investment to get is always the first one, and because investors are risk averse, few are willing to take a chance on you until someone else has committed.

- How many times have they done follow-on investments with startups? Can they lead you to other investors when you need to raise more capital?

Next, research how you can reach the investor directly. A solo angel investor might answer your phone call, while an angel group, accelerator, or incubator may ask for applications or ask you to come in to pitch at one of their monthly meetings. When pursuing a VC, you probably will have to plan on several meetings yourself, and then wait until the entire funding committee reviews your presentation. (This is especially true when the VC is writing you a big check.) I suggest you capture all of this information in a spreadsheet that you can refer to throughout the funding process.

Remember, the investors you choose will be part of the life and leadership of your startup for years to come, so it's wise to take the time up front to ensure they are the right people to help you build your business.

Step 4: Create and Follow Your Funding Roadmap

You're now ready to create a strategic plan to get in front of the investors that will fund your business at its current stage. As part of your plan, put together a timeline of how long you believe it will take you to raise the capital you need. Fundraising will be an important activity for your business during those weeks or months, just like marketing, sales, product development, and so on, and having schedules and benchmarks will help keep you on track. Select one person (usually the founder/CEO) to lead the fundraising campaign so everyone else at the company can keep working on building the business. Be aware, however, that the first time you approach investors for funding is usually the hardest and takes the longest. So plan your fundraising "campaign" with this in mind, and put contingencies in place to keep the business going if it takes a while to land your first investor.

Financing is organized in *rounds*, each of which has a dollar figure attached to it. The round you're in will depend on the stage of your business, the amount of money you want to raise, and the type of investors you intend to pursue. Startups typically go through several rounds of funding throughout their lifetime. You should do your best to take just enough money in each round to keep going and growing your business to the next stage.

The first funding round is usually a *seed* round. Note: In some businesses, such as technology, there may also be a *preseed* or *idea* round. Serial entrepreneurs with a proven track record may ask for funding to work on an idea for a product or service, and investors who have worked with these founders before may be willing to put up the money. However, most startup founders will start with a seed round.

Seed funding is just what it sounds like: money to grow the "seed" of your business until it becomes viable. The goal of seed funding is to cover your expenses so you can hit your milestones for the next twelve to eighteen months. Seed funding may help you turn your demo product into a more workable iteration, for example, or help you hire a key team member, or give you enough capital to grow your customer base beyond the first few currently signed up for your service.

Depending on your business, seed funding can be anywhere from $10,000 to $750,000 (that higher number would only be for complicated, expensive industries like biotech or medical devices). You're usually approaching angels and certain VC funds specializing in seed funding, and they may offer you convertible notes or safes (*simple agreements for future equity*, which you'll learn about in Chapter 10) rather than asking for a percentage of equity up front. Because the amounts are relatively small, the process may take only one or two meetings before you receive an offer. At this point most startups are prerevenue, so your ability to raise money will be due largely to your ability to communicate your story, your vision for the company, and the team you have in place. Unless you have a spectacular track record as an entrepreneur, you also can expect to hear a lot of *no*'s. That's why the seed-stage funding round is a great opportunity for you to test out your story and your business model and make significant revisions to both.

Seed-stage investors are betting on you and your team more than they are on your business, because they know how frequently seed-stage startups will pivot as they learn more about their market or further develop their product or service. They know the chances of one particular startup succeeding are slim, so as Andrew Goldner (founding partner of seed-stage venture fund GrowthX) puts it, they're looking not just for home runs but grand slams. To GrowthX that means a three times cash on cash return, but every investor's goals will be slightly different.[9]

Next is the *early-stage* round, also called an angel round. (Not all startups go through each round in turn. Some go straight to early-stage funding or even to series A, which I'll describe below. Others may be acquired after the early-stage round, or go out of business after raising a little seed capital.) Your startup is further along, with more customers, perhaps a product in its second or third iteration; perhaps you've already changed your business model at least once. But it's likely that your revenues are still not enough to cover expenses (which have risen), so you need more capital—maybe $500,000 to $1 million.

It's quite possible that you will need multiple investors to make up your early-stage raise amount. However, if you've gotten prior seed-stage capital and used it to hit the promised milestones, more investors will be willing to consider your startup at this stage. Some of your seed-stage investors also may provide you with follow-on investments, this time asking for equity instead of using a convertible note or safe. According to *The American Angel* 2017 report, "75.9 percent of investors made at least one follow-on investment, and 49.4 percent of angels have made three or more follow-on investments."[10]

Early-stage investors include angels, angel syndicates or groups, and some VCs. Because you are raising larger amounts here, the process often will take longer than a seed-stage round—from six to eight months. Angel groups or syndicates and VC firms will need to get to know you, like you, and trust you, and this takes time and research on their part. These organizations also have processes and pipelines of investments, and your funding request will be reviewed along with dozens of others.

Both seed-stage and early-stage rounds are designed to give startups the support to prove their ideas and get their businesses up and running. In the next funding round, *series A*, your business concept should have been proven and your ideas validated. Investors are less likely to pay for a lot of experiments and more likely to look for strong growth, a working product, an expanding customer base, a demonstrated ability to hit most of your major milestones, and oh yes—profitability if at all possible. Investors should believe that your company is on the path to an acquisition or IPO.

Series A focuses primarily on VC-level investment of $2 to $5 million and up. (After this point, funding rounds are designated by the letters B, C, and so on.) While some super angels (ultra high net worth individuals who invest their own money) and angel syndicates may invest in series A rounds, most of the time the money will come from (1) VC funds that invest other people's money, (2) corporate VCs that use the organization's capital, and (3) family offices. Depending on the size of the funding request, it's also possible that a VC who participated in your early-stage round may continue to invest and bring in other VCs to fill in the remaining capital need in what's called a syndicated round.

In series A, your startup's valuation should have risen enough to make pursuing another round of capital (and giving away more equity) worthwhile. The capital you're requesting will be used to grow the business into one that can be acquired or go public within the next five to seven years and provide series A investors with significant returns. Competition for series A funding is fierce, and it can take quite a while for you to get in front of a VC, much less get offered a deal. In 2014, Sean Jacobsohn, a venture partner at Emergence Capital, described the firm's pipeline as follows: "In order to make 10 investments, the average venture capital firm reviews approximately 1,200 companies . . . [which leads to] approximately 500 face-to-face meetings with someone on the investment team. Yet only 10 percent progress from that stage. . . . In a typical midsize venture firm, the fifty companies may generate ten investments."[11]

It should be clear that in any funding round you'll hear *no* frequently: it's just easier for investors who see hundreds of startups a year to turn you down for any reason at all. Don't let it get to you. Learn any lessons you can and move on to the next meeting. And remember: Founders who are better prepared with a great story, solid financials, and traction get funded fastest. In Part II you'll learn how to make yourself more attractive to investors at any stage.

Because you are dealing with institutional investors and teams of people who make decisions, you will need to find a champion for your startup— one partner who will advocate for you in the committee meetings with other VCs. You also can expect a more thorough process than you experienced in earlier rounds. VCs and other investors will question your assumptions and verify your numbers even before offering you a deal. And

VCs talk with each other. They'll want to know who you've already approached for funding and if the other VC has offered you a deal. This is positive in that if one VC thinks you're worth funding, others may be happy to make you an offer too, and you can play one off the other to get better terms. On the other hand, if one VC turns you down, others will hear about it. If someone says *no*, find out why, and then address those concerns before you reach out to the next investor.

Here are a few final notes on your funding roadmap:

- Know when to stop. It's easy to get caught up in the process and keep going, either because you're getting lots of offers or you're not getting enough. Once you've hit your funding goals, you're better off taking the money and putting it to work in your business before you go back and raise any more. Your business will be in better shape and you'll get better terms. After you've approached all of the investors on your original list plus a few more, if you're not getting enough offers to reach your goal it's probably a sign that you need to stop fundraising and go back to work—either revising your business, or your pitch, or your funding assumptions. Do whatever it takes to bootstrap a little longer and see if you can get more traction to make you more attractive to investors.

- Try to avoid tranched investments. A tranche is where investors dole out parts of the total committed capital according either to a schedule or your meeting certain milestones. While it may seem logical (you receive money, put it to work, get a result, and then you get the next piece of funding), a startup is a fluid environment, and the milestones needed for you to grow the business may change significantly. If investors insist on using tranches, suggest a convertible note instead.

- If you are raising $250,000 and above, you are likely to need investments from at least a few sources. Watch your equity distribution, and don't give too much away. Use your waterfall chart to run various scenarios to ensure you keep enough equity to make the deal worthwhile for you and your employees.

- Don't reject an acceptable offer hoping that a better one is around the corner. And don't assume that once an investor makes you an offer that everything is done. Deals fall through at every stage, and nothing is guaranteed until the money is in your account.

While fundraising should never be the primary focus of your business, it is something that you should always keep in mind. Even after you've just completed a round, keep in touch with possible investors on a regular basis. Maintain and nurture those valuable relationships so that the next time you go to the market for capital, you'll have investors lined up and ready to see what you have to offer. And keep building your company: That's the best guarantee of funding that you could ever have.

5

NETWORK YOUR WAY
TO THE RIGHT INVESTORS

Driven people with great ideas find a way to investors.[1]
—**ASHTON KUTCHER,** actor and investor, Sound Ventures

When Paul Revere and William Dawes both rode out on the night of April 18, 1775, they sounded the alarm that the British were planning a surprise attack outside of Boston. Dawes rode south while Paul Revere rode north, and both went through the same type of villages. But most of the citizens who fought at the battle Lexington and Concord had been alerted due to the ride of Paul Revere—not William Dawes. Why? *Paul Revere was well-connected.* He knew a lot of powerful people and had friends and acquaintances throughout the area. And during his ride that night, he sought out other well-connected people and asked them to spread the word in their towns.[2]

As you begin your own funding "ride," you too must seek out well-connected people who can help you reach the investors you need. But it's not enough simply to knock on doors: You need to knock on the *right* doors, to get you in the *right* rooms, in front of the *right* investors. Strategic networking helps startup founders solve the tough problems, like getting funded. *Strategic networking is your key to success.*

I spend a lot of time advising founders and entrepreneurs about strategic networking because I've made a study of the topic. I'm known as the woman with the platinum Rolodex because of my extensive connections in business, government, industry, finance, and yes, in the angel investor and VC worlds. My business is based around connecting people with the resources and individuals they need to get funded fast. Over and over I've seen the truth of the statement, "Your network equals your net worth." A robust network can provide you with greater information, leverage, status, borrowed credibility, access, and power. Every strategic relationship you develop connects you to an entire web of people that you can call upon as needed. With a diverse network of strategic relationships, if one connection doesn't lead to the person or resource you need or wish to share, you have ten others to call upon. And with some careful planning and targeted outreach, you can utilize your current network while adding to it selectively, so you can reach the investors you want.

Because the investment community is a highly interconnected world, most investors understand the power of strategic networking. In venture capital, your network is one of the most valuable assets you own. Investors know each other; they talk with each other; and they actively build and maintain their networks because that's where their best deals will come from. They get referrals from other investors, entrepreneurs they've worked with in the past (especially those that have made them money), current portfolio companies, other entrepreneurs they know and respect, top-notch service providers (attorneys and bankers, for instance), academics, industry experts they've met at conferences or demo days, and so on.[3] And investors expect entrepreneurs to make the effort to reach them through their networks rather than a cold call or email.

The interconnectivity of the investment world has its upside and downside for startup founders. The upside is that once you secure investors, they will typically use their networks to open other doors for you. The larger their networks, the more connections you can access for future funding rounds—plus, you will have the power of the investors' personal introductions behind you. In addition, your strategic relationships with investors may well help to sway future funding decisions in your favor. A 2012 study cited in *Inc.* magazine stated that social ties between venture capitalists and entrepreneurs seeking funding are more important in the funding decision than whether a prestigious VC firm has already committed to the deal.[4] Your investors' credibility and reputation will make your startup seem attractive to others.

The downside is that unless you can obtain a personal introduction to an investor, it can be difficult to get your foot in the door. "If you have no track record and you cold call an investor, you have huge reputational obstacles to overcome," writes David Hornik, general partner at VC firm August Capital. "Many investors will assume that you were either unable to find someone to make the introduction or too naive to realize the importance of an introduction."[5]

The focus of this chapter is how to build a strong, strategic network that you can use to reach investors via a "warm" introduction from someone they know. You'll learn to think strategically about the connections you need to make—who those people are, where they can be found, and how best to connect with them—so you can reach the right investors in the right way.

Who's in Your Network Already?

When Tony Robbins was just beginning to build his personal development empire, one of the richest men in Canada gave him some excellent advice. "Tony, because you know so many people in the entertainment industry you could get a movie made in a heartbeat," the billionaire said. "But how many investment bankers do you know? If you want access to capital, you need to spend time with people who operate in that world."

Many startup founders know a lot of people just like them—young, entrepreneurial, maybe well-connected via university or graduate school—but they lack ties to the VC and angel investment worlds, nor do they have many contacts with bankers or other high-level professionals. They may not even know people from the other startups in their geographical area because they're been too busy to network, or they consider other startups as their competition. But as the Canadian billionaire pointed out, the people you know will determine your ability to access the important resources you and your company need. You must actively seek to build a network of high-quality connections of people who can help you, and whom you can help as well.

You start by knowing who's already in your network. Let's do a variation of an exercise recommended by Brian Uzzi, professor at Northwestern University Kellogg School of Management.[6] Begin by making a list of the people you interact with regularly, both personally and through your business. Put a star next to the names of those with whom you have strong relationships. The cofounder of your startup, for instance, would rate a star; your dry cleaner may not.

Now, organize your list using the following form.

1. Your Top 25–50 Connections	Rank (1–5)	2. Past Interactions and Value Given & Received	3. Possible Networking Opportunities
1.			
2.			
3.			
4.			
5.			
6.			
7.			
8.			
9.			
10.			
11.			
12.			
13.			
14.			
15.			
16.			
17.			
18.			
19.			
20.			

In column 1, write the top twenty-five to fifty connections on your list—the people you believe will be of the greatest help to you in reaching investors. Next to their names, put a ranking on a scale of 1 (least) to 5 (most) according to the amount of influence, gravitas, wealth, expertise, or connections this person has. Those with a ranking of 4 and above are the VIPs in your network.

In column 2, write where you met this person and/or where you interact with them. At your workplace? At church? Through sports? Via your kids? Through university? Make notes about the things you have in common, as well as any value you have exchanged lately in terms of favors, recommendations, resources, and so on.

In column 3, brainstorm potential networking opportunities these VIPs could provide. Can they introduce you to their bankers, attorneys, CPAs? Do they know investors? Do they live in places like New York or northern California where many angel investors and VCs reside? Who might they know that could help you reach investors?

Now, go back to your original list of everyone in your network and highlight anyone you would consider a "superconnector." Superconnectors are really good at putting people in touch with one another. They may not be the most influential in terms of social status or wealth, but they seem to know a lot of individuals from diverse groups. More important, they like making connections between the people they know and the resources those people may need. For example, when you were looking to buy a house, maybe the soccer coach for your daughter's team introduced you to a great realtor, then put you in touch with her bank for the mortgage, and finally gave you links to research about different neighborhoods where you might like to move. Superconnectors focus on providing value for people they know—and they can do the same for you in your search for investors. These are some of the first people you should approach with a simple question: "Who do you know that might help me connect with investors?"

As important as superconnectors are, however, *anyone* in your network may provide the introduction you need. A few years ago Wendy Keller, my literary agent, called me and said, "You need to know Mike Muhney—he's the founder of ACT! Software." When Mike came up to Salt Lake City to meet with me, I said to him, "I've never heard of your software, what are you doing to build your brand?" He told me, "If I could just get in *Success* magazine, it'd be a lot easier for me to grow my visibility." I said, "Well, have you asked Wendy to introduce you to Darren Hardy? He's a friend of hers, and he happens to be the founder and publisher of *Success* magazine." Mike almost fell out of his chair.

I see so many entrepreneurs looking for funding who haven't bothered to share their story with the people in their own network, and therefore they are missing out on the contacts that might lead to investors. Often it's the friends of friends of friends (what are called second or third level connections on LinkedIn) that will connect you to a particular resource. So your first step on the funding journey is to let everyone in your network know that you are looking for investors, and ask who they know that could help. You might be surprised that your cousin Bob is good friends with a VP of an investment bank, for example, or his college roommate is now an angel investor. (Make sure all of the team members of your startup ask their own networks about connections to potential investors too. You never know whose contact will lead to a warm introduction.)

And don't be surprised if some of the people in your own network say, "I might be interested in investing myself. Tell me more." As you learned in Chapter 3, initial funding for most startups comes from founders themselves, and after that from their friends and family. Depending on where you are in your funding roadmap, you might find your next investor is in your current network already!

Who Do You Need to Add to Your Network?

Once you know who is in your current network, you must add to it strategically, with the goal of reaching the investors and groups that are on your funding roadmap. Here are five ways to add the people you need.

First, *go to what I call the "right room"*—meaning, the professions or industries related to your company. If you're a mobile app startup, get to know key people within the mobile world. If you're in medical devices, reach out to people in biomed, including academics from prominent universities. Many of these people have important information or connections that can help you develop your business and reach investors.

Second, *find the key players in your community or geographic area*. A community bank is more likely to give you credit when you're first getting started, and (as you learned in Chapter 3) three-quarters of angel investors put their money into companies in the same state where they live. Get to know local bankers, attorneys, CPAs, politicians—any of them may provide critical introductions as well as information about resources for your business. When super angel investor David Berkus first decided to become an investor, he didn't know how to find startups to fund. So he visited both a key local banker and a VC who lived in the area, and said, "Give me the startups that can't get money from your bank or VC because the deals are either too small or too risky." Because the banker and VC knew David, they gave him the referrals, and his deal flow started immediately. If you know your local bankers, investors, or other prominent citizens, even if they can't fund your business themselves, they may know where to send you.

Third, *network with other founders*. Attend any startup meetings or conferences in your local area. In the startup world, other companies are more likely to be potential allies rather than competitors, so reach out to other founders, talk to them about their businesses, and ask about their investors. They may be able to give you the "inside scoop" on particular angel investors or VCs that will help you decide whether it's worthwhile to approach them for funding. They also can tell you what it's like to work with particular investors—how much expertise they contribute, how easy they are to work with, what's important to them, and so on. You may even be able to ask another startup entrepreneur for a warm introduction to the investor you want to reach.

Fourth, *seek out people who are centers of influence*—meaning, they are well connected and well respected in their professions. Attorneys at top law firms, investment bankers, local bank presidents, corporate CPAs, business professors from prestigious universities, or people who run the top entrepreneurial programs in your area qualify as centers of influence. Many such individuals are easier to reach than you think; indeed, someone in your current network may already know them and be happy to introduce you. Simply put, it's more likely that these centers of influence can connect you with investors.

Fifth, if you identify someone you would consider a powerful advocate for you and your company, consider *asking that person to become your mentor*. Mentors should be people with whom you feel a strong connection, and whom you believe can open doors for you and your business. Great mentors will have quality networks and be willing to introduce you to the people you need to know to get funded. If your mentor has significant "clout" or connections in your particular industry, enrolling her in the success of the company through a formal advisor role (and giving her a small amount of equity) can be a good move. By definition, mentors are people further along the path than you in experience and connections, and when they vouch for you, it means something. "In the business world, reputations are paramount," observes David Hornik. "When well-respected individuals vouch for an up-and-comer, it is meaningful."[7]

How to Network Effectively (Even If You're Not a Natural)

Networking is not a natural activity for many people. I get it—I was horribly shy growing up and worked hard to overcome my natural introversion. The turning point for me was reading the book, *How to Win Friends and Influence People*. I started saying hello and just smiling and talking to people. And the most interesting thing happened: I found out that people weren't that scary. Moreover, they liked me and I liked them! Now I meet regularly with VC executives who have billions of dollars under management, as well as top politicians, businesspeople, and academics around the world.

Like any skill, networking can be learned. You start by overcoming any feelings of shyness or introversion that you may have. Statistics show that approximately 42 percent of the U.S. population self-reports as shy (a number that has held remarkably steady for more than thirty years).[8] And many entrepreneurs just want to work on building their businesses; they have no desire to "waste" time talking to people simply to build connections with them. But as you should see by now, creating a strong strategic network is never a waste of time—especially if you can do it efficiently.

I developed an easy four-step process to feel comfortable approaching anyone.

1. If possible, *do your research*. Find out as much as you can about the person you will be meeting.

2. *Start the conversation by asking a question.* Stay away from the trite "What do you do?" and instead, ask something designed to focus the other person on the positive. "What are you enjoying about the conference?" for example, or "Why did you get into your business?" or "What's the most exciting deal you've done lately?" Then listen carefully to what they tell you; this information can help you figure out how to add value to them later.

3. When the other person finishes talking, he will usually ask you a question in turn, so *be ready to share a little about yourself and your business.* Keep what you say short and positive. Be enthusiastic, or proud, or passionate—whatever suits your personality best. If you would like this person's help with something, don't ask for it directly. Instead, put your request at the end of your share. For example, "I founded a startup specializing in digital training for customer service personnel, delivered internationally via a proprietary customizable software program. We're already in four countries in Europe and we're looking for funding to expand into Asian markets."

4. Before you leave the conversation, *ask what I call the two golden questions.* The first question is, "What other ideas do you have for me?" (Don't ask for money—that will come when you meet with investors for a pitch presentation.) The second question is, "Who else should I talk to?" These referrals may prove valuable and lead to the investor you are trying to reach.

The biggest secret to successful networking is to do whatever you can to *add value to the other person.* Before people are willing to help with the big things, they must know you, like you, and trust you, and that happens as a result of regular, value-added contact through time. You need a plan for connecting and adding value to your network regularly, to create a connection based on mutual support, respect, and liking. And whenever you encounter someone new, keep this thought in mind: "How can I help this person today?"

You probably know about the influence principle of reciprocity: When we are given something, we feel obligated to repay the favor in some way or other. But if you really want to tap into the principle of reciprocity, you will do your best to give the other person something that she wants or needs or will find valuable. Value comes in many forms and is determined by the needs of the situation and individual. But even the most well-situated investor needs more and better (1) information, (2) income, (3) key contacts, (4) favors, and (5) introductions.

No matter how new you are to business or to entrepreneurship, you have access to resources that this investor won't have. So keep your eyes and ears open, and watch the investor's presence on social media. Look for information about outside interests, as well as his business, or the companies in which she's already invested, to see if there are any ways you can add value in those areas, such as the following:

- Every investor is looking for quality deal flow. Do you know of other startups that might be suited to this investor, or perhaps for one of his colleagues?

- Do you have a contact in your network that can help the investor learn about new ideas from universities, laboratories, etc.?

- You may have access to information in your particular area of expertise that's not been made public yet. Can you point the investor toward some new technology that might represent a funding opportunity?

- If you share a particular hobby or charitable interest, can you provide some ideas or tips on that topic? Could you meet them at a function tied to that hobby or charity? Many a business deal has been started on the golf course or tennis or squash court, or at a fundraiser or an arts event.

The easiest way to add value to investors is to make a practice of becoming a conduit of information, connection, and introductions, not just for the people whom you need but also for everyone in your network. The real power of your network comes from creating interrelationships between the people you know and the people you are trying to reach. See if you can facilitate an introduction between the investor and someone she would like to meet.

How to Connect with Investors

In Chapter 4 you created a list of investors that you want to target for your funding round(s). With the above information in how to network, let's talk about other ways you can reach investors. First and most important is to get a warm introduction from someone the investor knows, either personally or by reputation. As I said earlier, few investors will even look at you unless you can get someone they know to connect you with them.

However, some introductions will be "warmer" than others. Y Combinator founder Paul Graham lists five strong sources for warm introductions, and I've added some ideas of how you can reach these people.[9]

Five Warm Introduction Sources

1. A well-known investor who's already put money into your company. Whenever someone invests in your startup, ask them for referrals to other investors for current or later rounds.

2. The founder of a company the investor has previously funded. Get to know other startup founders and ask them to put you in touch with angels and VCs.

3. Other angel investors and VCs. Even if a particular investor doesn't fund your type of startup, they will know others in the angel investing or VC community that do. If you or your network know any angels or VCs, ask for their advice in reaching the investor you are targeting.

4. Centers of influence known to the investor. Can you connect with the investor's attorney, CPA, financial planner, or investment banker? Or does your attorney/CPA/planner know his service provider? These kinds of professional connections can provide you with a qualified introduction.

5. Friends or colleagues of the investor. If possible, ask them to place a call to the investor for you, or send an email on your behalf (see below). If they seem reluctant, request permission to use their name when you

call or email the investor. The more frequently an investor hears about you from people she knows, likes, and trusts, the more interested she is likely to be in your startup.

Reaching Investors at Conferences

Another way to connect with investors in person is at entrepreneurial conferences, competitions, capital conferences, panels that feature investors, and venture fairs run by different angel investment groups or VCs. You can go to "demo day" events held by incubators and accelerators—there are over a thousand of these in the U.S. There also are industry conferences and symposia in your particular field happening throughout the year. These kinds of informal meetings will pay off later when you reach out to investors. Being able to say, "I met you at the Disrupt SF conference last year," or "I saw you speak at the Biomed 2018 conference in Boston" can create a point of commonality that sets you apart from other startup founders. (At any conference or meeting, just make sure to spend your time talking with people in addition to attending sessions.)

Using LinkedIn and Social Media

You also can reach out to investors via social media and LinkedIn. Remember, it's often the friends of friends that are your best connections to the people you wish to reach, and the LinkedIn platform is perfectly designed to maximize these connections. Start with the list of possible investors that you created as part of your funding roadmap, and review their LinkedIn profiles. Then check to see if any of the people in your current network are first-, second-, or third-degree connections with those investors, and then request a LinkedIn introduction from your connection.

Even if you don't have someone in common to introduce you, there are other ways you can connect with potential investors via social media. Do they blog? Comment on their blogs, ask or answer questions, and start a dialogue with them. Are they on Twitter? Respond to their tweets and retweet what they post. Do they write articles that appear on LinkedIn, or in places like *Forbes, Inc.*, or *Entrepreneur*? Comment on their articles, or if there is a contact address listed at the end of the article, send them a thoughtful email. Do they recommend other people's blogs or articles? Read those articles, too, and add your own comments. The author of the piece may turn out to be the person who introduces you to the investor. Engaging with investors via social media *before* you approach them for funding will allow them to get to know you (and vice versa) before you ask for a meeting.

Having an active social-media presence yourself is an excellent way for investors to find out more about you too. David Pakman, partner at Venrock VC, once said, "I find social media (where people's points of view, reputation, and activity are quickly validated) to be a great way to 'meet' new entrepreneurs. I still love to read something written by the person, like a blog or Medium post, so I can understand the way this person thinks."[10] And as Mark Suster points out, since most investors' emails are usually overloaded, connecting with them via LinkedIn direct message, or a Facebook private message, or on Twitter, may help you stand out from the rest.[11]

Effective Email Strategies

In the course of networking with investors, you are likely at some point to connect with them via email. (Note: Do everything you can to avoid sending an unsolicited email. Investors' mailboxes are jammed with junk emails and spam, and you never want your email to fall into those categories.) Before you send an email, however, be sure to make contact with the investor one of three ways.

First is a personal connection at a conference or meeting where you got their business card. Then you can reference the specific meeting in the subject line of your email.

Second is having interacted sufficiently via social media that the investor has a sense of who you are. Again, make specific reference to your interactions in the subject line of your email.

Third, and the vastly preferred way, is for the person who has given you the "warm" introduction to send an email to the investor and copy you on it. (I have found this three-way introduction email to be extremely effective.) Once the investor has received the email from your contact, follow up with your own email to the investor, and copy your contact. I suggest putting your contact's name in the subject line ("Following up on Suzy

Smith's email to you") to decrease the likelihood of the investor deleting it without reading.

Keep the body of your email short and to the point, a few sentences at most. Start with one or two intriguing sentences about your startup, including any significant facts and figures that demonstrate traction. Then make a clear request: for the investor to read your executive summary, to set up a brief phone call or meeting, and so on. Do *not* ask for money; at this point you want a meeting or phone call, nothing more. Tell the investor that you will follow up within a few days to confirm any next steps, and thank them for their time. Finally, if there's a way you can add value to the investor in the email—with an article, referral, resource, etc.—do so in a postscript.

If you don't get a response right away, be persistent until you get either a yes or no. But always be polite, and always add value if you can. The investing world is a small community, and how you interact with its members will quickly become known. The investors who won't give you the time of day in your first funding round may jump on the bandwagon after you close your first deal, or the angel investor whom you turned down because they didn't seem right for your company may know someone who is. So always stay professional, and keep in touch with any investor throughout the funding process.

Remember, when investors put money into your company, it is the beginning of a multiyear relationship between you and them. "You, the founder, are starting a long-term, committed relationship with your investors, and that requires cultivation and nurturing," writes Eden Shochat of Israeli VC fund Aleph.[12] Your networking and relationship-building skills will be critical throughout the lifetime of your business—not simply to reach investors but also to keep them involved and engaged in your company.

III
WHAT INVESTORS ARE LOOKING FOR

As an entrepreneur, the question you should ask yourself is—have you realized the full potential of the business you have created, and do you have the right team which can deliver this dream?[1]

—RENUKA RAMNATH, founder, Multiples Alternate Asset Management

6

THE RIGHT FOUNDER AND
THE RIGHT TEAM

> Having the right team determines the path and outcome of a new
> venture more than any decision in the lifecycle of a company.[1]
>
> **—BERND SCHONER,** cofounder, ThingMagic

When seeking funding, the importance of having the right founder and the right team should not be underestimated. A 2014 study by students from Stanford Graduate School of Business in conjunction with AngelList demonstrated that the average early-stage investor responded most strongly to information about the founding team (their experience, entrepreneurial background, education, and so on) rather than data on traction or existing lead investors. "Our findings suggest that the characteristics of the founding team are important for fundraising, and thus ultimately for firm success," the study authors conclude.[2]

Here's an example of the power of having the right founder and team. When Desktop Metal (a maker of office-friendly 3D printers) did its first round of fundraising in 2015, the company had no website and no prototype. What it *did* have was a team composed of several MIT engineering professors and a cofounder who had been a general partner at a VC firm. On the strength of its team and founder, Desktop Metal raised $14 million in that initial round. Less than two years later, Desktop Metal's 2017 series D raise put the company into "unicorn" status, with a billion-dollar valuation.[3]

On the other hand, according to a review of 253 startups that had to close their doors, of the top twenty reasons the founders cited for their failure, four had to do with human capital: not the right team (23 percent), getting sidetracked or losing focus (13 percent), disharmony with a cofounder or investors (13 percent), and burnout (which was attributed to lack of a strong team) (8 percent).[4]

In this chapter, Dr. Annette Lavoie and other experts cover the key characteristics of successful startup founders and teams. I met Annette not long after she had sought funding for her medical device company. (You can read that story below.) For the last several years she has provided mentoring and coaching to startup companies. You can use her insights to help you build an effective team.

Annette Lavoie: The Importance of Your Team

Judy and I met when I was trying to a raise the first round of funding for my medical device startup company. I'd spent years honing my pitch and meeting with various venture capital investors, dedicating scarce time (and scarcer capital resources) to fly to these meetings. But even though I had a compelling story of a market need and a product solution, I wasn't getting funded. Every VC told me the same thing: "We love your technology and your market—come back when you're raising a series B."

I was so excited: all I had to do was raise the A round and the rest was in the bag! I had no idea that what I was really hearing was venture-speak for "No way." What's worse, I didn't know *why* they weren't interested.

Judy helped me to realize that all of my scientific expertise wasn't enough to fund my company if I wasn't pitching in the right room and, more important, *if I didn't have the right team*. At the time, I didn't know how to build a team without money to pay them—until Judy taught me the power of well-placed equity incentives. With those in place, I was able to attract engineers who worked on their evenings and weekends to help me build and test the prototype.

I also found doctors and medical entrepreneurs who were willing to give me advice about the product and the markets I was entering. I recruited business leaders who had walked the path before me and knew where the landmines were buried. Armed with my newfound knowledge, and finally backed by a credible team, it wasn't long before I was pitching to a boutique venture fund that invested in early-stage technologies in my industry. I had the right team, and I was finally in the right room.

I secured the funding for my team and me to prove the viability of our product. Not long afterward we were acquired by a large medical device company, which had the internal resources to take the product through clinical trials to market. While it was hard to let go, I appreciated the lessons I had learned. I'd been able to keep the company alive long enough to implement a successful exit for my investors, my team, and myself. But ultimately, it was our internal and external teams that made all the difference.

Just about everyone in the startup world talks about the importance of teams. I've heard investors say they would rather invest in an "A" team and a "C" product than the other way around. Serial entrepreneur Andy Miller has a formula: "People + Execution = Success." Notice that there's no mention of a great product in his formula! Regardless of how the picture is painted, the message is clear: *teams do matter.*

I see it over and over again, particularly in startups. Scientists or engineers like me are certain that our latest idea is so revolutionary, with such potential to change the world, that we believe the device is our primary responsibility and the greatest asset in the company. I honestly thought that *my* job was the technology, to develop it and to make it perfect; it was the investors' job to put money in and mop up the pesky business details.

I learned quickly that I was wrong. Investors are counting on the startup team to create and execute on the business plan that will make money for the company regardless of what gets in the way. The primary role of the founding team is to plan a road to market that avoids potential roadblocks, and then to navigate a changing path to market when unanticipated roadblocks appear. GrowthX founding partner Sean Sheppard puts it this way: "Most companies and innovations fail, and the reasons have to do with markets and the behaviors of the people who are running them, not the products themselves."[5]

Let's go through the different components of a startup team: the founder, cofounders (if any), first hires, subsequent hires, and outside advisors. (Eventually investors also will form part of the startup's team, but in this chapter we'll focus on the team that will attract those investors.)

Founder = Leader = Visionary

A startup's team begins with a founder. Usually this is the person with the idea for the product or service in the first place. Founders are the cornerstones of their respective startups. "The skills and traits of a company's founders are irreplaceable," says entrepreneur Bernd Schoner. "No one can speak to investors or customers with authority like a founder. It's a great asset to have at the beginning and hard to add later."[6]

To build a successful startup, I believe founders must take on three key responsibilities. First, *founders must be leaders.* When a startup launches, the "team" may only be the founder and a product (or the idea of a product). But the founder must quickly become a leader for the company's "outside team" of customers, suppliers, advisors, and investors. The founder also must inspire possible "inside team" members to join the company even when there isn't one. In 2015 Noam Wasserman (author of *The Founder's Dilemma*) wrote in *The Wall Street Journal,* "Founders believe in their ideas so strongly they throw aside comfortable jobs and risk their life savings to chase their dreams. They have such contagious enthusiasm they can convince others to sign on, whether it's cofounders or venture investors or early-adopting customers."[7]

As part of leadership, founders must be comfortable with risk. This is usually not a problem: Anyone founding a company who hasn't quit their day job to do so is a "wantrepreneur," not an entrepreneur. And investors who see that you have everything at stake in this company usually believe that you will do everything it takes to make it a success. Founders also must have confidence in their ability to overcome adversity. The good news is that the pressure of having everything on the line breeds creativity and confidence to make things happen regardless of what stands in the way!

Second, *founders must set the values for the company and shape the company culture.* What will be the company's top priorities? Innovation? Profit at all costs? Market share? Social good? Pulverizing the competition? Diversity? Teamwork? Revolutionizing the industry? "[Values are] things that you're not willing to compromise on if you get into a conflict over them," writes CEO of Business & Investor Labs Martin Hoffman.[8] Values will shape the company's priorities while attracting specific categories of customers, advisors, and investors. Because company values are important for founders to determine, it's best to make the decision about them early—and consciously.

Values also will directly affect company culture, defined as the "personality" of the organization. Is your company laid back? Driven? Informal? "Techie"? Fun? Does it welcome alternate points of view? Is it open and transparent—in other words, is information shared freely among the team? Company culture is a big factor in the work atmosphere and can determine which employees are attracted to your startup.

Third, *founders must have a vision and be able to communicate it clearly to both internal and external teams.* Founders usually start a company *because* they have a vision: They have a great product or service and feel called to create a company to bring it to the marketplace. But to make the vision real, founders need to be able to (1) create a roadmap that gets the product or service from vision to market, and then (2) communicate that vision and roadmap to customers, team members, advisors, and ultimately, investors.

Communicating a clear, compelling vision with energy and enthusiasm is often the founder's most important job. It starts with recruiting potential team members, who must be inspired enough by the startup's potential to leave their current jobs for an uncertain future. "Vision is the most important trait of a startup leader," says Russell Kommer, founder of eSoftware Associates Inc. "The ultimate test, though, is . . . encouraging the people around you to believe in your vision and quest. A consistent message and constantly renewed energy will help others to live your passion."[9]

Choosing Cofounders

Sometimes the founder who will lead the company isn't the inventor, but someone who believes in the idea early on and is willing to put her future on the line to turn that idea into a successful company. This type of cofounder can be successful—try to imagine Steve Wozniak starting Apple without Steve Jobs! A great cofounder can increase the potential for your startup's success by providing strengths and experience that the founder may lack.

People often ask me how they can recognize a great cofounder. We've all heard of people like Richard Branson, who started his first company at age eleven: but what if you don't know anyone like that in your industry or area? That's what your network is for. Especially if you are a technical expert, or you have a great idea but little business experience, ask your network connections for their recommendations. Look for people who have worked in startups before, particularly as early hires—meaning, they were some of the first team members brought on to the startup. Then you can use these three criteria to evaluate potential cofounders:

1. *Do their skills, abilities, and experiences complement yours?* Few founders are well rounded enough to be great at everything, and cofounders can fill those gaps. For example, Steve Wozniak was a great computer engineer while Steve Jobs was a great visionary and market developer. The skills, abilities, and experiences of one complemented the other. The problem is that many founders are drawn to partners that are just like themselves, with the same background, skills, and personal qualities. Instead, you should try to choose people who have skills that you lack, or whose background is in a different industry, or at least in a different part of the business. If you're a technologist, find an entrepreneur. If you're an entrepreneur, find a great product developer or marketer. Your startup will be stronger as a result.

2. *Are your values, goals, and expectations aligned?* Even though your goal is to bring on cofounders with complementary skills and experience, they still need to be on the same page concerning the startup's values, mission, goals, and timeline. They also need to be clear as to what will be expected of them. Are they looking for a lifestyle business while you want a quick exit so you can build another company? Do you both have similar values around customers, business ethics, finances, and teamwork? Do you agree about the company's mission? If you want to save the world with your product or service and a cofounder wants profit at all costs, there could be some serious arguments ahead. While some of these concerns can be outlined in a cofounders' written agreement (which you *always* should insist upon having), it's more important that you discuss these matters before you become partners. Putting all of

your expectations, values, goals, and mission in writing may help keep things smoother when the going gets tough—which it will.

3. *Are you compatible? Can you work together over the short and long haul?* Many people recommend you "vet" a cofounder as thoroughly and carefully as you would (or should) a life partner. Lindred Greer is a professor at Stanford Graduate School of Business, where she offers a course on the psychology of startup teams. "If you're starting a business and choosing cofounders and making your first hires, you're looking at one of the most intense relationships you're going to have in your life," she comments. "With a startup, it's more of a life-or-death situation. Issues around power and fairness are bigger, because your entire life is probably vested in the business."[10] Professor Greer suggests that founders spend months with possible cofounders before bringing them on. Checking references is also a good idea, especially if cofounders have participated in previous entrepreneurial ventures.

Remember, the most important feature of cofounders is being able to work together. If you can trust and count on each other, then your company foundation will be strong.

Your Startup's First Hires

Like most founders, I wore multiple "hats" in my startup company, and I worked hard to learn everything I could about business. But ultimately I discovered that it's impossible to wear *every* hat: I had to hire a team to help me realize my vision. For your company to grow, you too will need to assemble a team of employees who will provide the skills to execute your business plan. Recruiting employees also shows preliminary viability to seed-stage investors, proving that you're not the only one that believes in your vision.

However, it's easy for founders to make mistakes with early hires for four reasons. First, because startup teams are usually small in number, every hire you make is critical, and one mistake can have big consequences. As Sam Altman, president of Y Combinator, says, "Mediocre people at a big company cause some problems, but they don't usually kill the company. A single mediocre hire in the first five will kill a startup."[11]

Second, startup companies rarely have human resource directors so founders are usually doing the hiring, and they may or may not know what to look for in these critical first few employees. As they did with cofounders, they may end up hiring people that are too much like themselves, rather than looking for individuals who bring different and complementary abilities, attitudes, and experiences to the team.

Third, founders may not know how to go about finding the right employees. They may only look among the people they know personally ("Sam's a coder—I'll bring him on") or take recommendations from others already on the team without doing any real vetting. For most founders, hiring is just one of the thousands of urgent tasks on their plates, so it's no wonder they look for as many shortcuts as possible.

Fourth, founders may make unwise choices when it comes to employee compensation. It may be tempting to low-ball salaries and tie compensation to company equity to save precious capital early on. But as you'll see in Chapter 9, such a practice can backfire when you're seeking funding.

With a little preparation, founders can avoid these hiring traps and pull together a great core team. Here are five suggestions.

1. Know Thyself—and Know Who Else You Need on Your Team

Most startup founders have at least one core "strength" and perhaps a few additional strengths they've developed along the way. I was the "technician" of my startup, the lone inventor of an amazing technology; but I needed engineers to help me build a prototype, sales and marketing help to help reach my target customers, and so on.

To hire the people you need, make a list of your strengths and perspectives as well as those of your cofounders and any current team members. Then make a second list of what you believe is missing in terms of (a) core competencies (do you need financial expertise, or someone who can build prototypes), (b) experience (for example, if your product or service has a military application, perhaps you should hire a former military officer), (c) personal qualities (if you are an introvert, you might need someone more extroverted to handle sales), and (d) perspectives (people from different genders, ethnicities, countries, or backgrounds may provide valuable insights you could never have on your own). Each new hire is an opportunity to make your startup stronger by filling in gaps that may hold you back.

2. Look in the Right Places for Candidates

According to Sam Altman (who's seen quite a few startups go through the Y Combinator accelerator), the first hundred hires at most tech companies typically come from referrals.[12] However, don't hire people simply because they are recommended by someone you know. Have them go through your interview process (see below) to ensure they have the skills, abilities, experience, and above all, personality that will fit well in your company. Be aware that people who have spent their careers in big corporations may not be the best fit for a startup culture. Your first few employees will need to be "generalists"—meaning, they will have to do whatever's needed regardless of job description. This is a different approach to work than you find in most big companies.

Where should you look for new hires? At other startups. At entrepreneurial-based business programs. At trade shows and startup incubators. At local "coworking" office suites. Great startup team members rarely are found in traditional locations because their personalities are attracted more to innovation and risk than security. Startup employees also tend to be younger and at earlier stages in their careers, and less locked into the "big company" corporate culture. That said, make sure you never turn someone down because of their age, experience, or background. Sometimes the perfect candidate is someone who's fed up with their job at a big company or organization and ready to take a chance on your startup.

3. Put a Rigorous Hiring Process in Place

This one is challenging for startups: Usually when you need to hire someone, you need them *now!* But it can be difficult to fire an early hire, especially if their compensation includes equity. What's worse, within a short time a disgruntled employee can poison your entire team. So it's not surprising that the advice you hear from many investors is "Hire slow, fire fast." This means that you should (1) plan for your hiring needs far in advance (twelve to eighteen months), (2) put in place a thorough process for vetting potential employees, (3) calculate an average of six months to find and hire a new team member, and (4) always have candidates in the pipeline.

Your hiring process might include these elements:

- Check for ability and talent with an initial screen for the core competencies of the position. You can determine this through a candidate's résumé.

- Interview to get a feel for a candidate and assess "team fit" in terms of personal traits (see below). The interview also should include questions designed to see how candidates would deal with specific challenges. Most people working in startups spend the majority of their time handling problems and coming up with creative solutions. Using real examples of issues your company already has run into or you are facing now will give you a good idea as to the attitude and flexibility of the candidate.

- Thoroughly vet references.

- Spend time with candidates individually and as a team. You may see different personality indicators in social situations and in groups than you do in a formal interview.

On the flip side, whoever is doing the interviewing needs to communicate clearly the values, vision, and corporate culture of the startup. This is what should ultimately "sell" candidates on your company and make them excited to join your team. But more important, if a candidate isn't a good fit for the company's values, vision, and culture, then that person's skills and experience won't be enough to keep him engaged in a startup's fast-paced, stressful environment. Remember, your first employees will probably have many different responsibilities and may even have to create their own positions as they go along. The company's product, market, and premise may completely change overnight. The only thing that will keep the team moving in the same direction is the company's vision, values, and culture.

4. Look for Diverse Personalities

The first employees in a startup look different from those who are great at their jobs in an established company. Like founders themselves, these team members are usually more comfortable with risk, more optimistic, and more flexible when it comes to job descriptions and roles within the company. However, just as you need to balance the skills, background, and experiences of your team, you also need to balance personality traits. Take optimism: It's a common trait in most startup employees, but every company needs people who can be realistic or even pessimistic, especially when it comes to things like financial projections or market share. The people on a great startup team may be different from each other, as long as they share a commitment to the company's mission.

5. Compensate Intelligently

People attracted to working at a startup are rarely driven by high salaries: In fact, most entrepreneurs or startup company employees will take a pay cut for the opportunity to be in on the ground floor of an exciting new venture. Instead, they're typically motivated by some combination of long-term financial opportunity in the form of equity or stock options, and short-term lifestyle benefits such as flexible hours, autonomy, creative work environment, making a difference in the world, and pride of inventorship. It's important to understand these motivations and to be able to satisfy them in order to attract and keep your startup team.

But you shouldn't give away equity or participation in the company to everyone. Outsource rather than hire for noncritical skills or short-term needs. Think of accountants or attorneys, for example: They typically provide a valuable service to the company but they're not integral to the product being developed, so startups usually hire these services on an hourly basis. Sometimes this is harder to distinguish when the service *is* required for the product, such as building a mobile or web-based platform for your app or service. While programming is the backbone of the product, creating that backbone is not part of the "secret sauce" of the company and can be outsourced. Paying for services whenever possible is typically cheaper than bringing someone in and paying them with long-term equity options.

The value of equity can be illustrated by the artist David Cho, who opted to take payment in stock options for painting a mural on an office wall for Facebook. When Facebook went public, his shares were worth a staggering $200 million.[13] So don't underestimate the value of your equity. Just because your stock isn't worth much today, you should spend it to make progress, yes—but spend it wisely.

Hiring New Members as the Company Grows

One of the biggest challenges for startups isn't hiring core team members; it's the second wave of hiring as the company grows. These new employees can sometimes feel like second-class citizens, shut out of the camaraderie (and often the financial benefits) of the original team. It's critical for founders and longer-term team members to do whatever's needed to involve, engage, and enroll new employees in the mission and culture of the startup.

At this stage, communication becomes even more critical. As part of Professor Greer's class at Stanford, students go into early-stage startups (ten or fewer people) to study team dynamics. Consistently the biggest problem reported is a lack of team alignment around the company mission and vision. "You tell that to the CEO, and he or she will say, 'I told them six months ago what the vision was,'" Professor Greer reports. "It doesn't work that way, especially in startups. . . . You have to keep emphasizing in all your internal communications: 'Who are we and what are we doing right now? What is our goal?'"[14] From first hire to the person added to the team yesterday, founders need to continue to guide and inspire the startup team.

Your "Outside" Team of Advisors and Investors

Hopefully you now have a core team of enthusiastic, talented individuals who are motivated to work long hours to build your company. But typically, this team doesn't possess the depth of expertise that is key to navigating the path to market. The company usually can neither afford to hire this expertise, nor would such an expert typically work well in the trenches with the rest of the team. That's where advisory boards come in. Advisory boards are vital to expanding the broad knowledge and industry expertise of the team without creating imbalance in the team or on the books.

Think of advisors as providing the expertise you need but don't have in-house. For example, some technology companies will have plenty of technical and industry expertise but will need to bring on sales advisors to anticipate the process of taking the technology to market. Other founders will come from the sales and marketing channel, and need input on the technology side. Industry advisors are also important for their expertise (like military contracts, for example), connections to potential customers or acquirers, or for their influence, such as key opinion leaders in the industry. The types of advisors you bring on will depend on the type and the stage of the product, and will change as the company matures.

Because I was an academic researcher developing a medical device, I recognized the weakness of my team in several areas and chose to create both a medical advisory board and a business advisory board. Initially my advisors were all *ad hoc* and available to contribute over the phone as needed. Later, as the interactions between advisors became more important and it was more critical for me to hear these conversations, we scheduled advisory board meetings and conference calls, in which we asked advisors to address issues in their areas of expertise.

The primary responsibility of advisors is to help the founders run the business. This is a key distinction between boards of advisors and boards of directors. Advisors are important partners for the founder and are compensated with common shares similar to the management and the employees. Boards of directors are responsible to the shareholders, and therefore act as a boss to the founders. Their primary responsibility is to make money for the company—hopefully by helping the founders execute on their vision, but sometimes by replacing founders with more experienced management.

At some point as the company matures and brings in larger investors, it will be necessary to create a five-member board of experienced individuals that represent your investors, but until then it's best to keep most industry experts as advisors instead of directors. A startup board with two founders and one key advisor who share the mission and the vision for the company can be effective for getting the company off the ground in the early stages.

How to Keep Your Position as Founder as the Company Grows

Founders are often concerned about being replaced by their boards of directors, especially when venture capital is raised and a VC takes a board seat. I've been in the room when a VC stated that her first job following an investment was to replace the founder! The only way to make sure that you're not "fired" by the board of directors is to continue to create value for the company in whatever capacity you find yourself.

As a company matures from prerevenues to breakeven and sustainability to growth, the skillsets required of the CEO change. As a founder you're rarely the right person to take the company public, but if you can continue to contribute to the value of the company regardless of your title, then the chance that you'll stay involved in the company increases significantly. You need to be a team player, always. Try on the investor hat, see what you can do to make money for the shareholder, and just do it. Job security is never part of the startup world, but there are ways to improve your odds, and remaining valuable to the company is key.

Remember, the true value of any startup may start with a product or service, but that value is multiplied exponentially by what the founders and their team create together. That's why you must always be as specific and deliberate about building your team as you are about building your product or service.

7

THE RIGHT BUSINESS PLAN AND CLEAR FINANCIALS

Every business has to start with a plan.[1]

—WILLIAM BYGRAVE, professor emeritus, Babson College

The next element that must be in place for investors to fund your startup is an achievable *business plan* with *clear financials*. Your business plan is a road to market that charts a clear path to profitability.

Now, it used to be that every entrepreneur would be expected to develop a multi-page business plan and submit it to any investor or institution where they were seeking funding. And some sources (notably banks and government grants or lending programs) still require a business plan as part of the application process. However, the thinking about business plans has changed over the past several years, especially for startups and entrepreneurs seeking seed-stage or early-stage funding.

So why create a detailed business plan? Three reasons. First, there is a great deal of statistical evidence that entrepreneurs who plan their businesses are more likely to build successful ventures. For example, a 2010 study of companies bringing a new product or service to the market revealed that those with a written business plan had 33.4 percent higher annual average growth than those that didn't.[2] And a 2016 survey of more than 2,800 entrepreneurs showed that those who had completed a business plan were twice as likely to receive loans or investment capital.[3]

Second, entrepreneurs can benefit greatly from going through the process of developing a business plan before launching their companies. As you'll see later, the thinking that goes into a business plan requires you to understand every part of your business, from locating customers (and knowing who those customers are) to creating systems for sales, organizational, marketing, production, finances, and so on, to setting the goals and milestones required to keep the business on track. "While we think business plans prepared specifically for fundraising are a waste of time, we still believe that they are valuable documents for entrepreneurs to write while they are formulating their businesses," write VCs Brad Feld and Jason Mendelson.[4]

Third, when raising capital you need to be prepared to answer investor questions about every aspect of your startup. A 2010 study of VCs indicated that the VC's perception of an entrepreneur's preparedness, coupled with a strong business plan, is outweighed only by the evaluation of the business management team in the decision to offer funding.[5] Exercising the discipline of creating a business plan will help you walk into investor meetings prepared and with greater confidence of a favorable outcome.

Learning how to create a business plan is a valuable discipline. Still, there are shortcuts you can use to lay out the fundamentals of your startup. In this chapter we'll cover how to create a detailed business plan, and then financial and business expert Marilyn Magett will give you suggestions for creating a simplified plan as well as your basic financial numbers.

While investors may be intrigued and seduced by your business plan, they will *always* thoroughly review your financials to see if your startup is worth a second look. Marcia Nelson says of the entrepreneurs that approach family offices, "We want to see a well thought out business plan, solid financial model including sales data, two- to three-year projections, and information about what is valuable in the company. Can a founder articulate how they're going to make money and how we're going to get a return on our investment? If not, then they'll have a hard time raising capital."[6] To help you with your numbers, strategic financial expert David Meister will walk you through the kind of financials that investors want to see.

The Elements of a Business Plan

Having a comprehensive business plan is like having a GPS in your car or on your smartphone. You input where you are and where you want to go, and because the GPS has accurate maps of current conditions, it will provide you with various routes to get there. You can choose whatever route makes the most sense for you—the fastest, the one that uses interstates rather than surface streets (or vice versa), the most scenic roads, the routes that avoid rush hour traffic or accidents, and so on.

With a detailed business plan, you are loading your startup's "GPS" with the information needed to put you on the road to success, including things like your ideal customers, key competitors, organizational structure, production and distribution, revenue, costs, marketing, sales, personnel, and so on. Assembling all this information in one document will give you an opportunity to see where your initial assumptions about your startup may be faulty, and where you may need to pivot to create a viable business.

Let's divide the information of a business plan into eight sections.

1. Executive Summary

This is the first thing investors or lenders read (and it may be the last, if it's not done well). It should summarize the key elements of your business in one or two pages, describing them in a way that shows your passion as well as the significant financial opportunity your startup represents. You can use bullet points or narrative, just as long as your summary intrigues investors and makes them want to know more.

Include the following:

- The problem you're solving—and the more pain this problem is causing for your customers, the better.

- Your solution and why it is new/different/better.

- Your target market. Focus on the specific market segments you will serve, and how this group is large and growing.

- Your competition and your sustainable competitive advantage.

- An overview of your business and its management team. Provide a synopsis of your business model and show pricing and margins of your product or service. Describe your team and why it will make this business successful.

- Your business goals for the next one, three, and five years. Include major milestones you expect to hit and when.

- Financial highlights, including revenue, sales, profit margin, costs, cash burn, how much capital you are seeking, how you will use it, and how it will make your business profitable. Outline when and how investors will receive a return on investment, and how much they may expect to receive.

2. Company Description

This introduces investors to your company and business concept. Include the company mission statement, vision, and goals, as well as information about your corporate structure. Provide an overview of your industry, marketplace, and competition, showing how your company will be competitive. Describe your target market and the different categories of customers you will be pursuing.

3. Products or Services

This is the nitty-gritty of what you are selling and how you produce it. You should describe in detail the problem your customers have, and how your product or service solves it. This section should be written from the perspective of the customer and be benefit heavy.

List any product feature that will give you a competitive advantage over other companies. Also include your pricing strategy and methodology, how your price compares with other products or services, and how your strategy will attract customers.

4. Marketing Plan

This includes a more thorough description of your customers, where they are, and how you will reach them. Describe the size of your target market and the demographics, psychographics, and buyer personas of the different categories of your customers. Provide data from market research and customer interviews to substantiate your claims.

Outline the positioning of your product or service and the brand identity you wish to develop. Review your competitors, their strengths and weaknesses, and how you will capitalize on these weaknesses to take market share. Include information on industry trends, market size, and how much market share you can realistically gain. Describe any barriers to entering the market: Do you anticipate increased government regulation, or changes in technology that might affect your business?

The marketing section also covers distribution of your product or service to customers, as well as all marketing and promotional activities. It outlines your sales cycle and anticipated profit margins, and includes a twelve-month sales and revenue forecast. (Note: If your startup has sales, use those numbers for your projections. If you're prerevenue, estimate your forecast based on your market research, estimated market share, and sales figures from your competitors.) You'll use the sales and revenue forecasts in the financials section to calculate profit and loss and cash flow for the first year, and then project those numbers out three and five years. It may be tempting to create a rosy "hockey stick" sales forecast, but it's better to be realistic and even slightly pessimistic in your projections. Build at least one sales forecast that you feel you can meet no matter what.

5. Operations

This section covers the daily operations of your startup: production, quality control, inventory systems, and so on. If your business offers an online product or service, describe your system of delivery to customers, as well as the technology that backs up your product or service, and where it is stored—onsite or offsite servers, blockchain ledgers, etc. Include information on backup systems in case of disruptions or hacker attacks.

Also discuss the legal structure of your company, insurance, permits, licenses, patents, copyrights, or trademarks already secured or in the application process. Include information on personnel, current employees, hiring plans, training, and compensation. (Note: These employees are different from your management team, which is described in the next section.) Go through your key suppliers, what they provide, and how they are paid. Outline how customers will pay *you*, including your credit policies.

6. Management and Organization

Here you detail your company management team, including names, job titles, position descriptions, prior experience, and qualifications. If you have yet to fill a key management position, describe who you are looking for and when you expect to fill the role. Also provide information on any members of your board of directors or advisory boards, with their backgrounds and qualifications.

Outline the overall organization of the company, with an organizational chart that shows the divisions of the company and management responsibilities for those divisions. If you plan on adding departments or divisions in the next year to three years, represent those additions on your org chart with timelines as to when you believe those positions will be added.

7. Startup Expenses and Capitalization

From this point on, your business plan is all about the "numbers"—the money needed to open and run the business, and your estimated revenues, profits, and cash flow.

Section 7 is focused exclusively on the capital needed to open the business, including startup expenses, product development costs, overhead, and the opening day balance sheet. (If the business is already up and running, you can skip to the next section, which discusses capital needed for operating the company once it's open.) You should include personal financial statements for all founders and anyone participating in the business in a material way, as investors will expect the owners to use a portion of personal assets to provide initial financing for the business.

8. Financial Plan

This section is so important that we will cover it in depth later in this chapter. The financial plan covers the business's financial goals and presents an estimate of capitalization needs for its first three to five years of operations.

The three critical documents in your financial plan are: (1) the profit & loss (P&L) statement; (2) the company balance sheet; and (3) the cash flow statement. Unless your startup has already made some sales, all of the numbers in your financial plan will be projections based upon the suppositions you have made throughout the rest of your business plan. Therefore, it's vital that you keep detailed notes on these assumptions so you can answer any investor questions. Once your business is up and running, you should regularly update the numbers in your financial plan based on your actual results, and correct any inaccurate assumptions you may have made.

The final document of the financial plan section describes the capital your business needs in both the short term and for each of the next five years of operations, based upon the numbers shown in the three documents listed above. Outline how you will use this capital to grow the business, and include proposed milestones for tracking progress. State what percentage of ownership you are offering investors, and give an estimated return on investment and exit strategy options.

Appendices

This includes any supporting materials for your business plan, such as purchase orders or letters of intent from customers; URLs, trademarks, or patents already obtained; résumés of key management team members; press or advertising materials; market research; plans or blueprints; assets that can be used as collateral, and so on.

This is only a suggested outline; there are multiple business plan templates, software, courses, books, and online sources that will take you through the process of developing your business plan. But for the purpose of this book—getting funds from investors—remember to write your business plan with that "target market" in mind. It will be critical to show your business's (1) market differentiation, (2) path to profitability, (3) amount of investment needed, and (4) how investors will receive a significant return on their capital.

Above all, recognize that any business plan is a set of educated guesses that must be revisited consistently and updated to reflect reality. "Having a plan is less about accurately predicting the future, and more about setting regular goals and making changes to your business as you learn more about your customers," writes Noah Parsons, COO of Palo Alto Software.[7] "However, you shouldn't create a plan and follow it blindly. A good plan is one that you're constantly adjusting and refining as you gather more information about your business and your customers."[8]

Other Business Plan Options

While the process of creating a detailed business plan can help startup entrepreneurs organize their businesses, it can be a time-consuming exercise. What's more, many startups find that most (if not all) of their assumptions are either wrong or need to be changed dramatically. "The necessity of rapid-fire adaptation at the startup stage makes it so that business plans are almost always outdated from the minute they're committed to paper," writes Brian Hamilton, chairman of software company Sageworks.[9] That's why you may find it more effective to create a shorter version of a business plan, one designed simply to outline your basic presuppositions and evaluate the possible pluses and minuses of your business model.

There are several different planning templates you can use to lay out your business idea: The Business Model Canvas, Lean Planning approach, and the $100 Startup's one-page model are a few. I asked financial management consultant Marilyn Magett (principal, CRS Financial Management Solutions) to describe how she would advise a startup entrepreneur to create a business plan and set up financials correctly. Here is her stripped-down process for creating a plan for your startup.

Marilyn Magett: Creating Your Business Plan and Financial Forecast

There are three things the founder of any startup needs to know:

1. *The vision:* what the principals are trying to accomplish
2. *The business plan narrative:* to define the strategies to be utilized to accomplish the vision
3. *The financial forecast:* for operating and capital raise purposes

Your vision should start with a narrative about the business itself. This narrative is important in both creating your business plan and a thorough financial forecast for it. In your mind, go over every aspect of the business and write down a statement about each. (You also can brainstorm this narrative statement with your team.) This narrative doesn't have to be pretty or grammatically correct, but it does need to be as thorough as possible.

Include the following:

- Business name
- Mission statement
- The problem being solved and the solution being offered
- The target market and its size in number of prospects
- The value of the market
- The competitors and how your solution is better than theirs
- Sales channels
- Marketing activities
- Key business activities
- Key resources
- Key team members and their roles and responsibilities
- External key partners and their roles
- The different revenue streams, sales cycles, and service delivery methods
- Anticipated cost structure and types of costs involved
- Initiatives necessary to get the business started

- Required fixed assets and equipment purchases, office space, manufacturing space, warehousing, technology, etc.
- Any other startup costs

Make a copy of your narrative, and then reorganize it into the following sections. These sections form the outline of your business plan.

- Marketing
- Sales
- Operations
- Direct expenses (expenses that would not exist if there were no sales, including personnel necessary to create the product or deliver the service)
- Operating expenses (expenses that would still exist even if there were no sales, such as office space, telephone expense, your salary and the salary of other personnel, etc.)
- Startup costs
- Buildings, equipment, technology, and other assets

The Financials Section

Start by going back through your narrative and creating a budget for your first year of operation. (Note: If you are already in business and have financial reports for the prior year [or partial prior year] and/or the current year to date, you will use those reports as a template to create a forecast that shows both the historical data and projections for the next three to five years. If you are not yet in business, you'll begin by creating projections without historical data.)

1. Estimate costs for all direct expenses, operating expenses, startup costs, purchase or rental of assets, cost of producing your product or service, cost of sales and marketing, and so on.

2. Estimate revenues based on anticipated sales on a month-to-month basis for your first year. These numbers will be used to create your initial financial documents.

You will have three financial templates (as well as a lot of backup documentation) in your business plan. The templates are:

1. A profit & loss (P&L) statement
2. A balance sheet
3. A *cash flow statement* that summarizes the P&L on the top line (cash flow from operations), and then lists line items for changes in balance sheet items.

Use your narrative for each area to help you determine your target figures for the current year as well as forecast years one through five. If you have no data of your own to draw on, you can use industry statistics to help you determine what the appropriate relationships between the figures should be. For instance, if in your industry gross profit is typically 40 percent, then total cost of goods sold is 60 percent. Any deviations from industry norms should be justified by either scale or disruptions to industry norms spelled out in your narrative.

Let's go through an example. Say you started a business in June 2018 and it's now June 2019. Your revenues for the last six months of 2018 were $400,000. This year (2019) you want to double revenues over 2018's annualized figures. That would mean in 2019 you'd need to make *four times* what you made in the last six months of 2018. If revenue doubles again in Forecast Year 1 (2020), that year's total revenue would be $3,200,000. It looks like this:

Revenues for 6 months 2018:	$400,000
Annualized revenues for 2018:	$800,000
Double annualized revenues for 2019:	$1,600,000
Double annualized revenues for Forecast Year 1 (2020):	$3,200,000

Now let's look at how you can estimate gross profits for this business by using the industry standard number of 60 percent for cost of goods sold.

	Prior ½ Year	Current Year	Forecast Year 1	Forecast Year 2	Forecast Year 3	Forecast Year 4	Forecast Year 5
Revenue	$400,000	$1,600,000	$3,200,000				
Cost of Goods Sold (60%)	$240,000	$960,000	$1,920,000				
Gross Profits (40%)	$160,000	$640,000	$1,280,000				

If your cost of goods sold is consistent with your industry at 60 percent, then the prior year cost of goods sold would have been $240,000, and the gross profit $160,000. The current year cost of goods sold would be $960,000, and gross profit would be $640,000.

For each line item in your P&L, determine and fill in what you anticipate the total expense to be, based on your narrative about each respective area. When you have completed all of this, your forecast will tell you if you are profitable or not.

Similarly, complete the forecast for your balance sheet using current balances, and adjust each year based on the activity for that year. Once you have completed both the P&L and the balance sheet, you will know how much capital is required and when.

By the way, I would recommend not doing this alone. Hire a consultant for a few hours to help you with it.

———

David Meister is a strategic financial executive who has over thirty years' experience advising scores of public and private companies in diverse industries. He's raised debt and equity worth more than $800 million and worked on over fifty M&A transactions with an aggregate value of $1 billion. He will walk you through the kind of financial information that investors and institutions want to see when considering your startup.

David Meister: What Investors Want to See in Your Financial Plan

Almost all entrepreneurs seeking funding think that the most important way to demonstrate the viability of their project is by showing its enormous revenue potential. It is surprising how many entrepreneurs believe that their product or service will take off in an ever-increasing way. They sometimes show a chart that plots accelerated revenue growth over a period of time, usually five years. (This is called "hockey stick" revenue growth.) Unfortunately, some of these entrepreneurs do not focus on, or ignore entirely, the costs of producing their product or service, or how long it will take to break even, let alone make a reasonable profit. Since they haven't figured out the costs, they don't know when (or if) their business will become cash flow positive, and how much capital they need. And even if these entrepreneurs know how much it costs to make the product, sometimes they don't know their overhead costs. (Note: Overhead costs are also known as selling, general, and administrative costs, or *SG&A*. They do not vary with the level of sales, as do *cost of sales*, which are the direct costs of making and selling the product.)

You cannot expect investors to get interested in your product without cost and profit information. That's where the profit & loss (P&L) statement comes in. It is one of the basic financial statements that all businesses need, because it measures *revenues*, *costs*, and *profits*. Here are the basics of the P&L for any business:

Financial equation 1

- ► Revenues minus costs of making and selling product = profit or loss
- ► Profit occurs when revenues exceed costs = good
- ► Loss occurs when costs exceeds revenues = bad

Financial equation 2

- ► Revenues minus cost of sales (direct costs of making/selling the product) = gross profit
- ► Gross profit minus overhead costs (SG&A) = operating profit

Here is a sample P&L showing revenues and costs in the year 2018 for "Startup Company, Inc.":

STARTUP COMPANY, INC.	
Profit & Loss Statement	
For the year ended December 31, 2018	
Revenues	$ 100,000
Cost of Sales	$ 52,000
Gross Profit	$ 48,000
Gross Margin	48%
SG&A Costs (overhead)	$ 40,000
Operating Profit (Loss)	**$ 8,000**
Other Expenses:	
Depreciation & Amortization	$ 2,500
Interest Expense	0
Income Taxes	$ 1,500
Net Income (Loss)	**$ 4,000**

This P&L shows there is $4,000 in net income that Startup Company, Inc., will be able to use—right? Not so fast. This is a snapshot of just *one year* of profit and loss; it doesn't take into account company history. You see, in the early years of most startups, the business will probably generate losses; it might not be until its second or third year of operations (if ever) that the business begins to make profits. That $4,000 Startup Company, Inc., earned in 2018 may need to offset expenses from 2017 or 2016.

The lesson? Most startups need capital to fund their early-year losses.

Additionally, depending on the type of business, you might not be able to collect revenues right away. This is called "accounts receivable" and is shown on the balance sheet (which we'll review later). It is not until you collect monies owed that you turn accounts receivable into actual money in the bank. Depending on your business, your customers will pay you in thirty, sixty, or ninety days, or more, or not pay at all. Of course, with B2C startups you can have your customers pay by credit card when they purchase your product, and you'll receive the cash from the credit card company in three business days. But in B2B, where your customers are businesses, you will wait to be paid. And if your customer is a large company, you could wait quite a while before they pay you. After all, you will not refuse to sell to them, and they know it, so they will take their time paying you. Furthermore, your employees and vendors want to be paid weekly, and you have to pay them before your customers pay you, or even before you make the first sale!

I think you can see why startups need to raise capital from investors: to fund losses in early years, to pay employees and vendors, and to fund accounts receivable until they start collecting payments from customers.

What if your startup is "capital intensive"—meaning, you need to invest in machines, computers, equipment, furniture, office leases, security deposits, patents, or other assets that have to be paid for before you start generating revenues (and hopefully profits) with them? Then you'll need to raise additional funding from investors to cover those expenditures. What's worse, these items do not show as expenses on the P&L, so the entrepreneur will be understating the amount of capital needed if they just consider the P&L and avoid the balance sheet and statement of cash flows.

Let's review what investors want to see in your startup's financials, and what conclusions your financials need to show so that investors will give your company a second look.

How the P&L Statement, Balance Sheet, and Cash Flow Statement Work Together

Investors want to see financial projections showing how your startup will perform over the first three to five years of operations. Intuitively, entrepreneurs know they need a P&L, even if they don't know the proper name for it (the formal name is "statement of operations"). They might have heard of a balance sheet but might not know exactly what that is, and almost all have never heard of a statement of cash flow.

But here's a question: What's more important—revenues, profits, or cash flow? (Hint: This is a trick question.)

As a friend of mine, a third generation CEO of a contracting company, once told me, "Revenues are vanity, profits are sanity, but cash flow is reality!" The importance of cash flow to businesses in general cannot be understated. To a startup, it is the essence of corporate life. After all, what do you need investors for? *To fund the business.* How much funding (i.e., cash) do you need? That is where the balance sheet and cash flow statement come into play in conjunction with the P&L.

In my opinion, the cash flow statement tells much more about the health of a startup business than the P&L and balance sheet do. In fact, when you are seeking funding, the cash flow statement is indispensable in determining how much funding you need and when you will need it. In a business plan, the P&L is an illustration of the economics of your venture, and the balance sheet shows, among other things, how much the company owns, how much it owes, the level of debt (if any), and how much existing investors have invested already. But the determining factor in how much capital the venture needs and when (key questions for investors) comes from the cash flow statement.

At a minimum, investors want to see financial projections that include an integrated P&L, balance sheet, and cash flow statement. You also should have spreadsheets, charts, and analyses that explain how you derive your numbers—revenue growth and market share, for example. The following is a sample integrated financial projection for five years. Notice how the numbers from the P&L flow to the balance sheet and cash flow statement, and changes in the balance sheet accounts flow to the cash flow statement. Finally, the ending cash balance in the cash flow statement flows to the cash balance line in the balance sheet. Changing one number anywhere changes all relevant numbers in any of the statements automatically.

This is a sample of the financial projections investors are looking for you to provide. We'll review each element and show you why this is a company that investors might find attractive.

SAMPLE INTEGRATED FINANCIAL PROJECTIONS CHART

STARTUP COMPANY, INC.

Financial projections for years ending December 31.

Profit & Loss Statement	Year 1	Year 2	Year 3	Year 4	Year 5	CAGR
Revenues	$ 100,000	$ 300,000	$ 750,000	$ 1,350,000	$ 2,000,000	111%
% Increase	N/A	200%	150%	80%	48%	
Cost of Sales	$ 90,000	$ 250,000	$ 350,000	$ 475,000	$ 600,000	61%
Gross Profit	$ 10,000	$ 50,000	$ 400,000	$ 875,000	$ 1,400,000	244%
Gross Margin	10%	17%	53%	65%	70%	
SG&A Costs (Overhead)	$ 100,000	$ 150,000	$ 210,000	$ 425,000	$ 600,000	57%
Operating Profit (Loss) (EBITDA)	$ (90,000)	$ (100,000)	$ 190,000	$ 450,000	$ 800,000	
Operating Margin	-90%	-33%	25%	33%	40%	
OTHER EXPENSES:						
Depreciation & Amortization	$ 2,500	$ 5,000	$ 5,000	$ 5,000	$ 5,000	
Interest Expense	0	0	0	0	0	
Income Taxes	0	0	0	$ 108,125	$ 198,750	
Net Income (Loss)	$ (92,500)	$ (105,000)	$ 185,000	$ 336,875	$ 596,250	

SAMPLE INTEGRATED FINANCIAL PROJECTIONS CHART *(continued)*

STARTUP COMPANY, INC.

Financial projections for years ending December 31.

Balance Sheet	Year 1	Year 2	Year 3	Year 4	Year 5	CAGR
Cash	$ 3,000	$ 5,000	$ 2,500	$ 102,500	$ 256,875	
Accounts Receivable	$ 100,000	$ 300,000	$ 712,500	$ 1,147,500	$ 1,700,000	
Prepaid Assets	0	0	0	0	0	
Fixed Assets	25,000	25,000	25,000	25,000	25,000	
Accumulated Depreciation	(2,500)	(7,500)	(12,500)	(17,500)	(22,500)	
Other Assets	0	0	0	0	0	
Total Assets	$ 125,500	$ 322,500	$ 727,500	$ 1,257,000	$ 1,959,375	
Accounts Payable	$ 38,000	$ 100,000	$ 140,000	$ 225,000	$ 240,000	
Accrued Expenses	0	0	0	$ 108,125	$ 198,750	
Debt	0	0	0	0	0	
Owners' Capital	$ 180,000	$ 420,000	$ 600,000	$ 600,000	$ 600,000	
Accum Deficit/Retained Earnings	$ (92,500)	$ (197,500)	$ (12,500)	$ 324,375	$ 920,625	
Total Liabilities & Equity	$ 125,500	$ 322,500	$ 727,500	$ 1,257,500	$ 1,959,375	

SAMPLE INTEGRATED FINANCIAL PROJECTIONS CHART *(continued)*

STARTUP COMPANY, INC.

Financial projections for years ending December 31.

Cash Flow	Year 1	Year 2	Year 3	Year 4	Year 5	CAGR
Net Income (Loss)	$ (92,500)	$ (105,000)	$ 185,000	$ 336,875	$ 596,250	
Depreciation Expense	2,500	5,000	5,000	5,000	5,000	
CHANGES IN BALANCE SHEET ITEMS:						
Accounts Receivable	$ (100,000)	$ (200,000)	$ (412,500)	$ (435,000)	$ (552,500)	
Accounts Payable	$ 38,000	$ 62,000	$ 40,000	$ 85,000	$ 15,000	
Accrued Expenses	$ -	$ -	$ -	$ 108,125	$ 90,625	
Cash Flow from Operations	**$ (152,000)**	**$ (238,000)**	**$ (182,500)**	**$ 100,000**	**$ 154,375**	
INVESTING ACTIVITIES:						
Purchase of Fixed Assets	(25,000)	0	0	0	0	
FINANCING ACTIVITIES:						
Funding Contributed from Investors	$ 180,000	$ 240,000	$ 180,000	$ -	$ -	
Change in Cash	$ 3,000	$ 2,000	$ (2,500)	$ 100,000	$ 154,375	
Beginning Cash Balance	$ -	$ 3,000	$ 5,000	$ 2,500	$ 102,500	
Ending Cash Balance	**$ 3,000**	**$ 5,000**	**$ 2,500**	**$ 102,500**	**$ 256,875**	

Profit and Loss Statement (P&L)

Look at year 1: the P&L shows revenues of $100,000, cost of sales of $90,000, giving a gross profit of $10,000, or a 10 percent gross margin. (Note: If you do a projection that shows a loss for gross profit and a negative gross margin, then something is wrong with your business model and/or spreadsheet model.)

Now look at year 5. Revenues increased from $100,000 in year 1 to $2 million in year 5, a compound annual growth rate (CAGR) of 111 percent. Investors want to see strong revenue growth because that demonstrates the potential viability and market acceptance of your product. Of course, the growth has to be backed up by rational assumptions and reasonable premises that can pass muster under scrutiny.

Over the five years of the projection, gross profit increases from $10,000 in year 1 to $1.4 million in year 5, enabling the gross margin to increase from 10 percent to 70 percent. A business that achieved this kind of growth would be attractive to investors.

Now look at the overhead costs (SG&A), which include things like payroll, benefits, rent, insurance, marketing, technology (internet access, website, and telephony), training, recruiting, and any other costs that do not directly vary with revenues. (Note: You should have backup schedules that detail these costs and tie into this line in your integrated financial projections.)

In the example, overhead costs are $100,000 in year 1 (100 percent of revenues), and they grow by six times to $600,000 in year 5 (30 percent of revenues). These costs are usually a big percentage of revenues in the early years but decline over time as a percentage of revenues, even though the total dollar amount increases. Overhead costs are subtracted from gross profit to derive *operating profit*, also known by the acronym EBITDA—Earnings Before Interest, Taxes, and Depreciation and Amortization expenses.

Operating profit is a key measure of the profitability of the business and factors into the valuation of the business and its available capital structure. A consistent and growing operating profit enables the company to raise debt, in addition to equity, which can also fund the growth of the company. In our example, there are operating losses in years 1 and 2 even though there is gross profit in those years. But by year 5 operating profit grows to $800,000, or 40 percent of revenues. If the venture achieves these amounts of operating profit, they could consider raising debt in year 6 or 7 (or even earlier) if they need more capital to grow the business at that point.

The expenses below the operating profit line are generally depreciation and amortization, interest expense, and income taxes. Investors like to see these below the operating profit line because they are not controllable in the short run, and because it makes it easy to see EBITDA. It is an important measure of profitability and is used for valuation purposes. In this example, in year 5 the venture achieves EBITDA of $800,000. There are several valuation techniques for businesses (and Judy will discuss a few of them in Chapter 10), but a common rule of thumb is that the business is worth some multiple of operating profit, or EBITDA. Bankers might survey other companies in your industry to get the range of multiples that might apply, and adjust as deemed necessary for your particular venture.

For our discussion, let's say the multiple to use is five times. That means this business could have a value of $4 million after the fifth year (EBITDA of $800,000 times the multiple of five). Compared to the total capital invested ($600,000), this would be a nice return for the investors. (You'll see the valuation calculation in greater detail after we review the cash flow statement.)

Balance Sheet

The balance sheet is a statement of what the company *owns* (assets—things like cash, accounts receivable, fixed assets like equipment, and intangible assets like patents), what the company *owes* (liabilities), and how much the existing investors have *invested* in the company (owners' equity or capital). The balance sheet, as its name implies, balances.

Notice that in our sample balance sheet the cash balance in the first three years is nominal, even in year 3 when the net income is $185,000. This is because there is still $712,500 of accounts receivable (i.e., sales that have not been collected yet) at the end of year 3. That is almost the amount of total revenues for year 3 of $750,000. It is not until years 4 and 5 that the cash balances increase to workable levels.

As a result, this startup company needs capital in years 1, 2, and 3, totaling $600,000. This can be seen in the "Owners' Capital" line in the balance sheet. In year 1 it is $180,000, in year 2 it increases to $420,000, and in year 3 to $600,000. It is not until years 4 and 5 that the business is self-sufficient.

Statement of Cash Flow

We determine the total amount of capital needed and the timing of the capital contributions from the cash flow statement. Take a look at our example. A cash flow statement starts with the net income (loss) from the P&L. In year 1 our example shows a loss of $92,500. Added back to this amount are non-cash expenses like depreciation and amortization. In year 1 this amount is $2,500.

Now the balance sheet comes into play, as the net income (loss) amount is further adjusted by changes in certain accounts on the balance sheet—the so-called "working capital" accounts. In our example, they are accounts receivable (AR), accounts payable (AP), and accrued expenses.

Since this is the company's first balance sheet, the beginning balances of these accounts are naturally zero. At the end of year 1, AR is $100,000—that is the total of revenues for year 1 that have not been collected as of the end of the year. An increase in AR is a negative adjustment to the net income (loss, i.e., because the revenues have not been collected), while a decrease in AR would be a positive adjustment. On the other hand, AP increased to $38,000 during the year; this increase is a positive adjustment to cash (i.e., because this amount has not been paid yet). All of this totals a "cash flow from operations" number of negative $152,000. This means that in the first year of the startup they are projecting the business to consume $152,000 of cash.

Here is a summary of cash flow for year 1:

Net loss	$ (92,500)
Add back noncash expenses:	
Depreciation	$2,500
Adjustments for changes in balance sheet items:	
Accounts receivable	$ (100,000)
Accounts payable	$38,000
Cash flow from operations:	$ (152,000)

Other uses of cash in year 1 include a projected expenditure of $25,000 on fixed assets (probably desks, computers, and other office equipment). Adding this $25,000 expenditure to the $152,000 needed to run the business gives us a cash need of $177,000 for year 1. This cash need is also called "cash burn," which is the term you'll hear most often from investors. Let's round the cash need for year 1 up to $180,000 so our cash balance is not zero at year-end. Therefore, we project asking our investors to fund $180,000 in year 1.

The same exercise is done for years 2 through 5 in the example projection. In year 2, the need is for an additional $240,000 of capital, and in year 3, another $180,000. Notice in years 4 and 5, the cash flow from operations is projected to be positive, and there are no further fixed asset expenditures that require cash, so there is no further need for investor capital. In fact, the venture is projected to generate $100,000 of cash in year 4, and $154,375 in year 5, which totals a cash balance of $256,875 by the end of year 5.

Valuation and Return on Investment

As discussed above, the cash flows to the investors are negative in the first three years, as follows:

Year 1	$ (180,000)
Year 2	$ (240,000)
Year 3	$ (180,000)
Total	**$ (600,000)**

The cash flows are deemed negative because the investors have to give to (fund) the business for the first three years, as opposed to investors receiving funds from the business (e.g., dividends). In the remaining years, the cash flows to the investors are zero in each year: They neither have to fund the business nor are they getting a return from the business.

How do we value the projected business in this sample scenario? For illustration purposes I will show the use of projected cash flow valuation with an assumed "exit" after year 5. To do this we assume the business will be sold at the end of year 5 (the exit). As I said earlier, a common valuation metric is the use of a multiple of operating profit, or EBITDA. Using the five times multiple, that gives a value of $4 million after year 5—meaning that presumably a willing buyer would agree to pay the investors $4 million for this business after year 5.

What are other sources of cash for the investors who are selling the business? They are shown on the balance sheet. In year 5 there is cash of $256,875, which the investors will distribute to themselves before the sale of the company. There is also something called "working capital," which is accounts receivable minus accounts payable and accrued expenses. In our example the numbers look like this:

Accounts receivable	$1,700,000
Accounts payable	$ (240,000)
Accrued expenses	$ (198,750)
Working capital	**$1,261,250**

Therefore, upon a sale the investors will receive the following:

Sale proceeds from buyer of company	$4,000,000
Ending cash balance of company	$256,875
Working capital of company	$1,261,250
Total cash to investors	**$5,518,250**

The investors would get back $5.5 million after five years on a $600,000 investment. That is an incredible return. Remember, however, that startup investing is risky. Most startups do not survive. When I was in venture capital we understood that in a portfolio of ten investments, six would not provide a positive return, three would be mediocre returns, but one could be a grand-slam homerun—and the return on the grand slam would more than make up for the losses and mediocre returns on the other investments.

For those that want a return on investment (ROI) calculation, the ROI in our example is better than 50 percent. (Note: For calculation purposes,

I assumed the sale of the company would close by the end of year 6.) This return compares to the long-term return of publicly traded stocks of approximately 10 percent per year.

Once you understand the type of financial information that must be prepared for investors, you will have a better chance of raising the funds necessary to get your startup off the ground. That, and having a great financial consultant to help you prepare them!

8

SECRETS OF CREATING AND DELIVERING A COMPELLING PITCH

Pitching your idea to investors is daunting. But when you have a great idea, a smart business plan, and amazing people backing you up, you can wow investors and get the financial backing you need.[1]

—ZEYNEP ILGAZ, entrepreneur, former member, Tech Coast Angels group

A pitch is a presentation where you have anywhere from ten to forty minutes to sell investors or organizations on the idea that you, your team, and your company represent an opportunity for them to reap significant returns. Your pitch deck and presentation are usually the first things that an investor sees to learn more about your company. Angel investors and VCs hear thousands of pitches in a given year. However, on average, only 1 percent of pitches ever get funded. The other 99 percent fail because the presentations are unclear, confusing, and not backed up with logical projections, or the founders simply fail to persuade investors of the viability of either the business or the team.

For most investors, a truly good pitch stands out like a lighthouse casting its signal. "The best pitches are when you walk into a room without much of a preformed opinion and meet an exceptional entrepreneur who convinces you within ten minutes that he or she is building a fundamentally important company to address a crucial problem that they're uniquely positioned to solve," says Matt Turck, Managing Director, FirstMark Capital (early-stage VC). "It's sort of magical when everything clicks."[2] Creating that kind of magic takes a great business, a great business plan, and a lot of preparation to deliver a pitch that will sell it easily to investors.

There's a good reason that *Inc.* magazine called John Livesay "the Pitch Whisperer": Helping entrepreneurs create great pitches is his special genius. John is an exceptional coach and mentor for entrepreneurs. He helps them take complex ideas and complicated data and turn them into a compelling story, so that investors are intrigued and want to know more. In this chapter he'll teach you how to build a powerful pitch deck and then create and deliver a knockout pitch presentation.

John Livesay: Pitch Perfect—How to Be Irresistible to Investors

The first part of a perfect pitch is to be in the right room with investors who have money and are interested in what you are doing. And the best way to reach those people is with a warm introduction from someone they know. As an investor once told me, "If you can't figure out a way to get a warm introduction, you probably can't figure out how to get to your customer either."

Once you receive that warm introduction to an investor, follow up promptly with an email outlining your business idea and then asking for a meeting. Keep asking until you get a yes or no. If it's a no, ask for feedback as to why, then thank the investor and ask, "Who else do you know that I should talk to?" Investors know other investors, and that third-degree connection may be the one that funds your business.

Eventually you'll get an investor to say *yes* to a meeting. Congratulations! Now the *real* work begins—finding out as much as possible about who will be in the room. Investigate the individuals (VCs or angels) and organizations (family office, angel group, incubator, accelerator, bank, even the judges of a pitch contest). Research the kinds of deals they've done and the size, the deal points they seem to favor (e.g., a particular equity or debt arrangement, seats on your board), and so on. If you're smart, you'll dig a little deeper to discover what gets the investors excited outside of work, to see if there's a connection between you or your business and that activity.

If an investor loves rock climbing, for instance, and you have an app that helps people find and arrange their perfect vacation, you might emphasize how the "outdoor travel" segment of your market uses your app to plan trips to places like Yosemite. Research your investors the way you would your ideal customers: The more you know, the easier it will be to customize your pitch and get closer to a yes.

However, a pitch is *not* designed to raise money. *The whole purpose of your pitch is to get the "second date"*—that is, a follow-up meeting where your business will be discussed in greater detail. On a first date, you don't want to overwhelm the other person by telling them your entire life story; in the same way, you are *not* explaining everything about your business in your pitch. Your goal is to intrigue and interest investors with just enough juicy information that they will want to know more.

A great pitch answers two key questions. First, "*Why you?*" What makes you and your team uniquely qualified to execute this idea? I've seen far too many entrepreneurs waste half of their ten-minute pitch with a five-minute product demo or description. But investors care more about why you and your team are so passionate about this business, the type of traction you have, how you will make money and scale the business, and how they will get a great ROI.

The second question is, "*Why now?*" Timing is important. If so many people didn't have smartphones by 2009, Uber would not have worked. If the economy hadn't been in trouble in 2008, a lot fewer people would have been open to renting a room or their home to strangers to get more income, and Airbnb would never have been viable. It is important to address why now is the perfect time for your idea—not too early or too late.

But that's not enough: there are three *unspoken* questions that need to be answered, not by the data of your presentation, but by the investor's perceptions of you and your idea.

1. *Unspoken Question #1.* "*Do I think this will work for me?*" This is a head thing. Investors need to see how your startup fits with the other companies in their portfolios. They also need to know they can bring value to the table beyond just money.

2. *Unspoken Question #2*. *"Do I like you?"* This is a heart thing. Investors know that they are potentially entering into a three- to five-year (or more) relationship with you and your company. Will they like spending time with you? Do they feel you have empathy for your customers, understanding their problems on an emotional level? When you connect with your customers' problems, investors are more inclined to believe in your solution.

3. *Unspoken Question #3*. *"Do I trust you?"* This is a gut thing. Investors are taking a large risk with you, as the number of startups that produce a significant ROI is small. So they need to feel like they can trust you to do whatever you say you will to the best of your ability. That means you must be honest and truthful in your pitch. If you get an offer to go into due diligence and investors find out you lied about anything, game over.

To answer all these questions successfully and get to the "second date," your pitch needs to be a combination of (1) a clear business plan as outlined in your pitch deck, wrapped in (2) a compelling presentation filled with interesting stories instead of dry facts, (3) delivered by you with confidence, passion, clarity—and brevity.

The Essentials of a Great Pitch Deck

A pitch deck is a series of slides created in PowerPoint, Keynote, or other presentation software. While your pitch deck is based on the information from your business plan's executive summary, it is supposed to be a *visual* (not digital) outline of your presentation. The biggest mistake many people make with their pitch decks is to have too many slides and too many words on those slides. *The goal is to show the essence of your business in ten to fifteen slides with few (or no) bullet points.*

Guy Kawasaki is a Silicon Valley based marketing specialist who came up with a formula for a good pitch deck: 10/20/30, or ten slides, presented in twenty minutes, using a thirty-point or larger font.[3] Having only ten slides forces you to focus on the essentials of your business. Keeping your presentation to twenty minutes or less keeps you from boring your audience with unnecessary details. And using a thirty-point font causes you to communicate visually using images and high-level information—a much more effective approach for your first meetings with investors.

Let's go through an outline of a successful pitch deck. We'll use as an example the deck for Cole Smith's Tresit Group. (You can find the entire deck in the appendices.) Their product is an app named "All is Well," a customizable software application to help schools, communities, airports, hospitals, and businesses handle emergencies. With his pitch deck and presentation, Cole was offered $1 million from a family office and $700,000 from a New York angel group.

Slide 1. Opening or title. Keep it simple and clean. Feature the name of your product or service, and if you have a tagline or "big idea" for your company, use that too. Cole's first slide featured the tagline, "Prevent—Notify—Respond": essentially the promise of his product in three words.

Slide 2. Summary/value proposition. Investors want to know quickly the value you are offering your customers and the value your business represents to them. This is a great place to show traction—previous sales, revenue, or purchase commitments, for example. Tresit's summary slide states that their technology is patent pending, the target market is $2 billion in size, the app is already in thirty schools, and it has been endorsed by law enforcement. There's also a great testimonial quote.

Slide 3. The problem. Your problem slide should define three distinct customer problems with an image for each. The problems that Tresit is looking to solve are a fifteen-minute response time to emergencies, delayed communication with first responders, and unknown locations of incidents, which delays responses even more.

Slide 4. The solution. This slide should offer a clear solution for each problem, listed in the same order. Tresit's solutions are a five-second notification via the app, instant communication with responders and other concerned parties, and maps within the app directing responders exactly where to go.

Slide 5. The product. This is where the description or demo of your product would happen in your presentation. It should feature what Kawasaki calls the "underlying magic" of your product—what you do better than anyone else. Cole used two slides to show how "All is Well" would work on a smartphone, and then included a diagram of all the different people who could be notified of an emergency in less than five seconds.

Slide 6. Business model. This slide shows who your customers are, the size of your target market, and how your company will make money (or has already made money). To show the size of the market, Cole used a map and statistics about the number of mass shootings, natural disasters, and medical emergencies that occur annually in schools, airports, hospitals, and government buildings in the United States. He followed this slide with Tresit's revenue model: a one-time installation fee, and annual renewal fees for each school or institution that purchased it.

You can include in your business model slide any commitments you have from customers, or sales you have already made. The "All is Well" app was already being used in thirty schools at the time, and Cole highlighted that fact here.

Slide 7. Go to market strategy. This explains how you will reach your customers and who is involved in the decision to buy. Tresit is a B2B company whose target customers are school superintendents, airport or hospital administrators, and possibly local governments. But others can influence the decision to purchase—local law enforcement, parents, other districts, and community influencers (ministers, nonprofits, etc.)— so they are listed as well.

Slide 8. Financials. This slide has the basics of your financial projections in simplified form, including a three-year forecast of sales, revenues, profit and loss, and key metrics like number of customers and conversion rate. (Note: Many investors will be interested in your monthly cash burn, so if you do not include this on your slide, be ready to discuss it in your presentation.) Tresit used a graph of projected revenues and EBITDA designed to give Cole a spot in the presentation to review his financials.

Slide 9. Competition/your unique advantage. You need to make clear to investors that you are aware of who your competitors are, what they offer, and the significant advantages of your product or service. I have found that the best way to do this is to use an x/y-axis grid with short, easy-to-read descriptions of the criteria. Your company should appear in the upper right hand quadrant as the best option, while your competitors are in the other quadrants.

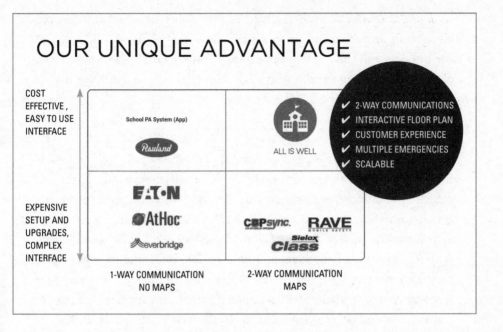

Here's how Tresit's competition grid was laid out. The *x*-axis (at the bottom) is one-way communication without maps, and two-way communication with maps. The *y*-axis (on the side) tracks both cost and ease of use.

Slide 10. The team. This slide should have a photograph of each executive team member, with titles and short descriptions of any valuable past experience. This is one of the most important slides, as your team can give investors greater confidence in your business. Tresit highlighted the law enforcement and school security experience of the founders, along with the web and mobile app design skills of the lead engineer. It noted that two team members had already worked on previous startups.

Slide 11. Funding request and use of funds. This slide outlines clearly where you are in your business development, your funding needs, what the funds will be used for, and a timeline for next steps. If you have other investors already, put those investment amounts on this slide.

Tresit emphasized the fact that its founders already had bootstrapped through two years and the creation of a minimum viable product (MVP), and were now seeking $700,000. Funds would be used to create a new version of the product and hire more key personnel, with the goal of increasing revenues to $6 million in two years.

Slide 12. Closing. The final slide has the business contact information along with any other images or testimonials that reinforce the value of the business and the exciting opportunity it represents to investors. Tresit closed with two powerful testimonials, one of which stated, "Not having Tresit is like not having 911."

You might want to have a few additional slides in your deck, to be used if investors have specific questions on your financials, for example, or the exit strategy you propose, or if you have any strategic partnerships in place. That way, if a question comes up you can simply bring up the appropriate slide as you give the answer. As part of your presentation, you also should bring with you a packet of supplemental information, including your Executive Summary and business plan, current financials with three- to five-year projections, recommendations or testimonial letters, and any detailed market research on your target market. If you already have purchase commitments from customers, bring copies of those letters or purchase orders.

A few final notes about your pitch deck. First, *keep your deck current.* Fundraising can take time, and you may end up going through multiple rounds—and startups have been known to pivot or change a business model in the process. To make sure you're presenting accurate information, update your deck at any point your company makes a substantive change.

Second, *you may want to have a more thorough version of your deck in PDF form* that you can leave with investors. This deck might include your supplemental slides, as well as any details you covered in person but are not on your slides: highlights of your financials, for example, or more data on your target market. That way, an investor who wasn't at the meeting can review the deck and get a sense of the content you covered in your live presentation.

Finally, remember: *the real goal of your pitch deck is to get a second meeting.* So keep your slides short, sweet, and to the point—just like your presentation.

A Great Pitch Presentation Tells a Great Story

You will use the slides of your pitch deck as the outline, but *you* have to fill in the facts, figures, and most important, stories that will compel investors to want to know more about you and your business. All of this in anywhere from ten to forty minutes!

Remember, investors see thousands of pitches in a given year, so they can quickly lose interest unless you have something that makes you and your company stand out. Therefore, the secret to a successful pitch presentation is to turn the facts and figures of your business into a great *story*.

Plato is supposed to have said, "People who tell stories rule society." That's because stories are far more memorable than plain facts and figures. When you start talking about numbers and how something works, you're tapping into the left brain/analytical side, and investors often will start critiquing your pitch. But if you say, "Let me tell you a story," they relax. They're in their right brain, their imagination, and suddenly you are making an emotional as well as a logical connection with them. Investors will need to see your numbers, but they will *connect* with—and remember—your stories. The stories told in your presentation should inform, inspire, and entertain while being both pertinent and persuasive.

Like a story, your presentation should have a clear beginning, middle, and end, with specific types of content that will tell the persuasive story of the value of your business idea. Using your slides as an outline, here are some important content points you should make, as well as a few suggestions of how to use stories in your presentation.

Your Opening

There's an important principle in journalism: "Never bury the lede." This means, put whatever you want your investors to remember up front. No matter how much or little time you are given to pitch, you have only ninety seconds to grab an investor's attention, so open with a declaration of who you are, what your company is about, and what you are looking for in funding. Follow this with a story, fact, or statistic about your company that will immediately engage the audience's interest.

Because investors often bet on founders as much as the company, if you have a great personal story, open with that. One of my clients, Martin, grew up in the Netherlands but is originally from South America. When he turned eighteen his parents took him back to South America and dropped him, naked, into the Amazon jungle to survive on his own for two weeks—in his culture, that is the rite of passage into manhood. When I asked him what three lessons he learned from surviving in the Amazon jungle, he said, "How to focus, how to persevere, and how to pivot when something wasn't working. I took those lessons from the Amazon jungle into the 'concrete jungle' of being an entrepreneur." That story became an important part of the opening of Martin's pitch.

Many founders appearing on *Shark Tank* start their pitch with a personal story of facing a particular problem themselves and caring so much about it that they had to come up with a solution. This story adds credibility (if they've had the problem themselves, then they understand their customers) as well as humanity to their presentations.

Another way to open your pitch is with a story about a specific customer. Tinder's original pitch featured a guy named Matt:

"This is Matt.

"Matt spots a girl he likes at a party . . . BUT, like most of us, Matt won't go over to say hello.

"He has the same problem most of us do . . . FEAR OF REJECTION!

"Meet the cure . . . Matchbox!" (Tinder's original name)

This opening (complete with photos of "Matt" on the slides) put the customer's problem front and center, and then positioned Tinder as the solution.[4]

You also can start with a "Did you know?" question that describes the problems you are solving in a way that surprises investors with new information.[5] Here's an example from the pitch for Walkabout Office:

"Did you know over 90 percent of remote business workers say the biggest issue they have is not being able to engage face to face or just being able to walk down the hall and knock on a colleague's door to ask a quick question?

Combine this with the fact that the majority of collaboration tools today tend to have poor adoption and can be confusing to use, you can see why the majority of managers say their remote teams are still falling short of their goals.

"Imagine if there was a simple to use, three-dimensional virtual workplace that made remote teams feel like they were physically together, made spontaneous interactions easy, increased employee engagement, created faster and better decisionmaking, and allowed them to actually exceed their goals.

"You don't have to imagine it. We have created it."

Because you should allow no more than ninety seconds for your entire opening, make sure that any story you tell is short and to the point.

The Body of Your Presentation

This is the majority of your presentation, which you will cover in ten to fifteen minutes. Start with your *value proposition*, your unique advantage in the marketplace, the size of the potential target market, and any proof of concept (traction). Let investors know right up front that you have something of value to offer and how excited you are about your company.

Next, tell a story of *the problems your customers are facing*, and how your product or service is the solution. Mary (a client of mine) has a company that helps banks use technology to deal with regulations efficiently so they won't get fined for noncompliance. We were trying to figure out a way to explain this to investors without getting too technical about the product or bank regulations. We used this story to describe the customers' problem:

"Do you remember the opening scene from the movie, Raiders of the Lost Ark? *Indiana Jones is being chased by a huge boulder that's rolling after him, faster and faster. He's running as fast as he can, and the audience is on the edge of their seats because they think he's not going to not make it. That's how banks are feeling today, because they are facing a 'boulder' of regulations bearing down on them all the time. Every day they're worried about making even the smallest mistake that might cause them to incur huge fines. And because regulations are constantly changing, no matter how fast the banks go, they still can't stay ahead.*

"That's why there is such a need for our services. We make it possible for the banks to easily stay on the right side of changing regulations and avoid paying thousands, if not hundreds of thousands, of dollars in fines."

When you paint a picture for investors using a visual image and a reference to a story they already know, investors instantly understand the problem you're solving.

Now you're up to the *product demo or description of what your product does*. You must walk a fine line here: You need to make clear what your product is and what it does in such a way that investors are intrigued but not overwhelmed. Keep your presentation high-level and clear, and deliver your product information or demo concisely and with enthusiasm. Do not let yourself get bogged down even in "cool" technical details, or the minutia of how your cutting-edge technology works. Focus instead on how your product or service is new, different, or better, and how it solves the customers' problems.

Keep two things in mind when preparing the body of your presentation. First, investors are not buying your product; they are investing in your company and your team's ability to make a profit. So the product demo is *not* the most important part of your presentation, and it should take no more than two to three minutes.

Second, make sure to test your product demo before the meeting to make sure everything works!

The next section of your presentation describes your business, which *is* what investors want to know about: your *business model, go to market strategy*, and *financials*. Your presentation will talk about how your company makes its money; who you sell to and how you reach them; what revenues you expect to make in the next one, three, and five years; your current monthly cash burn rate; and when you expect to be profitable if you are not already. If you've already made sales or have any traction in the marketplace, describe that here as well. Talk about any major goals you've already achieved, and the next steps you plan on taking. Make sure your numbers (including your projections) are realistic and backed up with data-driven assumptions. Your goal is to demonstrate that you know your business—and your numbers—cold.

The next area to cover is your *competition*. Investors want to know that you're aware of your competitors but not worried about them. If you have market research about your customers' primary concerns (cost versus value, speed, ease of use, and so on), use it to show how your company can beat the competition in those areas. If your competition has a particular weakness in an area where you are strong, cite that. And if there is an aspect of a competitor's product or service that's better than yours, mention it and say how you are either compensating for it or working to overcome it. Investors are likely to know about any competitor's advantage already, so better for you to bring it up first.

Next, describe the key members of *your team*, including their backgrounds and achievements, and why this is the best team to make your company successful. Often there is a great story to be told about how you and your team came together and started the company. If it's pertinent and it demonstrates team expertise or cohesiveness, tell it. But keep it short: You're close to the end of your presentation, and investors are ready to hear what you need from them.

Now it's time to make your *funding request*—clearly, specifically, and unapologetically. Ask for the money you need, and then immediately say exactly what milestones it will be used to accomplish: to upgrade a product, launch a new marketing campaign, hire key personnel, and so on. If you have other investors already on board, mention them and what they have received for their investment. Tell the investors what you are offering them for their money: a percentage of equity, convertible debt, a board seat, and so on. (While all of this will be up for discussion later, investors usually prefer founders to say what they are offering first.)

After your funding request, you can open the floor for any questions. (Note: It's possible investors won't wait until the end to ask questions. Don't let this throw you off—it's often a *good* sign, as it shows they are interested enough to want to know more.) When you're asked a question, remember that you know more about your company than they do, so answer with confidence. Also, you should have prepared supplemental slides for your pitch deck to help you answer certain questions. If there are things you don't know, say so, and tell them you will get the answer within forty-eight hours (or other reasonable amount of time). Then keep your commitment and provide the requested information by the deadline!

Your Conclusion

The *conclusion* of your presentation should be a confident declaration of the great potential of your company and how excited you are to move forward to the next phase, and then end with an invitation for investors to join you on the journey. Without stating it directly, make them feel you will be successful with or without their help, but they will be missing out if they don't come along.

Here are a few keys to remember when working on your presentation. First, *don't "boil the ocean."* Many founders try to tell investors everything they want to do now and in the future—in other words, "boiling the ocean." Your job is to take all of the information about your company and pull out only the "nuggets" that will make investors want to put their money in your "gold mine." Remember, the confused mind always says *no*. If you pitch your idea in a way that is too hard to understand, investors say *no*. If you can't answer investor questions, you will lose credibility and get a no. Be concise and clear in your thinking—and in your presentation.

Second, *prioritize the information in your presentation.* You may walk in for a meeting and find out you have ten minutes instead of the forty you were promised. Know what you can cut out of your presentation depending on the time you have, and what you absolutely need to keep in. And always take less time than you're given. The most valuable asset investors have is their time, and as entrepreneur Neil Patel points out, if you show respect for their time, they may equate that to a willingness to treat their investment with respect also.[6] So if you've been told you have fifteen minutes, take ten; if you're supposed to have thirty minutes, take twenty. When I gave my TEDx talk, "Be the lifeguard of your own life," they told me I could have up to eighteen minutes. But I only spoke for over eleven minutes because that is the exact amount of time I needed to get my point across. It must have worked, because my TEDx talk has over one million views.

Just because you're given a certain amount of time doesn't mean you need to fill it all up. The more clear, concise, and compelling you are, the better your pitch will be. Better to end early and have more time for questions than to have to rush through and forget something important.

Third, *make sure your stories are effective.* They must be clear, have an important point, take no more than thirty seconds to a minute, and produce either a strong emotion or greater understanding in the listener. Above all, remember to tell your stories with energy and passion. There are academic studies showing that investors respond more favorably to founders who demonstrate passion, because they believe these entrepreneurs are more likely to stay the course when their startups face tough times.[7] Don't be afraid to show investors your excitement about your idea, and your commitment to making this business successful.

Finally, you can have a great pitch deck and great content, but if you are uncomfortable or uncertain in your delivery, you're sunk. You need to *practice your presentation until it's second nature and then deliver it with confidence.* That's what we'll cover next.

Prepare to Deliver a Powerful Pitch

Investors want to see you have a vision for your business *and* the confidence to make that vision real. From the moment you walk in the room to begin your pitch, you have to exude confidence that your idea is going to work and investors are putting their money in the right place. And the only way to create this level of confidence is to prepare, prepare, prepare.

Tennis great Arthur Ashe said, "One important key to success is self-confidence. An important key to self-confidence is preparation."[8] Athletes don't wing it before they get to the Olympics—they practice. So do musicians; so do actors before getting onstage or in front of the camera. If they need to practice and rehearse, so do you. You must practice your pitch until it's second nature.

To practice effectively, do the following. First, figure out what works best for you when preparing your presentation. Some people write out every word, while others prefer to use bullet points. Whether you start with a written script or bullet points, eventually you should work without notes and use the slides from your pitch deck as a guide for delivering your pitch.

Once you have your presentation outlined or written, practice it with your pitch deck so you get used to delivering your presentation while running the slides at the same time. When you're somewhat confident with what you're saying and how you're saying it (while running slides), do your presentation in front of one person or a few people—team members, family, or friends. Make sure they are clear that this is *not* a feedback session; it's simply to allow you to get used to presenting to a live audience. Once you're feeling more comfortable, ask one or two people whose opinion you trust to give you feedback. You don't have to adopt everything they say, but listen to their input and see if it is valid. If so, change your presentation accordingly.

Finally, do a full-on dress rehearsal for a few friends or team members. Wear what you plan to wear when you present, and walk into the place you will be presenting as if it is the investor's office, and greet people as if they were the investors. (From the moment you walk into a meeting, you'll be evaluated on how you look, dress, shake hands, introduce yourself, and so on, so practice it all.) Set up your laptop, projector, and screen, and test your equipment just like you will in the real pitch. Then go through your presentation without stopping, just as you would do in front of investors. If anything goes wrong, deal with it and keep going. Make sure to include questions and answers as part of your dress rehearsal. Put together a list of the toughest questions you can imagine investors asking, and then have your friends or team members ask you those questions, so you can practice handling them effectively.

Do as many dress rehearsals as you need to feel confident. If you follow this schedule, by the time you walk into an investor's office or conference room to deliver your first presentation, it'll be easy, because you'll feel like you've done it a hundred times already.

A Few Tips to Speak More Effectively

Your goal with rehearsing your presentation thoroughly is to appear confident and natural, even if you've never spoken to investors before and it's not in your comfort zone. But while your presentation should feel like a conversation, your goal is to take people on a journey with you, to keep them engaged with what you are saying and showing them, and to persuade them to say *yes*. You can call it a "heightened" conversation—one with energy and impact.

To that end, when you practice your presentation, keep these tips in mind to be a more effective speaker.

1. *Before you enter the room, relax.* Don't try to get rid of the butterflies in your stomach: Recognize them as a manifestation of excess nervous energy. Try shaking your hands vigorously or doing a few head rolls to release tension. And instead of worrying about the outcome, focus on why you started your business in the first place.

2. *Stack your moments of certainty* (see Chapter 2 for this exercise). Review those moments, and remember how it felt when you succeeded. Focus on those thoughts and feelings instead of any negative self-talk. Think to yourself, "That confident person is my authentic self."

3. *For two minutes, stand in a "superhero" pose.* Imagine what Superman or Wonder Woman looks like, and adopt their body posture: stand tall, put your hands on your hips, put your shoulders back, and imagine a cape blowing in the wind behind you. This technique is also called "power posing" or the "expansive pose," and it's been shown to increase feelings of power.[9] Doing the superhero pose helped Mallory Dyer, founder and CEO of GraphLock, win a pitch contest in 2016. Right before she went onstage, she took a few moments to stand in her superhero pose and remember her moments of certainty. "The judges, the MC, and many people from the crowd told me my pitch was by far the best and I was the most steady and confident out of the eight," she said.[10] She also won two of three awards presented that night.

4. *When you walk in the room, own the space and fill the room with your energy.* Whatever your usual level of energy, increase it by 50 percent—especially if you're an introvert. (Make sure you practice your pitch with this heightened level of energy as well.) Let the people in the room know immediately that they will want to listen to what you have to say.

5. *Make eye contact.* A presentation is still a conversation, so look at the people, not your slides. However, don't freak people out by staring at them—keep it natural.

6. *Speak slowly.* This is counterintuitive, because it's easy to feel time pressure to cover everything in your presentation. However, speaking slowly gives you authority and makes it easier for investors to absorb what you have to say. So take three deep breaths before you begin, and speak slower than

you think you should. And never rush the end of your presentation. It's better to edit your content rather than speed up at the end.

7. *Vary your voice.* Think of your pitch as a piece of music and your voice as a musical instrument. Just like music has a variety of speed, tone, tempo, with pauses for silence, your vocal delivery should be the same. A monotone, robot-line recitation of facts is deadly. Instead, vary your pace, speak loudly and softly, and use pauses to emphasize your points.

8. *Move and gesture with purpose.* Purposeful movement or gestures can be great ways of emphasizing important points. Is there a spot where you could lean toward your listeners? Do you want to point at the projection of your slide to emphasize the size of your market or when you will reach profitability? Using movement and gesture naturally can be difficult for some people; that's why it's vital to rehearse movement and gestures so you will be comfortable with them. And if you're not comfortable, don't do it.

9. *No matter what happens, power through.* Don't apologize, don't explain, and don't let them see you sweat. Just keep going, and convey your total belief and passion about your business and the opportunity it presents.

A great pitch displays key business information with powerful visuals in a pitch deck. Then that information is wrapped in a compelling story and it's presented confidently by the business founder with passion and energy. But remember—you are selling yourself as well as your business, so create and deliver a pitch presentation that's right for *you*. It's far better for you to devise a presentation based on your own natural strengths than try to be someone you're not. As long as you have a strong business model and a cohesive story, and you've practiced your presentation enough that you have confidence in your ability to deliver it well, then you'll do fine.

The bottom line is, there's never just one way to deliver a great pitch. As VC Tomasz Tunguz puts it, "Some founders use data. Others use logic. Still others use emotion and passion to do it. But in the end, these exceptional storytellers make you want to believe, suspend doubt, and disregard the great risks that all startups face all along their journey, and get involved with the business."[11] Simply do your best—and then confidently ask for the "second date."

9

RISK MITIGATION
How to Make It Easy for Investors to Say *Yes*

> While unicorns as the focal point of most startup conversations illustrate the upside potential, battles are more often won by reducing the downside risk.[1]
>
> **—MARTIN HOFFMAN,** CEO, Business & Investor Labs

I f you followed the advice in Chapter 8, you delivered a great presentation to your potential investors—one that clearly described your idea, business model, customers, the quality of your team, financial projections, and request for funding. But that's still not enough to get the second meeting. Most investors have seen a lot of presentations, and they know that, despite how great the opportunity may seem, at least 70 percent of tech startups (and 97 percent of consumer hardware startups) fail, usually within twenty months of their first fundraising round. What's worse, those tech startups raised around $1.3 million each—money down the drain from the investors' perspective.[2]

Of course, investors know that startups are inherently risky, but they want to minimize or mitigate risk as much as possible. Therefore, while your pitch is painting a clear picture of how great your product or service is and how profitable you and your team are going to make the company, investors are listening for the ways you're protecting your business from failure and the resulting loss of their capital.

Risk mitigation is so important that the "dean" of early-stage angel investors, Dave Berkus, uses it as his primary means of valuing prerevenue tech startups. (We'll cover valuation models in Chapter 10.) As investors evaluate your pitch, they are looking for ways that your startup addresses five principal types of risk: *product risk, market risk, management (or execution) risk, financial risk*, and *competitive risk*. Especially during the Q&A, you need to be prepared to show how you have dealt with these risks or plan to do so as you grow.

1. Product Risk

Every great idea doesn't turn into a great product or service, and it's far too easy for founders to be so captivated by their "next big thing" that they ignore issues that will keep it from being the foundation for a profitable business. Therefore, you need to be able to answer these questions.

First, *is the product or service workable? Is it possible given today's technology?* Visionaries like Steve Jobs and Elon Musk may be great at envisioning a new product and then inspiring teams to create the technology needed to create it. But sometimes the promises outdistance the ability of the founder's company to meet them.

Musk's company, Tesla, Inc., is a great example. The Tesla Model 3 was supposed to be the inexpensive ($35,000 base price) "cash cow" that would take the company from the red into the black. As of August 2017, Tesla reported that more than 455,000 people had put deposits on the Model 3.[3] However, it took until mid-2018 for Tesla to hit its production goals of 5,000 cars per week, and by then the company had refunded almost a quarter of customer deposits.[4] The biggest delay may have been due to problems with the battery that powers the Model 3. Some analysts speculated the issue was with the chemistry of the new battery.[5] Others pointed out assembly issues at Tesla's battery production site in Nevada. But regardless of cause, issues with production of the Model 3 affected the price of Tesla stock.[6]

Of course, many startup products are still in development and may change dramatically over their lifetimes. To mitigate this risk, create an MVP (minimum viable product) before you start to raise funds, and when you pitch, bring a working prototype with you.

Second, *is the product user-friendly?* According to data on 243 startup failures collected by CB Insights, founders stated that 17 percent of their companies failed due to a user-unfriendly product.[7] In 2005, Wesabe launched as a web-based personal money management tool, and over the life of the company it amassed $4.7 million in funding. In 2007, Mint launched a competing financial management website. Despite entering the market two years after Wesabe, Mint had a better design and an easier user interface: Mint's users had to do almost no work at all to get their account up and running. Wesabe's cofounder Marc Hedlund freely admitted that his company "sucked at all that." Intuit acquired Mint in 2009 for $170 million, while Wesabe closed its doors in 2010.[8]

To mitigate this risk, do what Hedlund advised in a blog post entitled "Why Wesabe Lost to Mint": "Focus on what really matters: making users happy with your product as quickly as you can, and helping them as much as you can after that. If you do those better than anyone else out there you'll win."[9]

Third, *is it possible to produce the product or service at a price point that will cover costs while attracting the majority of customers in its target market?* Tyler Gaffney, sales expert in residence at First Round Capital, a seed-stage VC firm, cites four mistakes startups commonly make in their pricing: (1) conjuring prices without consulting their customers; (2) picking a price and sticking to it even as the business grows and changes; (3) setting the price too low; and (4) trying to innovate too much on their pricing structure (charging per call when your customers are used to a monthly fee, for example).

To mitigate this risk, be willing to adapt your pricing based on customer feedback. "Getting pricing right requires an experimental mindset and willingness to have an honest dialogue with potential customers," says Gaffney. "Each conversation is another signal telling you if you're moving in the right direction, or if you need to adapt and change."[10]

2. Market Risk

The top reason startup founders gave for failure (42 percent) was no market need for their product or service.[11] Even if you think your product is amazing, unless enough customers want it, your business will not survive. Is your product really something that your customers want and need? Does it solve the customers' problem and reduce their pain? If it is simply an incremental improvement on something that's already available, is it enough of a difference that people will pay for it?

Juicero sold a high-end juice press that featured proprietary juice packs and wifi connectivity, at a price point of $699 (juice packs extra). The company raised $100 million from investors, but consumers saw no reason to spend that much on a juice press, even with wifi connectivity. After it was revealed that the juice packs could be squeezed by hand as efficiently as with the press, Juicero shut down operations just sixteen months after launch.[12]

To mitigate this risk, do detailed market research so you can prove to investors that (1) the solutions provided by your product or service answer the pressing problems your potential customers are facing, and (2) these answers are good enough to justify your taking market share. Investors also like to see that you have customers already willing to purchase, so letters of intent from customers or previous sales are helpful in making your case. By the way, don't think you can prove market need because you've done a big (and expensive) marketing push to attract potential customers. Smart investors will look at your acquisition cost per customer to see if your model is sustainable. Remember, the "Holy Grail" of proven market need is organic growth driven by recommendations of happy customers.

Another market risk that investors want to avoid is a mistimed product. Is your product ahead (or behind) of what the market needs? In 1999 Netscape's Marc Andreessen and Ben Horowitz started LoudCloud, a site that hosted dot-com companies' websites and e-commerce—essentially, an early version of cloud computing. It was a great idea but ahead of its time, especially after the dot-com bubble burst in 2001. LoudCloud pivoted, becoming Opsware, which sold data management software to big companies. Hewlett-Packard acquired Opsware in 2007 for $1.65 billion.[13]

Another example of market mistiming is releasing a minimally viable product that's not quite "viable" enough. Keen Home markets products to help people make their homes more comfortable and energy-efficient, and its first product was the Keen Vent system. In 2013 cofounders Nayeem Hussain, Will McLeod, and Ryan Fant were given the chance to pitch their company at TechCrunch Disrupt NYC, and they decided to launch a crowdfunding campaign at the same time to take advantage of the publicity. However, Keen Vent raised only $40,000 on Indiegogo, a less than stellar demonstration of market demand. "In hindsight, our company/product was far too early-stage for us to instill the requisite confidence that we would be able to deliver a working product to backers," Hussain remembers.[14]

Luckily, bad timing for an MVP does not have to mean the end. Keen Home produced more than $2.6 million in sales in its first twelve months, and as of 2018 it had raised $9.5 million via five funding rounds, including two rounds of equity crowdfunding.[15] And it's better to launch an early-stage MVP and then adapt it based on customer feedback than to wait until the product is "perfect" to release it. But poor sales of an MVP will raise questions with investors—unless you can show your plans to either change the product or pivot to a new product altogether.

3. Management (or Execution) Risk

A great idea often fails due to the inexperience of the management team. This risk is also known as *execution risk*: Investors want to know if the team can execute on the startup's business model and plan. As CEO of Garland Capital Group Gary Holdren observes, "Business models and go-to-market strategies may change, but I want to know that the team has what it takes to deliver, and that should come across in a pitch meeting."[16]

Do you have the right expertise and diversity in your team to bring the product to market? Is your team open to feedback from its customers, or is it so in love with the product that it develops "tunnel vision"? Management or execution risk is one of the reasons that many investors like founders to have startup experience under their belts. Marcia Nelson of Alberleen Family Offices, says, "We want to see a team that has experience running a business, especially in a similar or related field. If we don't have faith in the current management team then we won't pursue an investment."[17]

Investors also should feel that the management team shares a unified vision for the company. Startups are stressful environments, and investors want to know that your team will be pulling in the same direction when things get tough. One way to demonstrate team cohesion is for cofounders and other management team members to be present when the founder pitches investors. They may be able to bring up data if you forget to mention it, or be available for questions following your presentation. And founders usually appreciate having "supporters" in the room.

A unified vision isn't enough, however. Investors want to be certain of the team's ability to pivot if the business model or plan isn't working. How flexible is your team? Are they able to change focus dramatically if the business model, MVP, or execution plan fails? Are they tracking the right metrics to accurately evaluate the need for a pivot? Investors know that it may take two to three pivots before a startup figures out how to make money, but the ability to pivot will depend on the quality of the management team. Because Venrock invests early in a company's life cycle, partner and VC David Packman has seen the challenges startup management teams may face. "The one mitigating factor for setbacks is a great team," he says. "We spend the most amount of time thinking about the founders and the early team before investing."[18]

4. Financial Risk

Running out of cash is second only to "no market need" when it comes to reasons for startup failure.[19] Do you have enough cash to make it until you receive investor funding? Remember, it can take upward of six to nine months to close a funding round, so you'd better have enough money in the bank to keep the doors open for a while.

"Running out of cash is the opposite of a milestone—it's the ultimate moment of vulnerability," observes Eric Paley, managing partner of seed-stage fund Founder Collective. "Vulnerable companies are simply unappealing to investors, and often cannot attract capital on any terms."[20] If you are close to being out of cash, any investors you're pitching to will be asking themselves, "If I put money into this deal, are the founders going to have to come back to me (or someone else) again?" They want to make sure your startup is going to be a viable investment—which means, you have enough money to keep going. That's why investors will always ask for your cash flow statement and want to know your cash burn rate.

Here are a few ways to mitigate financial risk:

- *Lengthen your fundraising timeline.* Don't wait until you have two to three months' worth of money left; instead, start pitching when you have cash to cover six to nine months of operating expenses.

- *Let a professional handle company finances.* If you're prerevenue, you may not want (or need) to hire a CFO, but founders should focus on making the business successful, not on tracking expenses. Hire an accountant or bookkeeper, or contract with an accounting firm to keep your books and provide you with regular financial reports. However, you need to monitor those reports (as well as sales, revenues, expenses, and above all, cash flow) weekly, if not daily. Watch your sales cycles and see how you can accelerate sales and payments. Watch expenses and cut out any waste.

- *Keep a cash reserve fund* of a few months' operating expenses. It will give you the flexibility to deal with emergencies or an unexpected but necessary pivot.

- *Get paid—regularly.* See if you can set up automated payments with your customers. If finances get tight, you might consider giving good customers a discount for prepayment.

- *Raise more money from current investors rather than seeking new ones.* If your startup is making good but not great progress and you find yourself in need of more capital, you might find it easier to "top up" your current funding round instead of going to a new stage. If you're in the seed stage, for instance, go back to seed-stage investors; don't start trying to raise series A funding until you have better milestones to report.

- *Have an action plan for a worst-case financial scenario* that shows how investors could recoup some of their money if your startup fails. While startups are by their nature risky investments, showing that you are conscientious about repaying investors if the business goes under will go a long way to mitigating financial risk in their eyes.

5. Competitive Risk

You talked about your competitive advantage in your pitch, but investors need to know exactly what you are doing to gain market share from companies that are already in your space. Are there "barriers to entry" (like a patent, or new technology) that will keep you ahead of the marketplace? Do you have resources or assets (a database of loyal customers, for example) that can protect you from being outcompeted? Conversely, do you have competitors with deep pockets that could replicate your product or service?

It used to be that being first to market was an almost insurmountable competitive advantage, but no more. "First to market seldom matters. Rather, first to product/market fit is almost always the long-term winner," wrote Andy Rachleff, cofounder and executive chairman of Wealthfront.[21] Rachleff points out that LinkedIn and eight other professional networking sites, including Jigsaw, Plaxo, and Six Degrees, were founded at about the same time. But because of LinkedIn's early traction and expert management team, it attracted funding from two top-tier VCs, Sequoia and Greylock. By the time it went public in 2011, LinkedIn had raised more than $200 million; its IPO sold $352.8 million worth of shares. In 2016 Microsoft bought the company for $26 billion.[22]

You mitigate competitor risk by things like:

- Proprietary intellectual property protected by patents
- Contracts with major clients already in place
- A database of customers with comprehensive information on their preferences

As Harvard Business School professor and entrepreneurial expert Howard Stevenson once wrote, "Reducing and eliminating . . . risk increases the valuation of the company . . . and also improves your chance of survival and growth." I recommend that you create a risk mitigation worksheet to use in your company. Then, be sure to address these five kinds of risk in your presentation, and be prepared to answer questions about them. Even if you don't have clear solutions for every risk, simply showing that you are aware and are making efforts to mitigate them will go a long way toward reassuring investors.

Five Questions You'll Need to Answer for Investors to Say *Yes*

There are several other issues investors are likely to raise following your pitch, and you must deal with them before you secure a second meeting. We'll cover ways to respond to those questions, and then talk about what to do when you are turned down. (I say "when" because rejection is a key part of the funding journey. To crack the funding code, you need to know how to respond to rejection and use it to keep you moving forward.)

When you are answering investors' questions, you may get some direct feedback. Beware of becoming defensive or discounting their advice. Robert Herjavec, one of the Sharks on *Shark Tank*, says, "Be open to other people's perspectives. When an entrepreneur doesn't hear us out and instead gets defensive or aggressive, I know we're not going to get a deal done."[23] Be receptive to investor feedback and listen to their ideas. Even if you don't get their money, you may be able to use their suggestions to improve your business and your pitch.

Question #1: What's Your Company's Growth Potential?

Remember, investors are looking for a five to ten times ROI in five to ten years, so they are going to need to understand how you plan to scale your business. Be ready to cover not just the three- to five-year numbers from your financial projections but also how your business plan can handle massive growth. You may want to use examples of other startups in similar markets to show how they were able to scale up (and possibly exit).

"Investors are looking to make ten times on their money within the lifetime of their fund. They know they are often betting ahead of the curve on a market and want to feel confident that if they are right there'll be a big payoff," observes Andrew Medal, founder, Agent Beta digital agency. "This is where having well-grounded metrics around the size of the opportunity are important. They want to see a large growing market for what you offer to be in the billions. This means that even if you don't execute perfectly the market momentum may carry them to a successful exit."[24]

Question #2: What Are the Details of the Investment You're Proposing?

You cover this in your pitch presentation, but investors may want to know more about what you are offering them for their money, and what that money will be used for. They may suggest changes to your offer ("Would you give us a board seat?" "We usually ask for *X* percent of equity in a deal like this," and so on). Asking for something specific is a *really* good sign, so don't give investors a hard *no*. Instead, let them know that you'll be happy to discuss terms in your second meeting.

Question #3: What Will the Money Be Used For?

Again, your pitch presentation should have outlined objectives to be accomplished with the requested capital, but investors may want to dig deeper into your planning and strategy. They want to see that you have a clear operational plan, with specific milestones and dates, so their money isn't wasted on nonessentials. Your three- to five-year financial projections will give them an idea of income, P&L, and cash flow, but be prepared to discuss how your operational plan will produce those numbers, and how the current round of funding will help you get there. Be realistic in terms of the milestones you say you plan to hit. Investors want founders to be confident and committed—not delusional. Be honest, and don't overpromise.

Question #4: How and When Will Investors Get Their Money Back?

You should have projections for three different scenarios: (1) if your business goes to plan, (2) if it goes better than plan, and (3) if it goes worse than plan. In all three cases, show investors how and when their investment will be repaid. If you're speaking with seed- or early-stage investors, be ready to show what will happen to their investment if (or when) you pursue further rounds of funding with bigger firms. (Of course, these terms are open to negotiation and will be part of the term sheet and final agreement.)

Question #5: What's Your Exit Strategy?

It's important that you show investors right away that you are planning for a successful exit that will produce the greatest return in that five- to ten-year window. Do your research on similar companies that have been sold, who bought them, and for how much. If any of these companies went public, research how much the IPO raised. In both cases, determine the returns investors received and the time between investment and payout, and use those numbers to help you estimate potential exit totals.

How to Read Investors at the Meeting

Let's say that you've finished your pitch to investors. You've addressed all five risks to the best of your ability and answered the five questions listed above. You feel like you've made a compelling case for your startup as a great opportunity to invest. How can you tell if you've made the sale?

Start by focusing on your audience and read their body language. If they're not listening, or if they're checking their phones, it's obviously not a good sign. However, interrupting you to ask questions is a positive, because it means they want to know more about a particular point—and that means they're listening.

Next, if the investors don't propose next steps, ask them directly: "When can we set a second meeting?" This is not a time to be wishy-washy and ask, "Do you need any more information?" or "Any more questions?" Better to get a clear indication now than keep pursuing them when they're just not interested. In all honesty, any response other than, "Yes, let's set a meeting" is not good. If they put you off, or say, "We'll get back to you," ask if you should bother following up with them or if there is something specific they need to know to set a meeting. If the answer is *no*, thank them and move on.

Finally, if they tell you they'd like to see you again after you've completed the milestones you outlined in your presentation, thank them and ask if they can recommend any other investors you should speak with now.

If they are willing to introduce you to people in their network, it demonstrates their belief in the viability of your startup. "Make sure you know the investors who have coinvested with them on past deals, and ask for specific introductions to two or three of these investors," writes Candace Sjogren, founder of two fintech companies and managing partner of CXO Solutions. "If investors like what you are selling, they will be eager to introduce you to their peers, allowing them to get credit for sourcing your company and providing themselves with peer backup and coinvestment, should they choose to sign a check."[25]

Dealing with Rejection

Even if you have the best pitch in the world, you are still going to be rejected—repeatedly. Don't take it personally: Investors have reasons for turning you down that may have nothing to do with your startup. When you are turned down, do three things.

First, if you haven't already done so, ask if they know other investors you should speak to and if they'd be willing to provide you with an introduction. If possible, get names and contact details before you leave.

Second, ask for their reasons for turning you down and/or how you could improve your presentation. See if you can get specifics. Was it your financials? Your business model? Your target market? Use the information to make your next presentation better.

Third, recognize that every no is another step toward a yes. VC investor Mark Suster tells a story of going out with friends when they were all in their early twenties. They were surprised when one guy who wasn't particularly handsome or charismatic did far better at getting women to dance with him and give him their phone numbers. When asked, his friend said, "The only difference between me and the rest of you is that I'm willing to hear 'no' fifteen times before I get a yes. But I don't let the 'no's' get to me. I just know that I'm not for everybody so when they say 'no' I just think I must not be their type."[26]

Not every investor is going to be a good match for you and your business (and you wouldn't want to partner with an unsuitable investor anyway). But the only way to get to the *yes* is to get in front of a lot of people who will tell you *no*. Fundraising, like sales, is a numbers game: The more people you get in front of, the more *no*'s you will hear—but the more quickly you will find an investor who will say *yes*.

Above all, keep going. Fundraising is never the main focus of a startup: Producing and delivering a great product or service is. Keep doing that while you continue reaching out to investors through your network. Hone your presentation as you update your financials, get more traction, reach more customers, and so on. Create a monthly investor mailing list and send them information on your progress; you might be surprised to find that they reach out to you in the future.

Remember: All it takes is one *yes* to get that second meeting, and you're one step closer to the funding you need.

IV

CLOSING THE DEAL

If there is ever a time to remember the adage "time is money," it's during the final inning of your fundraising efforts.[1]

—RYAN CALDBECK, founder, CircleUp

10

"I HAVE AN INVESTOR: NOW WHAT?"
The Valuation, Deal Terms, and When to Say *No*

> Don't think of [the term sheet] as a letter of intent. Think of it as a blueprint for your future relationship with your investor.[1]
>
> **—BRAD FELD** and **JASON MENDELSON,** *Venture Deals*

Congratulations! You have attracted interest from an investor. Now comes the stage where you set up a deal that will work for both sides. In this chapter we'll discuss how to vet your investors, understand term sheet basics and deal terms, establish your company's valuation, how to cost-effectively choose and use a lawyer to ensure the deal works for you, and when to walk away from a deal.

Jeffrey M. Harvey, Esq., will be our guide through this chapter. Jeff is a business attorney and general counsel who has served as legal and strategic advisor to private and public companies, private equity and investment firms, high net worth individuals and family offices, and entrepreneurs and small-business owners. Currently he is the vice president and general counsel to PrimeSource Building Products, Inc.

Jeff Harvey: Vetting Your Investors and Setting Up the Deal

Setting up the funding agreement for your startup should be a proactive milestone, one that you approach with the same confidence and assuredness that you have had in conceiving and developing your technology, product, or service, building your team, preparing and presenting your pitch deck, and attracting your first potential investor. Unfortunately, when a founder gets an offer from an investor, the natural inclination is to say *yes* immediately and hope the investor doesn't change her mind. All too often when entrepreneurs reach this point, they turn from trailblazers into beggars. But remember: *Your idea or product is good, it is sellable—and it is fundable.*

You should think of investors as candidates to evaluate just as rigorously as they are evaluating you. You might even find in this process that you have to say *no* to them, even when they want to say *yes* to you! Keep in mind that for startups, having the right investor is as important as having the right software developer, product engineer, or marketing specialist. "Entrepreneurs don't realize it but early investors can play a significant role in shaping a company," says Tony Conrad, partner at True Ventures and cofounder of About.me.[2] You are building a team that will help you grow the company, hopefully with the aim of a profitable exit for you and your investors. And your investors are critical to the success of that team.

Before they make any funding offer, investors have done some basic due diligence on you and your company. They've been reviewing company financials, checking your references, investigating market size, and so on—essentially validating all of the underlying assumptions of your presentation. As a smart businessperson, why wouldn't you do the same for your potential investors? Here are some of the questions you should be asking about the people on the other side of your possible deal.

- *Are these investors a great fit for you and your startup?* Are they excited by your business and enthusiastic about investing in you? Does the investor seem like someone you will be happy working with in the long term?

- *Do they share your vision for the business?* Are they willing to listen to your needs? If you have the goal of growing your company to a $1 billion enterprise over the next ten years while the investor is looking for a quick exit as soon as the company can be sold for a ten times multiple, then the difference in your goals could lead to significant conflict in the future.

- *Are they ready to contribute their ideas, thoughts, and connections to help you grow?* Are they doing research so they can ask good questions that perhaps you haven't thought about? Great investors come to the table with research, thoughts, and questions that can help make your business more successful.

- *Do they have startup experience or experience in your industry?* With any funding you also should be gaining access to the investors' expertise and networks. Will their experience be of value to you? Can they put you in contact with valuable resources in your particular field?

- *How many investments do they make in a given year?* Deal experience is preferred, as it will often make deal negotiations easier. But don't assume that because someone has invested frequently and had some successes that they will be a good fit for you. And be aware that if you are working with a new investor you both may be "learning the ropes" at the same time.

- *Are they leading the deal or do they need to confirm with a partner or their boss?* VCs usually have a process for vetting and closing deals; your investor may need to review the deal terms with a committee or boss before you close. Nothing wrong with that, but if the person in front of you can't say *yes* without checking to see if the numbers you're proposing are acceptable, your fundraising might take more time.

- *Are these investors responsive?* Just as you must be prepared to respond promptly to investors' request for information, you want your investors to be equally ready to provide assistance when you need it.

Once you've made your own evaluation of the investors, ask them to provide references from three to five entrepreneurs whose companies they have funded previously. Talk with the entrepreneurs and get their take on how the investors performed. You also might want to do your own research and contact other founders who worked with these investors—in particular, founders whose startups failed. Try to get as rounded a picture you can as to what your relationship with these investors will be like.

Let's assume you feel ready to proceed with this investor: Now it's time to review the agreement that outlines the essential and material terms of the investment. In venture capital and angel investing, there are a couple of different forms of this agreement: a *simple agreement for future equity (safe)*, and a *term sheet*. A safe is most frequently used in seed-stage fundraising only: Because the process and terms are not as comprehensive, deals can be done more quickly (appropriate in the fast-moving world of tech startups, where safes originated). We will go over safes briefly, and then dive more deeply into term sheets, as they are used in every other funding round (and sometimes in seed stage as well).

Unless you are experienced in the terms and conditions of funding deals, you always should review any investment agreement with an investment attorney. Please do *not* use your personal attorney for this. An investment attorney experienced with startups can save you from tremendous headaches later on. As soon as you receive a safe or term sheet, have the attorney review it to be sure it meets your interests, objectives, and expectations. However, the term sheet is fundamentally a business document, not a legal document, so *you* should control its substantive contents. You will involve your investment attorney more deeply when due diligence has been completed and the final investment agreements are drawn up.

Simple Agreements for Future Equity (Safes)

In Chapter 4, Judy discussed the different kinds of compensation investors can receive: debt and equity. With banks (and family and friends), debt may be in the form of a straight loan, with a set interest rate and date of maturity. Angel investors and VCs, however, often issue *convertible notes*—a form of debt that converts to equity at a later point in the startup's life (usually a future funding round).

A safe is an alternative to a convertible note. Because it is not a debt instrument, safes do not have interest rates or loan maturity dates (unlike most convertible notes). It is what the acronym stands for: a *simple agreement for future equity* in the startup.

Safe agreements are much easier to create and negotiate because there are only a few terms for investors and founders to agree on: (1) the investment amount, (2) the valuation cap (see below), and (3) the specific event (usually a later funding round) that will trigger the conversion of the investment amount into equity (typically preferred stock). The safe will then be represented on the cap table (see Chapter 4) like any other convertible debt already incurred by the startup.

Y Combinator has produced four different versions of a safe agreement that correspond to the four kinds of convertible notes: a safe agreement with a valuation cap; a safe agreement with a discount rate (applied when the investment converts into equity); a safe agreement with a valuation cap and a discount rate; and a safe agreement with "most favored nation" (MFN) status (this gives this investor the right to convert the agreement to match any more favorable terms a subsequent investor receives). You can find the templates on the Y Combinator website (the URL is listed in the resources section at the end of the book).

A word of caution: while safe agreements are not convertible notes, they may *act* like convertible notes when it comes time for the investment to be converted into stock. Safe agreements can give investors liquidation preference and pro-rata rights. Also, safes and other convertible notes can have a significant impact on dilution (particularly for the founders' ownership percentage) in future funding rounds.[3] Make sure your cap table is up to date and accurate so you can see the effects of a potential safe agreement down the road. And always have your attorney review any safe agreement thoroughly before you sign.

The Term Sheet

The term sheet outlines the important provisions of an investment at the start. It is designed to put you and your investor on the same page before due diligence (and the significant expense of drafting the final legal agreement documents). Investors and founders alike don't want to find themselves weeks or months and many thousands of dollars down the road, only to discover there's a potentially fatal misunderstanding. You want to know sooner rather than later if there is an issue, and a term sheet will make that apparent quickly.

Once finalized, the term sheet will serve as the outline for drafting final or definitive contracts and agreements that are binding on both the company and the investor. Remember, while most founders deal with relatively few term sheets during a funding round, angel investors and VCs issue term sheets all the time. They know the language and conditions of term sheets backward and forward: You don't. This lack of information puts you at a disadvantage—and you can't expect your potential investors to spend their time looking out for your interests. Indeed, their responsibility is to protect their investment by maximizing the value of their capital in terms of the amount of equity it purchases, while protecting themselves from any potential downside caused by the company's poor future performance or liquidation. Therefore, *it is vital that you review the provisions of any term sheet thoroughly and consult a qualified attorney to ensure that you understand what you are signing and that the terms work in your favor.*

By the way, don't assume your deal is done once the term sheet is signed. Term sheets are only the first step in cementing the deal with your investor. Next will come due diligence and a thorough legal review of all documents before you see a penny of investor money. So plan for a process that will take weeks, if not months, from start to finish. In 2018 the average amount of time VC firms took to close deals was somewhere between thirty and sixty days.[4]

The structure and complexity of a term sheet can vary, depending on the stage of your business or the funding round that you are in. For an extremely thorough discussion of term sheets, I recommend reading *Venture Deals: Be Smarter than Your Lawyer or Venture Capitalist*, third edition, by Brad Feld and Jason Mendelson (New York: Wiley, 2016). In this chapter, I will provide an overview of the basic terms and give advice to entrepreneurs on what to focus on during your review. (In the resources section, you'll find the URL for a template of a series A venture capital term sheet, created by the National Venture Capital Association, as well as the URL for an angel investor term sheet template. There will be samples and links to other resources on this topic to aid you as you anticipate and enter the term sheet phase.)

A term sheet can be anywhere from five to eight pages of stipulations, clauses, numbers, and legal language, but according to Feld and Mendelson, they all boil down to *economics*—what the investors will receive for their money—and *control*—how much influence investors will have over the running of the business. As you go through each topic listed below, keep in mind (1) you must do your best to provide accurate information when it comes to the finances of your company, and (2) if you're smart, you will choose your battles and focus on what's most important to your startup. "How a founder acts during this phase can have a significant impact on the relationship going forward," writes Matthew Bartus, attorney with Cooley LLP (an international law firm with clients that include Google, Facebook, and Qualcomm). "Show the VC that you will stand up for the important issues, and that you know what the important issues are."[5]

The first paragraph of most term sheets usually stipulates that the agreement is nonbinding and does not constitute a legal obligation to invest. However, a term sheet is considered binding in two ways that are designed to protect the investor. First, exclusivity (also called a "no shop" clause), which means that you agree to negotiate only with this particular investor, at least during the term sheet review. Second, confidentiality: You agree not to discuss the existence of the term sheet with anyone not directly involved in the deal until negotiations are completed (or the deal is called off).

Now let's get into key sections of the term sheet that focus on economics or control.

Offering Terms (Economics)

The offering terms usually begin with the amount of the potential investment the investor is making, and the type of security being offered by you in return. The amount is pretty straightforward (unless it is allocated in tranches, which you should avoid if at all possible—see the section on "When to Say No to a Deal" at the end of this chapter). What the investor receives for that amount will be listed either as (1) a purchase of equity or (2) a convertible note (a loan that will convert to stock in a future round of funding).

We will be covering term sheets for an equity purchase. However, in some cases (especially in a seed-stage round) the investors may be offering a *convertible loan* that later converts into equity, usually at the series A round when equity value may be more apparent. In the resources section, you can find the URL for a template for a convertible note term sheet.

The basic information you'll see in the section on equity will include:

- The *type of equity* (usually preferred shares—see Chapter 4)
- The *number of shares purchased*

- The *percentage of equity* (or ownership position) those shares represent (see below)
- The *total amount of investment*, also known as the "aggregate" if there is more than one investor (if so, each investor's contribution will be listed separately, next to their names)
- The *price per share*, based on the company's total number of shares and valuation (see below)

Sometimes the closing date is listed; if not, it will be found at the end of the term sheet. The closing date shows how long the offer is good, and indicates the amount of time investors believe the negotiation and closing process will take.

Valuation

The price per share will be based upon the *valuation* of the company at the time of investment. Valuation may be the most significant item to be resolved in the term sheet negotiation because it determines how much ownership or equity the investor will receive for his investment, and whether that ownership occurs immediately or upon the conversion of a loan into equity.

Strictly speaking, a valuation is simply a guess as to the economic value of your company, today and in the future. If your business already has sales and revenue, the valuation is at least an educated guess, because it is easier to extrapolate what the business will produce in terms of revenue and profits this year and several years into the future. In other cases, notably when a company is prerevenue, the valuation is a guess based more upon evaluating the risk factors your company faces and the potential revenue it represents.

When it comes to term sheets, it's the investors who establish the valuation of your company based upon what they think it will be worth. And if this is your first term sheet, you need to pay particular attention to the valuation, because that number will influence the valuation in every subsequent deal. And just as you need to pay careful attention to the pricing of your product or service, you also need to be able to set a valuation that is a fair representation of the value of your startup—ideally not too high or too low.

A too-low valuation can mean your investors get a bigger chunk of the equity "pie" for their capital, leaving less for you (as the founder), your key employees, and any earlier investors (like friends and family). On the other hand, a too-high valuation can set a price for your company that you will not be able to sustain. Then, if you enter into another fundraise, you run the risk of a "down round," where the valuation of your company comes in below its previous valuation. Investors do not like down rounds, and it will make them less likely to offer you more funding at acceptable terms.

It's best that you run the numbers on your business valuation prior to receiving the term sheet. In fact, you should have a suggested valuation number before you meet with investors. You can estimate your current valuation by looking at comparable startups when they were at the same stage of development as yours. According to Heidi Roizen, investment partner with Silicon Valley VC firm DFJ (Draper Fisher Jurvetson), "The important thing in choosing your valuation is not to over-optimize. The objective is to find a valuation with which you are comfortable, that will allow you to raise the amount you need to achieve your goals with acceptable dilution, and that investors will find reasonable and attractive enough to write you a check. . . . I really believe that clean and simple terms at rational valuations are the best healthy hygiene for any normal company that is out there to raise money."[6]

Investors use specific formulas to determine what they believe the company will be worth, and therefore what their shares in the company will be worth. We'll cover a few of them here just to give you some background; you can find detailed information for all of these methods online.

Valuation methods fall into two categories: *prerevenue* and *postrevenue*. Prerevenue valuation methods include:

- *The Berkus Method:* In 1996, early-stage angel investor Dave Berkus created a model for evaluating prerevenue startups by using both qualitative and quantitative factors to assign specific valuations based upon the ways founders reduce four kinds of risk: *technology* risk (by developing a working prototype), *execution* risk (by having a quality management team), *market* risk (by building strategic relationships with customers and suppliers), and *production* risk (with a successful product rollout or sales). Berkus also gave a certain amount of valuation credit to the founders for their original idea. In the Berkus Method valuation, $500,000 is the maximum that can be earned in any category, giving a maximum premoney valuation of between $2 and $2.5 million. Once a company produces revenue, the Berkus Method no longer applies. However, it is an excellent way for seed-stage angel investors to calculate valuation on prerevenue companies.[7]

- *Scorecard Valuation*: Created by Bill Payne, an active early-stage angel investor, this method begins with the industry average premoney valuation for recently funded companies in the region, and then compares the target company to that valuation based upon the following factors: strength of management team, size of the opportunity, product/technology, competitive environment, marketing/sales channels (and key partners), need for additional investment, and other factors such as geography. Each factor is given a specific weighted average, and the sum of all the factors is then multiplied by the average industry valuation to give the final valuation number for the startup.[8]

- *The Venture Capital Method:* This method calculates valuation strictly from the viewpoint of investor returns. It works backward from the anticipated sale value, or Terminal Value, of the startup (five or so years in the future). You determine Terminal Value by (1) estimating the company's earnings in the year of sale and (2) multiplying that number by the typical price/earnings ratio, based on industry-specific statistics. Then you divide Terminal Value by the investors' target ROI. This determines the postmoney valuation of the company. Subtract the amount invested in this round, reduce that amount by anticipated dilution (see below), and you get the current premoney valuation.[9]

Postrevenue valuations are easier to calculate, since the business has some actual sales, revenue, and expense data to use when calculating earnings per year. In this case, investors may use the *discounted cash flow* (DCF) method, which takes future cash flow projections and discounts them using various factors such as depreciation, capital expenditures, market growth, and historical operating profit. Other methods recommend using the DCF valuations to create worst-case, best-case, and normal-case versions.

However, angel and VC investors are most likely to use their experience in evaluating startups similar to yours. They will pull up valuations on comparable companies to estimate the potential of your startup. Or they will work backward from the potential exit using the Venture Capital method. Finally, they will estimate how much equity they believe you are willing to sell in this particular round—in other words, how much dilution you are willing to accept in return for their investor capital. That is a question you will need to answer in your own evaluation of the investment.

Investors often use more than one method to determine valuation. You, too, may want to go through any of the above methods to estimate the valuation you believe is fair, and then compare it to the figure that your investors submit on the term sheet. Ultimately, however, as soon as you accept the money investors are offering to purchase a certain percentage of equity in your company, the valuation is whatever number the investor puts on the term sheet. That's why it's so important for you to have a clear idea of what you believe to be a fair valuation, and be ready to back up your assumptions with facts and figures.

All of the above valuation methods are used to estimate the company's *premoney* valuation: what it is worth before you receive the investors' money. Once you add the investor capital, you have the *postmoney valuation*—meaning, what your company is worth *after* the investor's money lands in your company bank account. In future rounds, investors will often look to see if the current premoney valuation of your company is equal to or (preferably) higher than the postmoney valuation of your previous funding round. It's a quick indication that you have used the investor capital to grow the company and thus are a better investment risk.

Let's look at a simple example. Two investors send you a term sheet saying that they will give you $1 million for 10 percent equity in your startup. That means they are calculating a postmoney valuation for your company of $11 million. However, the premoney valuation would be $11 million *minus* $1 million, or $10 million.[10]

This number becomes important when calculating how many shares the investor will receive for that $1 million. Assuming you have issued shares to yourself, other partners or key employees, and previous investors, you would need to refer to your capitalization table, or cap table, to determine how many shares have been issued already and how much those shares are worth given the current premoney valuation. Let's assume that you have issued 1 million shares to date. At a premoney valuation, the current share price is $10: $10 million divided by 1 million equals $10 per share.

You use the current share price to calculate how many shares your investors will receive for their money. They are giving you $1 million, so with a current share price of $10 they will receive 100,000 shares: $1 million divided by $10 = 100,000. That will be the number of new shares to be issued to the investor.

Of course, ownership can only add up to 100 percent, so if you issue new shares to cover the investor's 10 percent stake, it will reduce the ownership percentage of all current stakeholders. You will use your current cap table to make this calculation.

Cap Table: Pre- and Postfinancing

Investors usually expect you to provide them with a copy of your current cap table, which shows who owns equity in the company at the time of this particular investment round. Then they will ask you to calculate a new cap table that shows the investors' equity stake. This new cap table will clearly lay out the dilution of owner's equity that will result from the shares that the investors will receive in exchange for their capital.

On the next page is a sample cap table representing the company's premoney and postmoney valuations. (This is based on the cap table from Chapter 4.) In this example, prior to the current funding round, the founders owned 41.6 percent and 37.5 percent of the company, represented by 950,000 shares. An earlier investor owns 50,000 shares, or 4.2 percent. The founders had established an employee option pool of 200,000 shares but had not yet issued any. (This is common in early-stage startups; options for shares are often used as incentives to attract top talent to what is essentially a risky venture.) This company does not have any warrants (or options for outside parties to purchase equity at a certain price). The total of premoney shares issued is thus 1.2 million.

However, observe what happens when the investors receive 133,200 shares to equal 10 percent of equity. The number of shares issued has to increase (to 1.332 million from 1.2 million), but as a result the percentage

Shareholder	Prefinancing		Postfinancing	
	Shares	Percent	Shares	Percent
Founder 1	500,000	41.6	500,000	37.5
Founder 2	450,000	37.5	450,000	33.8
Friend (investor)	50,000	4.2	50,000	3.7
Employee Option Pool: Issued	0		0	
Employee Option Pool: Unissued	200,000	16.7	200,000	15.0
Warrants	0	0	0	0
Series A Preferred	0	0	133,200	10.0
Total	1,200,000	100	1,332,000	100

of company equity held by founders and the employee option pool decreases. The founders now hold 37.5 percent and 33.8 percent of company stock, the friend owns 3.7 percent, and the employee pool is 15 percent. Their ownership stake is *diluted* by the investors' percentage. (The cap table shows the "fully diluted" ownership of the company—in essence, who owns what.)

When founders are looking at the cap table term sheet, they need to pay particular attention to the dilution of their ownership percentage that will occur as a result of this funding round. Especially if you are in the seed stage or early stage, you should try to hold on to a majority share of ownership if you plan to raise capital later through a series A round (and more rounds after that). This will give you greater decisionmaking power now, and greater flexibility when it comes to bringing more equity investors on board later.

Additional Investor Incentives

Depending on the deal, investors may ask for other economic incentives in the term sheet. These can serve to give them greater participation in future rounds at a preferred price, or at a discount, or on a pro rata basis. Investors may ask for future stock options. Or you may see anti-dilution rights, which give existing investors the right to additional shares in the event of a down round in the future. There are different types of anti-dilution provisions, including full ratchet (which allows investors to retain the same percentage of ownership if the stock price goes down) and different weighted averages. Or investor may ask for preemption rights, which means they have the right to invest in future funding rounds so as to maintain their ownership percentage in the company.

You also may see liquidation preferences, which might specify when these investors would get paid in the case of a corporate liquidation—typically, before the holders of common stock receive any money. The term sheet might indicate that these investors would receive a multiple of their initial investment in full before anyone else got paid. You can imagine how this might affect your returns, since most founders own common, not preferred stock![11]

Other financial rights that investors may request include:

- Participation rights: Does the investor get to participate in the proceeds early, or do they have to wait until other investors or note holders are paid first?
- The right to receive a return (this is often called a "coupon" when attached to equity)
- Cash distribution or dividend rights
- Right of first refusal—if a shareholder wishes to sell her stock, the investors would get first choice of buying those shares
- Conversion terms, whether it is the conversion of a loan to equity or preferred equity into common equity

The bottom line is that investors will write term sheets to protect themselves and their capital from as much of the downside as possible, while maximizing the value of their investment in your company. You simply need to review the financial terms thoroughly, and then create spreadsheets to see the effects of these financial demands upon the value of your company and the returns to you for all your hard work. Then you need to decide if you can live with the terms as laid out or you need to negotiate on certain financial stipulations. Ultimately, it comes down to three questions: (1) How badly do you need the capital? (2) Are there other investors or resources that would provide a better deal? (3) Assuming you take the money, will the growth you create with it be worth the equity you are giving away?

Investor Rights (Control)

Investors not only want to outline exactly how they will participate in the company through their equity, but they also want to exercise a certain amount of control over the company and its founders. They do this by stipulating certain rights, such as:

- Voting or control and consent rights
- Board participation
- The right to receive financial and operational information about the business in a timely manner
- What's called a "drag-along right"—meaning, if the board and a majority of shareholders holding more than 50 percent of shares vote to sell the company (typically in an acquisition deal), they can require other shareholders to sell their shares on the same terms

Even though you may feel that certain requests in the term sheet favor investors in the extreme, the majority of these conditions are normal for investors. But remember that a term sheet is an offer of terms—not a "take it or leave it" proposition. Angel and VC investors are used to founders asking questions and negotiating on certain terms. Do not hesitate to ask investors to explain precisely what they are asking for and why. If you have reasons to change or amend the terms, bring them forward in a calm manner. However, choose the battles you wish to fight: Select the three issues in the term sheet that you feel are most important to you, and focus on those. It will make the negotiation easier for you and for your investors.

When to Say No to a Deal

Remember, a term sheet is not a finalized deal, and you or the investor can pull out at any point. For investors, this often occurs during due diligence, if they discover something about the company (or its founders) that gives them pause. Sometimes a better startup comes along and the investors choose to put their money into that deal rather than yours. However, you too have the chance to cancel the deal at any time before final contracts are signed. As you enter or conclude the term sheet phase, keep these things in mind:

First, if the deal doesn't make sense in the long term, don't do it. Know your numbers and don't give away too much equity, especially in early rounds. Keep your cap table and waterfall chart (see Chapter 4) by your side at all times, so you can figure out how this deal will affect your ownership percentage. You need to know if the deal the investors are offering is worth the equity they are asking you to give them.

As Heidi Roizen observes, the cap table always adds up to 100 percent, and you as the founder are at the end of the line when it comes to realizing any returns from your business.[12] So you need to make sure that the percentage of equity your investors are asking for makes sense. Especially as you get into later funding rounds, be aware that you might be making a "devil's bargain" by giving away too much equity just to keep the doors open.

Second, if you don't want to be in a long-term relationship with this investor, pass on the deal. If an investor is too picky, especially before you go through formal due diligence, they are likely to continue picking apart whatever information you send them—and is that what you want? "If the investor is really not all that sure about you and your business, and chooses to wait, you probably don't want them as an investor anyway," says Danielle Morrill, cofounder of Mattermark and partner in XFactor Ventures. "Focus on the investors that are so excited about you and your startup that they're asking you how soon they can invest—not how long they can wait."[13]

There also are investors that seem to want to negotiate on everything. They push for a lower valuation so their investment dollars are worth more. They press you for better terms on even the most insignificant conditions in the term sheet. If you are negotiating a deal and an investor is digging his feet in on a provision that doesn't affect the economics or control, he is probably flexing his negotiating muscles simply because he feels he can. Just as you need to have a clear sense of what's most important in the deal, you want your investors to focus on what's most important, which is to help you grow the company so they can get a healthy return on their investment. You want investors to be your partners, not your adversaries.

To recap:

1. Get all of the material terms into the term sheet, so there are no surprises for you or the investor.

2. Have the term sheet reviewed by an attorney, but don't "over-lawyer" it.

3. Try to negotiate the term sheet with a single major investor, then require all other smaller investors to follow suit. One deal for the round, not a round of multiple deals.

4. Hold your ground: The terms of this deal become the starting place for future deals. Don't give away too much too soon. There's more than one investor candidate for your business and if this one doesn't work out, another one will.

Remember, getting a term sheet from an investor is a sign in her confidence in the value of you and your startup. Like everything else in business, you need to put in your time and energy to ensure that the value you are receiving is worth the equity you are giving in return. But don't agonize over the term sheet. Zero in on what's important, change what needs to be changed, agree on a deal that will work for you and for your investors, and sign the term sheet so you can move on to the stages of due diligence, final agreements, and getting the capital your startup needs to grow. As Y Combinator partner Geoff Ralston puts it, "Get the best deal you can get—but get the deal!"[14]

11

DUE DILIGENCE AND CLOSING

Experienced entrepreneurs recognize that they are preparing for due diligence and investor scrutiny from the very beginning, even at the concept stage.[1]

—TONY LETTICH, founder and managing director, The Angel Roundtable

Once you've completed and returned the term sheet, you're one step closer to getting the investors' money and putting it to work in your business. Before that happens, however, you need to go through due diligence. Investors already will have verified in a general way the statements you made in your presentation and checked your financial assumptions. But due diligence is a deep dive into every aspect of you, your history, your team, your business, your competition, your market, your technology . . . pretty much anything and everything that could affect the success or failure of your startup. For investors, the goal of due diligence is to find out as much as possible about your company, identify the key risks associated with investing in it, and develop a risk mitigation plan with you and your team so the investment can move forward.

It's strange to think that some investors don't believe that due diligence is important. Research shows that one-third of angel investments closed after only ten hours of due diligence, and the average is around twenty hours. Yet a 2015 study of data from the Angel Investment Performance Project showed that investments made after ten or more hours of due diligence were twice as likely to achieve returns greater than five times, compared to investments made after fewer than ten hours of diligence.[2] What's more, every increase in hours spent in due diligence correlated with a higher percentage of wins and lower percentage of losses. "Compared to spending five hours on due diligence, spending forty hours on diligence improves the probability of a big win by more than three times (8 percent to 26 percent)," writes A. J. Watson of Fundify. "It also decreases the percent of losses by almost 40 percent."[3]

The process of due diligence is never pleasant (an article by Bagchi Law calls it "the not-totally-painless corporate equivalent of a full cavity search").[4] You need to provide documentation for every aspect of your business from day one, have your business life and the life of your associates examined in detail, and have every assumption you've ever made about your market, financials, product, and so on questioned. What's more, the deadlines you are given are usually aggressive. You want to be responsive, yet you wonder sometimes if your investors (and their attorneys) know that you are trying to run a business too.

Remember, however, that due diligence has great value for the startup founder as well as the investor. Due diligence is simply "making sure that your business is what it appears to be," writes an attorney at Bagchi Law. "If there are problems with it, your investor wants to figure out what those problems are and see if they can be corrected before she invests. As a founder, your equity in your business is only worth what the business is worth. If your investor finds problems with your business, you should want them fixed as much—or more—than your investor does."[5] For you, making it through due diligence is a validation of almost every aspect of your business. It puts the "seal of approval" on your startup and makes you more investable, now and in the future. And of course, you must pass due diligence in order to get the check!

If you have been following the guidance in this book, you will have been preparing for due diligence all along the way. In this chapter, Dr. Annette Lavoie (whom you met in Chapter 6) will be your guide through the process. As an entrepreneur herself and the coach of startup founders, she can show you how to avoid any pitfalls and navigate your due diligence with as much equanimity as possible.

Annette Lavoie: Surviving Due Diligence

If you're in due diligence, congratulations! You know as well as anyone how hard you had to work to get here and how much work went into it—and there's still a lot more work to be done.

The purpose of due diligence is a final reality check between partners. It's a chance to identify the outstanding risks and confirm the value of the deal to both parties. Potential investors don't go through due diligence unless they intend to make the investment, so entrepreneurs should approach due diligence as a chance to show that they are people whom investors want to work with and trust their money to, and they are interested in making this deal a success for both sides.

The most important thing to keep in mind while you're going through due diligence is that this is the first time that you and your investor will be on the same side of the table. You should approach due diligence not as if you're working with an adversary but rather with a new executive or a new hire in your company. It's a chance for you to show that you are someone they want to work with, spend time with, and feel good about entrusting with their money. So it's important that you are prompt with all your responses and professional in all of your dealings with this new partner. Most of all, be personable: They're going to spend a lot of time working with you to make sure that this deal goes forward and that it is a success for both sides.

Investors are already excited about the *potential* of the opportunity; now with due diligence they're going to get into the *reality* of the opportunity. The good news is that they don't expect your company to be perfect. They know that there are all sorts of bumps and bruises along the way. It's what they find, how they find it, and how you handle it that will determine whether the due diligence process is a success. This process is your chance to build trust with the investor. They will look at your past and use what they learn to anticipate how you will deal with them in the future. Let's say that you had a bad relationship or partnership in the past. If you try and hide that from investors, they won't trust that in the future when something goes wrong, you'll come to them and use them as a resource to fix the situation. Even if they love the opportunity, they'll kill the deal if they don't trust you moving forward.

Going into due diligence, there are three things that I always encourage entrepreneurs to remember: they should be *prepared* with all the information the investor might need, be *honest* about any challenges the business might face, and be *open* to any questions the investor might pose.

1. Be Prepared

Every due diligence experience is unique. Investors all have their own checklists, their own expectations, and their own processes that work for them. Interestingly, what may cause one investor to turn your deal down at the end of due diligence may be fine with another investor. But there are many required elements that every investor will insist on seeing, reviewing, and approving.

Typically due diligence will take between sixty and ninety days. Don't try to rush it: Spending time with your investors is one of the things that can make due diligence successful. Take this opportunity to get to know your investors, and let them know you. The process itself will teach you a lot about how you will work together and whether the relationship will be enjoyable. That in itself is important, because you and your investor will be interacting for many years to come.

The reason due diligence takes so long is because of the depth of information you will be expected to provide. While every investor will have his own checklists, there are several basics that they all will want to know. In the appendices you will find a full set of due diligence questions and a checklist, but here is an overview of the major elements, and where the information will come from.[6]

- *Corporate structure and governance*: corporate documents and interviews with management, board, and advisors.

- *Financial assumptions and revenue sources*: financial documents provided by you. These can be updates of the financial plans you submitted as part of your pitch presentation and term sheet information.

- *Market assessment*: independent market analysis and customer references, if applicable.

- *Competitive arena*: independent competitive analysis.

- *Management team*: interview all team members and check key employee references to see if the team is up to the task. This will include internet searches, background checks, and checking references.

- *Technology assessment and protection of your technology in the form of IP*: this may require expert or professional assistance to determine the validity of the technology. However, equally important is investigating the company's IP to confirm both ownership and legal protection.

- *Operations*: review the processes and internal structure of the company.

- *Comparables*: research similar companies and compare based upon the above factors.

- *Compliance documentation*: if your industry is tightly regulated (pharma, biotech, and medical device manufacture spring to mind), you might need to show compliance with federal, state, and local ordinances and all the necessary permits to operate the business.

- *Disclosures of past litigation or other legal issues*: any past instances of regulatory issues, lawsuits, human resource problems, or anything that could affect the value of the company or the ability of you or your employees to work there needs to be disclosed.

In addition, you may be asked to provide the contact information of professional partners like your CPA and attorney, as well as suppliers, customers, board members, and other investors, all of whom may be interviewed. It's highly likely that your attorney will be deeply involved in the due diligence process as well as in reviewing all of the contracts with the investor. Make sure that she is fully prepared to answer any investor questions.

On the documentation side, you'll be expected to provide the paperwork for every aspect of your business, including all corporate and government filings, founders and operating agreements, loan documents from banks or other lenders, any documentation having to do with equity (warrants, employee option pool, cap table, shareholder contact information), organization charts, articles of incorporation, employee agreements such as NDAs, noncompete agreements, any joint venture agreements, and all patent, trademark, and copyright applications and confirmations. You also should provide copies of marketing and sales plans, product release plans, financial plans, manufacturing plans (including product development costs and per-unit cost), and key sales and supplier agreements. On the financial side you should make available all tax returns (corporate and also personal), corporate financial statements, balance and P&L statements for the past and current year, and any insurance policies.

According to Katherine Homuth, a serial entrepreneur and angel investor from Canada, investors also may ask you to create documents especially for due diligence. These include an overview of your customer acquisition channels, a spreadsheet with your company's core metrics (such as revenue, growth rates, customer acquisition cost and lifetime value, and cash burn rate), and financial projections for the next three to five years.[7]

As you can see, organizing all of this information in advance will help make the due diligence process easier. You can keep physical copies of everything in binders so the information can be copied and shared. However, you also should store copies of all documentation in electronic form, ideally in digital folders in a cloud-based data room that is encrypted and password-protected and made accessible to investors on an as-needed basis. Designate one person on your team to make sure documents are uploaded and updated consistently, and investor requests are responded to promptly. I suggest you prepare modules that can be shared independently if an investor wants something specific, or grouped together in a more comprehensive document or folder. For example, you want to have an outline of your milestones and the use of proceeds to reach them, but you want that document to be able to link with your financial projections, cash flow statements, balance statements, P&L statements, and so on.

You probably will have to customize many of these documents for your particular investors, but if you've got them in a basic format, it's much easier to collect the information, modify it, and get it back to investors promptly, which is key in building any new working relationship. For Marcia Nelson of Alberleen Family Office Solutions, taking too long to get her requested information could kill a deal. "If management is slow to get us information, what will it be like when we want quarterly reports and other information?" she asks.[8] Keep your investors up to date on your progress on due diligence documents, as well as any company developments (positive or negative) that occur during this time. Remember, investors are evaluating how easy it will be to work with you, and your quick, professional response will start you off on the right foot.

2. Be Honest

Up to this point in the process it's customary to focus only on the positives—"This is what we've done, this is how we're moving along, this is the progress we've made"—and not to address in any significant way the bumps you've had along the way. But the key to any good business working relationships is honesty. "The ask is to disclose everything," says Alex Iskold, managing director of Techstars. "Do not panic. Just provide the information."[9] If you've got skeletons in your closet, or hair on your deal, or things that you're not excited to share with a potential investor . . . well, this is your chance to do it in a way that builds their confidence rather than drains it.

If there are issues with a current situation, present it up front but with a solution. For example, "This is a contract that's being renegotiated," or "This is a vendor we've had issues with, so we're getting bids from these three vendors that can provide services without the problems we're having currently." Show that you know about the issue and you're not afraid to address it. Investors know there are going to be issues in the future, so if they can see a situation where you had a problem and you handled it appropriately, fixed it, and mitigated the risk, then they feel much more comfortable and they're happy to be your partner.

Investors will be looking at your documents to see if there is missing information or inconsistencies, as these are signals of potential problems. Any red flags from the past, such as liens, lawsuits, personal issues, regulatory fines, and so on, need to be dealt with clearly and honestly. If the issue is significant, investors could request a revision of terms. More often, it's something that just needs to be acknowledged, addressed, and dealt with before contracts are signed.

Remember, these investors are your partners moving forward, and it's in their best interest to help you overcome any issues you might face. They want to know that there is good communication between you about any potential problems that might come up. "Investors want our level of trust to increase with each interaction we have with the CEO and the team," says Rick Vaughn of Mid America Angels in Kansas. "If it doesn't, that can be a dealbreaker."[10] Being honest will help build a solid foundation for trust between you and your investor.

3. Be Open

Your investors should bring to the table a lot more than money: They should have expertise, connections, and experience that will benefit you and your company enormously. (If they don't have that to offer, you might want to consider whether this investor is truly a good potential partner.) You don't know everything: You never will, so be open to their suggestions. When you come across as having all the answers and unwilling to accept coaching, input, or alternative views around your business or product, many investors will feel you are not a good fit.

If your investors are bringing expertise to your business, they'll want to know that you're willing to hear that and take heed. During due diligence this could come in the form of a discussion around potential strategic partners, maybe a pivot in the future, or creating an additional vertical around your technology. Stay open to their ideas and suggestions. "Your investors understand your strengths and weaknesses from the due diligence process," Dave Clark, president of Clark & Company, observes. "They gave you a capital infusion and will mentor you because they want a return on their investment. That guidance can be invaluable . . . if you receive it with the right attitude."[11] Your investors' outside perspective and expertise can help you build your business faster and more efficiently, as long as you are open to hearing it.

Make Sure You Want to Work with This Investor Too

While you're busy preparing and providing due diligence documents for this investor, take the time to ask your own due diligence questions of them. Make sure that you have the common vision for the future, you're on the same page in terms of the roles and responsibilities that you expect from your new investment partner, and you have a clear channel of communication. Be aware of warning signs: for example, they're not returning your phone calls or emails, or you and your team are being treated poorly. I know it's tempting to ignore warning signs when you're in a deal and you think, "I just need to get to the money and then I can fix this." Trust me, a bad investor relationship can be more stressful than a bad marriage, and harder to get out of. It's definitely not worth ignoring warning signs just to get the dollars in the door.

So to get through due diligence smoothly, I recommend you be prepared, be honest and be open, and make sure that the potential partner knows that you're someone whom your investor wants to do business with—and vice versa.

Legal Review and Closing

Toward the end of due diligence, assuming nothing has come up to derail the deal, the investor's legal counsel will draft contracts based on what was already agreed to in the term sheets. Have your attorney go through these agreements carefully, as you need to be sure your interests are protected and there are no surprises. Once the legal review is completed and you have signed the contracts, the investors should send you the money within a few days.

Your first investment (and any subsequent investment, for that matter) is a cause for celebration and is usually accompanied by a feeling of relief. You now have the capital to keep doing what you love best: growing your business. But in reality, the funding process continues, only in a different form. First of all, you must create a plan to integrate your investors into your company's operations. "The first steps you take with your new investment partners will set the tone for your future relationship and how you work together through the challenges that inevitably lie ahead," writes Bob Ackerman, founder and managing director of early-stage venture firm AllegisCyber. "The road from startup concept through to your destination of a successful and viable business is akin to running through a minefield at night. You will improve your odds of success (both as a business and as an executive) by making your investors and board members true partners—leveraging their experience and resources—and bringing them into your inner circle of trust."[12]

Stay in touch with your investors with regular, written updates about your company, including news, product development, finances, additional fundraising, significant hires or departures, new clients or sales and marketing campaigns, and any important shareholder or investor relation information. Have frequent phone conversations, and schedule regular meetings with your investors. If they are on your board of directors, these should happen on a preset schedule, but informal lunches or meetings over coffee also are valuable for discussing the business. Use your investors as sounding boards to talk over issues you are facing and the strategic direction of the business. If there is any bad news, it's critical that you communicate it to your investors before they hear it from anyone else. As Bob Ackerman comments, investors don't like surprises; but they can become part of the solution to the problem if you give them the opportunity.[13] They may be able to use their connections to bring you help that you couldn't access on your own.

However, it's not enough simply to take care of the investors you have: You must prepare for your next funding round by identifying possible investors and reaching out to them through your network. Your current investors can be of great help in this, so don't hesitate to ask them for referrals to other investors in their network. You also should keep in touch with investors who passed on your current deal. The next time you need funding, your startup may be more attractive to them and more in line with their requirements. Send regular updates to anyone you approached in your funding journey to let them know how your startup is growing. Remember, if you continue to do well you may need to do another, larger funding round, and you will need strong connections to open more investor doors for you.

The best funding is always going to be revenues from a strong business that you love making successful. Yes, fundraising is an important skill, and finding investors to believe in you and provide you with capital are great validation for any startup founder. OPM (other people's money) is the fuel that will help you go further and grow faster, but you've still got to build the "car" of your business and keep it driving, straight and true, along the road to a successful exit.

In other words, celebrate your successful fundraise—and then get back to work. Good luck!

APPENDICES

ARE YOU A POWER CONNECTOR?
AN ASSESSMENT

Please read each statement and then select the one that best describes you. If none of the statements seem to apply to you, please select the one that is closest.

1. Your Networking Strategy

a. You have no real strategy. You accept invitations to LinkedIn, Facebook, or other social-media sites. You see it as overwhelming or a waste of time, certainly not a high value activity. You're more likely to post about your friends or weekend activities.

b. You collect people's business cards and sometimes type them into your address file, maybe with notes on who they are or what you talked about. You occasionally remember to post on social media but it seems to have no effect. You joined industry organizations with good intentions, but never have the time to leverage all that potential.

c. You actively build your network. You not only belong to industry organizations, but you also volunteer and/or serve on boards. You participate regularly. You stay in personal contact with lots of people and share relevant and valuable content on social-media sites. You figure if you do enough good, it will come back to you eventually.

d. You have a clear written strategy that helps you do three things: target who you want and need in your network; connect with them proactively; and add value to everyone within your clearly identified power circles. You are proactive in reaching out to your network with pertinent information.

2. Conferences

a. You don't attend a conference or professional meeting unless your boss sends you and pays for it. You consider it a perk.

b. You try to find time to attend monthly meetings of your professional organizations and make an effort to attend the yearly conference sponsored by your chapter. You have attended their national conference once or twice.

c. You attend monthly meetings for your professional organization, have given presentations, and attend all annual conferences. You get business cards at each conference, keep track of who is who, and stay in touch with the most valuable people you meet.

d. You carefully select conferences both for the opportunity to meet influential people in your field and to meet critical players in other industries and professions. You actively seek out key people at conferences, engage with them, and build rapport. You add those key people to your contact list, assess where they belong in your power circles, and maintain the relationship accordingly.

3. Wide, Deep, Robust Network

a. Most of the people in your network work in your organization, in your profession, and are at a peer level to you. You're not the kind of person the "big dogs" spend time with.

b. Most of the people in your network work in your organization and profession but you have made an effort to include people that are both higher and lower than you in your organization's hierarchy.

c. You have many people in your network that are at a different organization level than you, in different disciplines, and who have influence in their field or profession. You appreciate different perspectives and feel you can be more effective through diverse interactions.

d. You target key people in different disciplines, organizational levels, locations, ages and more. You make friends with people like you who are also competent, responsive, and well connected. You build strength in your network by making sure you have more than one contact in critical ecosystems (industries or circles of influence like politics, media).

4. Power Connecting

a. You rarely contact those in your network unless you need something like a job recommendation, to find out about job openings for yourself or a friend, or to share office or industry gossip.

b. You contact people in your network if you need to know something or have a question that they can help you with. People contact you in the same way. You try to help when you can, if you have time.

c. You have a decent network. If you sent an email asking for solutions to a problem, several people would respond. You keep in reasonably good touch and make sure that you thank people who help you, send you information, or include you in what they are doing.

d. People in your network trust you. When you send them a referral, they know that this person can help them or meet their needs. You are thoughtful about who you reach out to and always seek to create mutual value for all involved. You respond to most requests and communications within twenty-four hours.

5. Managing Your Network

a. You do not actively manage your network. You think you might have most people's current contact information, but it's hard to be sure.

b. You keep an address list of your connections with email, phone numbers, and other contact information. It is not current, and you also have a stack of the business cards you have gotten over the years.

c. You keep a list (electronically or on paper) of your connections. It's organized and as best as possible, up to date. You include notes on who is who, where you met them, and sometimes even physical descriptions.

d. You use a management system for all your connections. You have identified your power circles: your top five, key fifty, and vital one hundred connections. You review regularly and as you meet new people determine if they should move into your power circles. You have a system for staying in touch with all of them. You learn as much as you can about your connections so that you can add the most value to them and your network.

6. Your Share

a. When you meet new people you do not typically tell them about yourself beyond your name and title, unless they ask things like whether or not you have kids or your favorite sports team.

b. When meeting a new person, you tell them what you do but often feel like you are self-promoting and not accurately conveying your value or what you can do well.

c. When you meet someone you might want to add to your network, you have a concise, rehearsed "elevator speech" so that you can quickly let them decide if they want what you've got.

d. When you meet a person you have chosen to add to your network, you share your passions and some of the interesting things you have been involved in. You ask questions about their passions and actions too. You're a good listener, you smile, use open posture, and know how to quickly build rapport. Your goal is to engage them authentically, share your vision with them, and build a mutually beneficial connection.

7. Your Ask

a. You rarely ask for help, resources, or connections from your network. You wouldn't know where to begin or with whom.

b. You ask those in your network for help, resources, or connections. Sometimes they're helpful, sometimes not. You don't know the top people anyway.

c. You can use your network for information, resources, opportunities, or other connections. People in your network sometimes make suggestions, offer recommendations, or connect you with key people.

d. You are certain that you have a good relationship before making requests of anyone. You start with small requests and continue to add value to the relationship so that when you need something big, your connections will want to help. You are passionate about what you do and communicate that. You do not waste people's time.

8. Reconnect Immediately

a. It might take weeks, months, or even a year before you follow up with someone new you just met. You've got a lot on your plate.

b. You try to follow up and send emails within a week to people you have just met. But if you don't get around to it, you typically just let it go.

c. You almost always send an email to someone you have just met and want to stay in touch with. If you tell people you will send them something, you make sure to send it. You enter anything personal, any point of real human connection into your database so when needed you can use it to help refresh your memory or theirs about who you are.

d. When you meet a new person you contact him or her within twenty-four hours and send them something that they will find valuable like an article, a webcast, or a website. You start to immediately add value to the relationship. You become unforgettable.

9. Social Networks

a. When you add or allow someone into a social network, you use the default option. You rarely check any of those sites to post or see who has posted. Who has the time?

b. When you add someone to a social network you use the default request option. You regularly post your own stuff and occasionally comment on the posts of people you like.

c. When you add someone to a social network you always add a personal note. You regularly post and respond to what others have posted. You try to post things that others will find beneficial.

d. When you add someone to a social network you make sure that this is a person you want to be connected with. You always send a warm greeting to the person to build rapport. You also reach out to people you don't know and start adding value to them by sharing beneficial information. You comment regularly and work to build good relationships through your social-media outreach.

10. Understanding the Power of Networking

a. You don't really use networking. You are sure you don't really need a network unless you are looking for a job.

b. You know that networking is important. You just haven't gotten organized and finding the time is difficult.

c. You know that networking is critical to having opportunities, advancing your career, and opening doors. You have a good network and you work to make it viable and useful, both to you and those in your network.

d. Networking is a key part of your professional strategy. You know that it is through people that you will be successful. You also know that relationships are the key to effective networks, and you make sure to add value to everyone in your power circles, to know what those in your power circles are doing and who they are connected to. You have had many unexpected opportunities come your way because of your network.

Instructions:

▶ Each **a** statement equals 1 point
▶ Each **b** statement equals 2 points
▶ Each **c** statement equals 3 points
▶ Each **d** statement equals 4 points

Add up your points and see the chart below.

▶ 34–40 = power connector
▶ 26–33 = active connector
▶ 18–25 = comfort connector
▶ 10–17 = disconnected

Power Connector 34–40	You have a process to manage your connections, you are a problem-solver and resource for your connections, and you actively bring people together.
	You interact with respect and bring value to your relationships. You follow through, you keep your word, and people trust you. You can reach powerful people in most industries within twenty-four hours, and you create new value, opportunities, and knowledge through your network.
	Your connections are well connected, making your reach farther than your grasp. You understand the importance of getting, keeping, maintaining, and bringing value to your network.
Your next steps	Read *How to Be a Power Connector: The 5+50+100 Rule for Turning Your Business Network into Profits.*
	Organize your connections into power circles.
	Learn to play 3D chess.
	Build your map links.
	Activate your power triangles.
	Multiply your value through regular communications.
	Use a CMS.

Active Connector 26–33	You are well-connected and stay in touch with your network. You have strong and weak connections, and you understand the importance of bringing value to your connections and being a resource. You are comfortable reaching out to those in your network.
	Broaden your network strength by learning how to bring value through connecting others with each other, being able to access networks of those who are in your network, and by formalizing your network through mindful and strategic relationship management.
	You will improve your networking by understanding social media and through strategic joining of associations and attendance of conferences.
	Add value to your networks through adding and sharing content through blogs, videos, online trainings, and information.
Your next steps	Read *How to Be a Power Connector: The 5+50+100 Rule for Turning Your Business Network into Profits.*
	Activate your power circles.
	Prepare your share, value add, and ask.
	Start adding value to your power circles.
	Set up regular communication routines.
	Start making connections within your network.
Comfort Connector 18–25	You have good connections and you reach out to them through LinkedIn and other networking sites. You stay in touch but not strategically or on a regular basis.
	Make your network stronger by assessing who you know now and who they are, what value you can bring to them, and what value they can bring to you.
	You will want to start regular outreach to your network and start to develop a plan to add width and depth to your network to make it robust.
	Implement the 5/50/100 power circles and start to proactively create your power connections.
	Improve your networking by understanding social media and through joining strategic associations and attending appropriate conferences.
Your next steps	Read *How to Be a Power Connector: The 5+50+100 Rule for Turning Your Business Network into Profits.*
	Assess your network.
	Start developing your power circles.
	Write down three to five goals.
	Attend professional associations and an industry conference.
	Prepare your share, value add, and ask.
	Start adding value to your power circles.

Disconnected 10–17	You have not yet tapped into your potential network. You have a lot of opportunities that you are not currently aware of.
	First look at possible barriers that could be preventing you from bringing value and getting value from the people you know.
	You will want to learn how to present yourself and put your best foot forward by doing a personal assessment of your strengths, skills, knowledge, and areas for improvement.
	Start the process of building your network by writing down the people you currently know and assessing their current value and connectedness.
	Identify your goals so that you can start to clarify who you need in your network in order to achieve your goals.
Your next steps	**Read *How to Be a Power Connector: The 5+50+100 Rule for Turning Your Business Network into Profits*.**
	Do a personal inventory.
	Review the barriers to connecting and apply the suggested remedy.
	Make a list of everyone you know or have known.
	Identify your core values.
	Write down three to five goals.
	Assess your network.

JUDY ROBINETT'S
TOP TEN POWER-CONNECTING TIPS

1. Start with the Three Golden Questions: How can I help you? What other ideas do you have for me? Who else do you know that I should talk to?

2. If you're not succeeding, you may be in the wrong room. Don't get stuck looking for love in all the wrong places.

3. Your problem is someone else's solution. Money, ideas, and opportunities are attached to other people.

4. Measure relationships not by net worth, but by their integrity. Do they have a good head, a good heart, and a good gut?

5. "Strangers are dangerous" is a fallacy. Watch for warning signs, but this doesn't work when you are an adult.

6. People must know you, like you, and trust you before sharing valuable social capital. Your network is golden, use it wisely.

7. Don't get lost in the crowd. A robust, wide, and deep network will make you stand out in a crowd.

8. Introductions are your most valuable resource. Use them to create win-win value propositions for both parties.

9. Keep the Rule of Two: Give favors twice before asking for one.

10. If you can only remember one rule, it is this: Engage in small acts of kindness. What you think is a small act may have enormous impact for others.

SUCCESSFUL PITCH DECK EXAMPLE

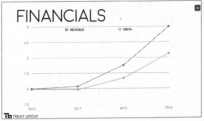

(continued on next page)

(continued from previous page)

DUE DILIGENCE QUESTIONS

ISSUES TO CONSIDER IN DUE DILIGENCE

Corporate Structure and Governance
(Review Documents and Interview Management, Board, and Advisors)

- What is the company's corporate structure? C corp., S corp., LLC, or LP? Does this model allow for a liquidity event and/or return on investment?
- Is there an exit strategy?
- Is the corporate structure overly complicated? If so, why, and might it be simplified?
- How many existing shareholders? Too numerous, and, if so, why?
- Does the corporate structure fit with the business model?
- Does the corporate structure allow for growth?
- What is the founder share allocation? Do they have a large enough stake to have the incentive to succeed, but not so large as to ignore board and other advisors? Is the founders' stock vested over time?
- Who is on the board of directors? Do they have the right background for the company? Is there a sufficient number of outside directors? How are board members compensated?
- Does the company have a board of advisors and, if so, who is on the board? Do the advisors actively participate in the company's development? How are advisors compensated?
- Has the company been involved in any litigation or been threatened with litigation?
- Does the company have all required permits and licenses?

Financial Assumptions and Revenue Sources
(Review All Financial Documents)

- Has the company completed one-, three-, and five-year financial projections?
- Have the financial documents been properly developed according to applicable accounting rules?
- Has the company used an outside, independent accounting firm to compile, review, or audit financials?
- How good are the assumptions (rate of growth, acceptance rate, pricing, multiple revenue streams, costs)?
- Are revenues realistic?
- When does the company reach cash flow positive, and what cash requirements will it take to get there?

- Has the company already received funding, and, if so, how much; what are pre-money valuation and terms?
- What are the follow-on funding requirements and sources? Has the company properly anticipated future needs, and is it already working on those?
- Have all tax returns been properly filed?
- What is the company's debt carry? What are the ratios?
- Is the company's current valuation aligned with its current stage of development and market potential?

Market Assessment
(Do Independent Market Analysis and Require Customer References if Applicable)

- Does the company's product or service address a new or existing market?
- Is the product or service platform-based, with the opportunity for additional products or services? Or is this potentially a one-trick pony?
- Does the company have a well-thought-out sales and marketing plan?
- Does the company have key relationships in place, or is it working on the same, with marketing and/or sales partners?
- Does the company have or need key joint venture relationships?
- Is the company focused on the appropriate market development, or are they trying to do too much at one time?
- Have they chosen the right first market?
- Does their product or service represent a market push or pull?
- What is the potential market size?
- Have they conducted thorough market research to support their financial assumptions, revenue model, and valuation?
- What is their stage of development? Concept, alpha, beta, or shipping?
- If the company has already introduced its product or service into the market, what is the number of current and potential customers?
- What is the length of its sales cycle?
- What are the channels of distribution?
- Does the company's product or service have a seasonal aspect?
- Is this a stable market and are COGS stable?

Competitive Arena
(Do Independent Competitive Analysis)

- Who are the company's competitors?
- Has the company realistically assessed its competitors?
- What is the company's market differentiator? Is this enough to make them superior to competition from the customer's perspective?
- Is this a market or product consolidation?
- How entrenched are the competitors?

- What is the financial stability of competitors?
- What does the market share look like?
- How will this company win?
- Has the company done a detailed feature-by-feature analysis?

Management Team
(Interview All Team Members and Key Employee References)

- What is the caliber/pedigree of the team?
- What is the team's overall track record?
- Do they have the combined requisite skills and experience?
- Do they recognize limitations in management, and are they seeking candidates?
- Is the management open to discussion and suggestions on improvement to their business model?
- Has the management team been previously funded?
- How are management and all other employees being compensated?
- Does the company have an option plan, and have options been granted to all employees? What percentage do the founders have as compared to other key management?

Technology Assessment
(May Need Expert or Professional Assistance in Technology Assessment)

- Do they have market requirements and functional specifications?
- At what stage is development? Concept, alpha, beta, shipping?
- Does the company have any usability studies?
- Does the company have adequate intellectual-property protection? Does it need it?
- Is the company relying on being first to market, rather than on any IP position, for competitive advantage, and is this realistic?
- What is product quality assurance like?
- Is it proprietary architecture or open-source code?
- Do they have adequate systems in place to identify and protect IP?
- Who in the company is focused on these issues?
- Has the company properly set up relationships and documentation to ensure ownership of all intellectual property?
- Does the company own all necessary intellectual property through internal development or licenses?
- Do any other companies have potential claims to the IP resulting from previous employment relationships or for any other reason?

Operations

- Does the company have an operating plan or outline of the same if early stage?
- Has the company considered all aspects of operation to successfully launch a product or service?

- Does the operating plan anticipate growth? Is anticipated growth realistic?
- Has the company received any citations or notices of violation?
- For more mature companies, does each division of the company have an operating plan, and are they compatible?
- Does management meet regularly to ensure compliance with plan or make needed adjustments?
- Has the company been able to stay on plan?
- Does the plan take into consideration all cash needs and anticipated cash flow?
- Does the company have an alternative plan if assumptions do not hold, such as for product rollout, cash needs, and market response?

Comparables:

- Recent IPOs (10Ks, annual reports)
- Recent companies funded in this space
- Third-party (including government) databases, reports, publications, and market analysis
- Comparable financial models

What to Watch Out For:

- Unrealistic valuation (or revenue model)
  - Affects percentage ownership
  - Affects possible subsequent rounds
  - May end up with "down-round" on next financing
- Complicated investment terms
  - Preferred fine, but be careful of other complicated features such as rights of first refusal; onerous liquidation preferences; registration rights; no lock-ups; co-sale
- Heavy debt
  - New investment dollars should be used for advancing the company, not for paying old obligations
- Missing key assumptions about market or financial model
- One-trick pony (one-product or -service company)
- No board per se
- Inexperienced management
- Poor advisors

Source: Susan L. Preston, *Angel Investment Groups, Networks, and Funds: A Guidebook to Developing the Right Angel Organization for Your Community* (Kansas City, MO: Ewing Marion Kauffman Foundation, 2004), 8.1–8.6.

DUE DILIGENCE CHECKLIST

The documents and materials itemized below constitute a list of materials which should be reviewed for any financing. Keep in mind that many early-stage companies will not have some or many of these documents, as certain events may not have occurred. Requests should be made for all documents or disclosures listed below.

Title of Section & Subsection	Documents Requested	Should Have	Date Received	Date Delivered	Reviewer's Initials	Comments
I.	**General corporate materials (the company, all subsidiaries, partnerships, and joint ventures).**					
A.	**Business Plan,** including executive summary, market analysis and plan, operational plan, and complete financials.					
B.	**Minutes**					
1.	Minutes of stockholders' meetings, including those of any predecessor corporations.					
2.	Minutes of board of directors, including those of any predecessor corporations.					
3.	Minutes of permanent committees of the board, including those of any predecessor corporations.					
4.	Authorizing resolutions relating to this offering and related transactions.					
C.	**Charter Documents**					
1.	Articles or Certificate of Incorporation, as amended to date, including current drafts of pending charter amendments and recapitalization documents.					
2.	Drafts of documents related to proposed reincorporation.					

Title of Section & Subsection	Documents Requested	Should Have	Date Received	Date Delivered	Reviewer's Initials	Comments
3.	Bylaws, as amended to date.					
4.	Good standing (and franchise tax board) certificates.					
5.	List of jurisdictions in which the Company or any of its subsidiaries or affiliates is qualified to do business.					
D.	**Corporate Organization**					
1.	List of officers and directors.					
2.	Management structure organization chart.					
3.	Stockholders' lists (including list of optionees and warrant holders), including number of shares and dates of issuance, and consideration paid.					
4.	Information regarding subsidiaries, i.e., ownership, date of acquisition of stock and/or assets, all closing binders relating to acquisitions.					
5.	Information regarding joint ventures or partnership, i.e., partners, date of formation, all closing binders relating to joint ventures or partnerships.					
6.	Agreements relating to mergers, acquisitions, or dispositions by the company of its subsidiaries or affiliates of companies, significant assets or operations involving the company or any of its subsidiaries or affiliates since inception, including those of any predecessor or subsidiary corporations.					
E.	**Capital Stock**					
1.	Stock records, stock ledgers, and other evidence of securities authorized and issued.					

Title of Section & Subsection	Documents Requested	Should Have	Date Received	Date Delivered	Reviewer's Initials	Comments
2.	Agreements relating to the purchase, repurchase, sale or issuance of securities, including oral commitments to sell or issue securities.					
3.	Agreements relating to voting of securities and restrictive share transfers.					
4.	Agreements relating to pre-emptive or other preferential rights to acquire securities and any waivers thereof.					
5.	Agreements relating to registration rights.					
6.	Evidence of qualification or exemption under applicable federal and state blue sky laws for issuance of the Company's securities.					
7.	Documents relating to any conversion, recapitalization, reorganization, or significant restructuring of the Company.					
II.	**Litigation**					
A.	Any litigation, claims, and proceedings settled or concluded, including those of any predecessor corporations and subsidiaries.					
B.	Any litigation, claims, and proceedings threatened or pending. Please include potential litigation—e.g., employees who may be in breach of non-compete agreements with prior employers.					
C.	Any litigation involving an executive officer or director, including executive officers or directors of predecessor corporations and subsidiaries, concerning bankruptcy, crimes, securities law, or business practices.					

Title of Section & Subsection	Documents Requested	Should Have	Date Received	Date Delivered	Reviewer's Initials	Comments
D.	Any consent decrees, injunctions, judgments, other decrees or orders, settlement agreements, or similar matters.					
E.	All attorneys' letters to auditors, including those of any predecessor corporation and subsidiaries.					
III.	**Compliance with Laws**					
A.	Any citations and notices received from government agencies, including those of any predecessor or subsidiary corporations, or with continuing effect from an earlier date.					
B.	Any pending or threatened investigations and governmental proceedings.					
C.	All material governmental permits, licenses, etc., of the company presently in force, together with information regarding any such permits, licenses, etc., which have been canceled or terminated, required to carry out the business or operations of the company or its subsidiaries or affiliates, including such permits, licenses, etc. required by foreign, federal, provincial, or local authorities, and any evidence of exemption from any such permit or license requirement.					
D.	All documents filed with the SEC or any state or foreign securities regulatory agency, if any.					
E.	Any material reports to and correspondence with any government entity, municipality or government agencies, including the EPA and OSHA, including those of any predecessor corporations or subsidiaries.					

Title of Section & Subsection	Documents Requested	Should Have	Date Received	Date Delivered	Reviewer's Initials	Comments
IV.	**Employee Matters** (including items regarding any predecessor or subsidiary or affiliated corporations and all items presently in force and drafts of any pending amendments or new items)					
A.	Employee agreements.					
B.	Consulting contracts.					
C.	Employee benefit and profit-sharing plans, including stock option, stock purchase, deferred compensation, and bonus plans or arrangements.					
D.	All other employee compensation, bonus, incentive, retirement, benefit (e.g., life or health insurance, medical reimbursement plans, etc.), or similar plans.					
E.	Employee Confidentiality and Proprietary Rights Agreement.					
F.	Officers and directors questionnaires.					
G.	Contracts with unions and other labor agreements.					
H.	Loans to and guarantees for the benefit of directors, officers or employees.					
I.	"Key person" insurance policies.					
J.	Listing of employees by office and department.					
K.	Affiliation agreements with advertising agencies or public relations firms.					
L.	Stock ownership of directors and of the five most highly compensated officers.					
V.	**Real Property**					
A.	Deeds.					
B.	Leases of real property.					

Title of Section & Subsection	Documents Requested	Should Have	Date Received	Date Delivered	Reviewer's Initials	Comments
C.	Other interests in real property.					
D.	Any documents showing any certification of compliance with, or any deficiency with respect to, regulatory standards of the company's or any of its subsidiaries' or affiliates' facilities.					
E.	Financing leases and sale and lease-back agreements.					
F.	Conditional sale agreements.					
G.	Equipment leases.					
VI.	**Intellectual Property Matters**					
A.	List of all foreign and domestic patents, patent applications, copyrights, patent licenses and copyright licenses held by the Company.					
B.	List of any trademarks, trademark applications, trade names, or service marks.					
C.	Claims of infringement or misappropriation of others' patents, copyrights, trade secrets, or other proprietary rights.					
D.	Copies of all agreements in-licensing or acquiring any technology, including without limitation software licenses, patent licenses, or other technology licenses, or any development or joint-development agreements.					
E.	Copies of all agreements out-licensing or selling any technology, including without limitation any software licenses, patent licenses, or other technology licenses, or any distribution, OEM, VAR or sales-representative agreements.					

Title of Section & Subsection	Documents Requested	Should Have	Date Received	Date Delivered	Reviewer's Initials	Comments
VII.	Debt Financing					
A.	All debt instruments, credit agreements, and guarantees entered into by the company, including lease financing, which are currently in effect.					
B.	All material correspondence with lenders, including all compliance reports submitted by the company or its accountants.					
C.	Any loans and guarantees of third-party obligations.					
D.	Any agreements restricting the payment of cash dividends.					
VIII.	Other Agreements					
A.	Marketing agreements.					
B.	Management and service agreements.					
C.	Forms of secrecy, confidentiality, and nondisclosure agreements.					
D.	Contracts outside the ordinary course of business.					
E.	Indemnification contracts and similar arrangements for officers and directors.					
F.	Agreements with officers, directors, and affiliated parties.					
G.	Any agreements with competitors.					
H.	Any agreements with governmental agencies or institutions.					
I.	Any agreements restricting the company's right to compete or other agreements material to the business.					

Title of Section & Subsection	Documents Requested	Should Have	Date Received	Date Delivered	Reviewer's Initials	Comments
J.	Any material insurance arrangements (including property damage, third-party liability, and key employee insurance).					
K.	Agreements requiring consents or approvals or resulting in changes in rights in connection with change-of control transactions.					
IX.	**Financial Information**					
A.	Audited/unaudited financial statements, including those of any predecessor corporations.					
B.	Interim financial statements.					
C.	Budget plan, including revisions to date with respect to the budget plan for the current fiscal year for the company and its subsidiaries and affiliates.					
D.	The company's long-range strategic plan, any other documents concerning its long-range plans, and any information concerning the company's compliance therewith.					
E.	Disclosure documents used in private placements of the company's or any of its subsidiaries' or affiliates' securities, or institutional- or bank-loan applications since inception.					
F.	Any other material agreements with creditors.					
G.	Significant correspondence with independent public accountants, including management letters.					

Title of Section & Subsection	Documents Requested	Should Have	Date Received	Date Delivered	Reviewer's Initials	Comments
H.	Any reports, studies and projections prepared by management on the company's or its subsidiaries' or affiliates' business, financial condition, or planned operations, including business plan.					
I.	Any reports and studies prepared by outside consultants on the company's or its subsidiaries' or affiliates' business or financial condition.					
J.	Reports and materials prepared for the company's board of directors or a committee thereof.					
K.	Contracts with investment bankers and brokers.					
X.	**Tax Matters**					
A.	Federal, state, and local tax returns, including those of any predecessor corporations.					
B.	Audit adjustments proposed by the IRS.					
XI.	**Acquisitions/Divestitures**					
A.	Acquisitions or divestitures (including related documentation).					
B.	Current plans or negotiations relating to potential acquisitions or divestitures.					
XII.	**Public Relations**					
A.	Annual reports and other reports and communications with stockholders, employees, suppliers, and customers.					
B.	Advertising, marketing, and other selling materials.					
XIII.	**Press Releases and Clippings**					
A.	Analyst reports.					

Title of Section & Subsection	Documents Required	Should Have	Date Received	Date Delivered	Reviewer's Initials	Comments
XIV.	**Miscellaneous**					
A.	Supply copies of all market research or marketing studies concerning the company's business conducted.					
B.	Significant agreements currently in draft stage.					

Source: Susan L. Preston, *Angel Investment Groups, Networks, and Funds: A Guidebook to Developing the Right Angel Organization for Your Community* (Kansas City, MO: Ewing Marion Kauffman Foundation, 2004), 9.1–9.8.

RESOURCES

"ACA Member Directory," ACA Member Directory. Accessed July 28, 2018. https://www.angelcapitalassociation.org/directory/.

Angel Investor Forum, "AIF Generic Term Sheet," February 28, 2014. Accessed September 5, 2018. www.angelinvestorforum.com/wp/wp-content/.../10/AIF-Generic-Term-Sheet.docx.

"For Entrepreneurs: Connections, Knowledge and Empowerment," *Tech Coast Angels*. Accessed July 30, 2018. https://www.techcoastangels.com/for-entrepreneurs/.

Harris, Aaron and Jason Kwon, "YC's Series A Due Diligence Checklist," *Y Combinator blog*, February 22, 2018. Accessed August 3, 2018. https://blog.ycombinator.com/ycs-series-a-diligence-checklist/.

Harroch, Richard, "The 10 Commandments for Obtaining Angel Funding for Your Startup." *All Business*. November 08, 2015. Accessed July 28, 2018. https://www.allbusiness.com/angel-funding-startup-21773-1.html.

Harroch, Richard, "50 Questions Angel Investors Will Ask Entrepreneurs." *All Business*. July 19, 2016. Accessed July 28, 2018. https://www.allbusiness.com/50-questions-angel-investors-will-ask-entrepreneurs-106619-1.html.

Lee, Aaron, "30 Legendary Startup Pitch Decks and What You Can Learn from Them." *Piktochart*. Accessed July 30, 2018. https://piktochart.com/blog/startup-pitch-decks-what-you-can-learn/.

"LinkedIn Pitch Deck," Pitch Deck Examples. January 29, 2016. Accessed July 30, 2018. https://pitchdeckexamples.com/startups/linkedin-pitch-deck.

National Venture Capital Association, "NVCA Model Term Sheet," updated June 2013. Accessed September 5, 2018. In "Model Legal Documents," https://nvca.org/resources/model-legal-documents/.

O'Brien, Paul, "Who Is the Best VC That Blogs (vs. Blogger Who Invests)?" *Quora*. July 4, 2018. Accessed July 28, 2018. https://www.quora.com/Who-is-the-best-VC-that-blogs-(vs.-blogger-who-invests).

Preston, Susan L., "Due Diligence Questions" and "Due Diligence Checklist," in *Angel Investor Groups, Networks, and Funds: A Guidebook to Developing the Right Angel Organization for Your Community* (Kansas City, MO: Ewing Marion Kauffman Foundation, 2004). Accessed June 1, 2018. https://www.angelcapitalassociation.org/data/Documents/Resources/AngelCapitalEducation/Kauffman_-_StartGroup_Guidebook.pdf.

Prince, Russ Alan, Richard J. Flynn, and Bruce Rogers, *Raising Capital from Single-Family Offices: Considerations for Financial Firms* (New York:

Rothstein Kass, 2011). Accessed August 3, 2018. RothsteinKass_
RaisingCapitalfromSFOs_June2011.pdf.

Prive, Tanya, "20 Most Active Angel Investors." *Forbes*. October 18, 2016.
Accessed July 28, 2018. https://www.forbes.com/sites/tanyaprive/2013/12/
16/20-most-active-angel-investors/#685fd4a4566a.

"Sample VC Due Diligence Request List," *Cooley GO*. July 2014. Accessed
August 3, 2018. https://www.cooleygo.com/wp-content/uploads/2014/07/
Cooley-GO-Tip-Sheet-Sample-VC-Due-Diligence-Request-List.pdf.

Shontell, Alyson, and Andrea Huspeni, "The 50 Early Stage Investors in Silicon
Valley You Need to Know." *Business Insider*. July 23, 2012. Accessed July 28,
2018. https://www.businessinsider.com/sv-angel-50-2012-7.

"Startup Documents," *Y Combinator*. February 2016. Accessed April 30, 2018.
https://www.ycombinator.com/documents/. Includes documents on Simple
Agreements for Equity (safes).

Tech Coast Angels, "TCA Sample Term Sheet Convertible Debt," May 2016.
Accessed September 5, 2018. https://www.techcoastangels.com/wp-content/
uploads/2016/05/TCA-Sample-Term-Sheet-Conv-Debt.pdf.

"The National Venture Capital Association—NVCA," *Crunchbase*. Accessed
July 29, 2018. https://www.crunchbase.com/organization/national-venture-
capital-association.

"The Periodic Table of Venture Capital Blogs," *Corporate Innovation Trends*.
July 20, 2017. Accessed July 28, 2018. https://www.cbinsights.com/research/
venture-capital-blogs-periodic-table/.

"Timely Reads," *Home | ACA*. Accessed July 28, 2018. https://www.
angelcapitalassociation.org/books/.

"Top 50 Venture Capital Blogs, Websites & Newsletters in 2018 | VC Blogs,"
Feedspot (blog). July 06, 2018. Accessed July 28, 2018. https://blog.feedspot.
com/venture_capital_blogs/.

"Trends and Issues: Top 10 Compensation Committee Agenda Items for 2012,"
Pearl Meyer & Partners, LLC, March 12, 2012. Accessed May 19, 2018.
https://www.nacdonline.org/files/PMP-TI-TopTenCCitemsfor2012-3-12_
1344957564109_1.pdf.

"Venture Capital Directory—Angel Investors Listing," *Associations Directory—
Media Broadcast Industry*. Accessed July 29, 2018. http://www.boogar.com/
resources/venturecapital/angels.htm.

REFERENCES

"17 Statistics Every Business Owner Needs to Be Well Aware Of," *Fundera* (blog). Accessed September 4, 2017. https://www.fundera.com/blog/small-business-statistics.

"253 Startup Failure Post-Mortems," *CB Insights Research Briefs*, April 17, 2018. Accessed May 1, 2018. https://www.cbinsights.com/research/startup-failure-post-mortem/.

4Q 2017 PitchBook-NVCA Venture Monitor. Seattle, WA: Pitchbook Data, Inc., 2018.

Ackerman, Bob, "You've Got the Money—Now What?" *Venture Beat*, May 1, 2013. Accessed April 10, 2018. https://venturebeat. com/2013/05/01/youve-got-the-money-now-what/.

Advani, Asheesh, "How to Value Your Startup" (originally published as "What's Your Biz Worth?"). *Entrepreneur.com*, December 21, 2004. Accessed May 15, 2018. https://www.entrepreneur.com/article/72384.

Amis, David and H. H. Stevenson, *Winning Angels: The Seven Fundamentals of Early-stage Investing*. London: Pearson Education, 2001.

"Appendix 8: Issues to Consider in Due Diligence," *Angel Capital Association*, no date. Accessed April 1, 2018. https://www.angelcapitalassociation.org/data/Documents/Resources/AngelCapitalEducation/Angel_Guidebook_-_Due_Diligence_Questions.pdf?rev=C7C4.

Arora, Punit, "5 Questions Every Startup Should Ask before Choosing a Incubator." *Entrepreneur*, November 13, 2013. Accessed September 4, 2017. https://www.entrepreneur.com/article/229856.

Balachandra, Lakshmi, Harry Sapienza, and Dennie Kim, "How Critical Cues Influence Angels' Investment Preferences." *Frontiers of Entrepreneurship Research* 34:1 [2014], p. 9. Accessed June 10, 2018. https://digitalknowledge.babson.edu/fer/vol34/iss1/1.

Barnett, Chance, "The All-in-One Startup Funding Guide." *Startup Grind*, last modified September 7, 2016. Accessed May 24, 2018. https://medium.com/startup-grind/the-startup-funding-guide-pitch-deck-term-sheets-investors-equity-crowdfunding-a212ba9cdab7.

Bartus, Matthew, "Negotiating Term Sheets: Focus on What's Important." *CooleyGo*, no date. Accessed May 1, 2018. https://www.cooleygo.com/negotiating-term-sheets/.

Belsito, Mike, *Start Up Seed Funding for the Rest of Us: How to Raise $1 Million for Your Startup—Even Outside of Silicon Valley*. Seattle, WA: Amazon Digital Services, LLC, 2015. Kindle edition.

Berkus, Dave, "After 20 Years, Updating the Berkus Method of Valuation." *Berkonomics* (blog), November 4, 2016. Accessed May 1, 2018. https://berkonomics.com/?p=2752.

Berkus, Dave, "Take Only 'Smart Money' Investments." *Berkonomics* (blog), February 13, 2018. Accessed May 1, 2018. https://berkonomics.com/?p=3293.

Bernstein, Shai, Arthur Korteweg, and Kevin Laws. "Attracting Early Stage Investors: Evidence from a Randomized Field Experiment." *The Journal of Finance* 72:2 (April 2017), pp. 509–538. Accessed June 11, 2018. https://doi.org/10.1111/jofi.12470.

Bukszpan, Daniel, "10 Key Elements of a Perfect Investor Pitch." *Entrepreneur*, January 13, 2014. Accessed April 8, 2018. https://www.entrepreneur.com/slideshow/230715.

Burke, Andrew, Stuart Fraser, and Francis Greene, "The Multiple Effects of Business Planning on New Venture Performance." *Journal of Management Studies* 47:3 (2010), pp. 391–415. Accessed May 2, 2018. https://doi.org/10.1111/j.1467-6486.2009.00857.x

Bussgang, Jeff, "Getting Introductions to Investors—The Ranking Algorithm." *Seeing Both Sides* (blog), June 12, 2014, accessed May 4, 2018. http://boston-vcblog.typepad.com/vc/2014/06/getting-introductions-to-investors-the-ranking-algorithm.html?utm_source=feedburner&utm_medium=feed&utm_campaign=Feed percent3A+typepad percent2FnqcX+ percent28Seeing+Both-+Sides percent29&utm_content=FeedBurner.

Carayannis, Elias G., and Maximillian von Zedtwitz, "Architecting gloCal (Global–Local), Real-Virtual Incubator Networks (G-RVINs) as Catalysts and Accelerators of Entrepreneurship in Transitioning and Developing Economies: Lessons Learned and Best Practices from Current Development and Business Incubation Practices." *Technovation*, February 2005, 25:2, 95-110. Abstract accessed September 4, 2017. http://www.sciencedirect.com/science/article/pii/S0166497203000725.

Carducci, Bernardo J., Quentin L. Stubbins, and Michael R. Bryant, "Still Shy After All These (30) Years." Poster presentation at the American Psychological Association115th National Conference, Boston, MA, August 17, 2008. Accessed May 1, 2018. http://psibeta.org/site/wp-content/uploads/APA2008-Carducci-Stubbins-Bryant-2008.pdf.

Chen, Xiao-Ping, Xin Yao, and Suresh Kotha, "Entrepreneur Passion and Preparedness in Business Plan Presentations: A Persuasion Analysis of Venture Capitalists' Funding Decisions." *Academy of Management Journal* 52:1 (2009), pp. 199–214. Accessed May 7, 2018. https://doi.org/10.5465/amj.2009.36462018.

Clark, Dave, "Dilution: The Real Meaning of Funding Success," *FundingSage*, April 16, 2018. Accessed May 9, 2018. https://fundingsage. com/dilution-real-meaning-funding-success/.

Clark, Kate, "Airbnb, Instacart and 8 More Companies that Sprinted to $1B Valuations." *Pitchbook,* April 27, 2018. Accessed May 8, 2018. https://pitch-book.com/news/articles/airbnb-instacart-and-8-more-companies-that-sprinted-to-1b-valuations.

Cuddy, Amy J., S. Jack Schultz, and Nathan E. Fosse, "*P*-Curving a More Comprehensive Body of Research on Postural Feedback Reveals Clear Evidential Value for Power-Posing Effects: Reply to Simmons and Simonsohn (2017)." *Psychological Science* 29:4 (April 1, 2018), pp. 656–666. Accessed June 15, 2018. https://doi.org/10.1177/0956797617746749.

Davie, Alexander J., "Venture Capital Term Sheet Negotiation—Part 2: Valuation, Capitalization Tables, and Price per Share." *Strictly Business Law* (blog), October 14, 2013. Accessed May 8, 2018. https://www.strictlybusinesslawblog.com/2013/10/14/venture-capital-term-sheet-negotiation-part-2-valuation-capitalization-tables-price-per-share/.

Espinal, Carlos Eduardo, *Fundraising Field Guide*. London, UK: Reedsy Ltd. 2015. Kindle edition.

Evarts, Eric C., "Study Shows 23 Percent Cancellations on Tesla Model 3 Deposits." *Green Car Reports*, June 4, 2018. Accessed May 2, 2018. https://www.greencarreports.com/news/1117043_study-shows-23-percent-cancelations-on-tesla-model-3-deposits.

Fabric Ventures and Token Data, *The State of the Token Market 2017: A Year in Review & an Outlook for 2018* (white paper). Downloaded June 4, 2018. https://static1.squarespace.com/static/5a19eca6c027d8615635f801/t/5a7369 7bc8302551711523ca/1517513088503/The+State+of+the+Token+Market+-Final2.pdf.

Fairlie, Robert W., Anobio Morelix, and Inara Tareque, *The Kauffman Index Startup Activity: National Trends 2017*. Kansas City, MO: Ewing Marion Kauffman Foundation, 2017.

Feld, Brad, and Jason Mendelson, *Venture Deals: Be Smarter Than Your Lawyer and Venture Capitalist*, 3rd edition. New York: Wiley. 2016.

Ferris, Robert, "Tesla Battery Production Is the Real Bottleneck, Not Model 3 Production, Analyst Says." *CNBC,* April 18, 2018. Accessed May 2, 2018. https://www.cnbc.com/2018/04/18/tesla-battery-production-is-the-real-bottleneck-not-model-3-production.html.

Gaffney, Tyler, "Pricing Lessons from Working with 30+ Seed and Series A B2B Startups." *First Round Review*, May 3, 2018. Accessed May 12, 2018. http://firstround.com/review/pricing-lessons-from-working-with-30-seed-and-series-a-b2b-startups/?utm_campaign=new_article&utm_medium=e-mail&utm_source=newsletter.

Gladwell, Malcolm, *The Tipping Point: How Little Things Can Make a Big Difference*. New York: Little, Brown and Company, 2000.

Gobry, Pascal-Emmanuel, "10 Brilliant Startups that Failed Because They Were Ahead of their Time." *Business Insider*, May 4, 2011. Accessed May 1, 2018. http://www.businessinsider.com/startup-failures-2011-5.

Gompers, Paul A., Anna Kovner, Josh Lerner, and David S. Scharfstein, *Performance Persistence in Entrepreneurship*, Working Paper 09-028. Cambridge, MA: Harvard Business School, 2008.

Graham, Paul, "How to Raise Money," *Paul Graham* (blog), September 2013. Accessed May 10, 2018. http://www.paulgraham.com/fr.html.

Hagen, Jean, "Top 12 Reasons Why Businesses Fail." In Eric Koester (Ed.,) *What Every Engineer Should Know About Starting a High-Tech Business Venture*. Boca Raton, FL: Taylor & Francis Group, 2009.

Hamilton, Brian, "Your Startup Doesn't Need a Business Plan." *Inc.*, March 12, 2015. Accessed April 8, 2018. https://www.inc.com/brian-hamilton/why-your-startup-doesn-t-need-a-business-plan.html.

Hansell, Saul, "Marc Andreessen's LoudCloud Finally Rains Money." *New York Times "Bits"* (blog), July 23, 2007. Accessed May 1, 2018. https://bits.blogs.nytimes.com/2007/07/23/marc-andreessens-loudcloud-finally-rains-money/.

Hawk, Steve, "How to Build a Better Startup Team." *Insights by Stanford Business*, December 14, 2016. Accessed April 30, 2018. https://www.gsb.stanford.edu/insights/how-build-better-startup-team.

Hedlund, Marc, "Why Wesabe Lost to Mint," *Marc Hedlund's Blog*, October 1, 2010. Accessed April 22, 2018. http://blog.precipice.org/why-wesabe-lost-to-mint/.

Henricks, Mark, "Do You Really Need a Business Plan?" *Entrepreneur*, December 2008. Accessed May 1, 2018. https://www.entrepreneur.com/article/198618.

Herzog, Alain, "Where to Play: A Practical Guide for Running Your Tech Business." Press release, September 26, 2017. Accessed June 1, 2018. https://actu.epfl.ch/news/where-to-play-a-practical-guide-for-running-your-t/.

Hoffman, Martin, "Is Your Startup Worth the Risk? 5 Questions You Need to Answer." *Entrepreneur*, March 9, 2018. Accessed May 1, 2018. https://www.entrepreneur.com/article/309893.

Homuth, Katherine, "Ask an Investor: How Do I Prepare for Due Diligence on My Startup?" *Canadian Startup News*, February 3, 2017. Accessed April 3, 2018. https://betakit.com/ask-an-investor-how-do-i-prepare-for-due-diligence-on-my-startup/.

Hornik, David, "Startup Advice: How Entrepreneurs Gain Credibility" *VentureBlog*, January 21, 2011. Accessed May 4, 2018. http://www.ventureblog.com/2011/01/startup-advice-how-entrepeneurs-gain-credibility.html.

Horowitz, Benjamin, and Patricia R. Olsen, "The Boss: Making Peace with Risk." *New York Times*, July 15, 2007. Accessed May 1, 2018. https://www.nytimes.com/2007/07/15/business/yourmoney/15boss.html.

"How to Avoid Presenting a Flat Tire for a Buyer to Kick: A Guide to the Venture Capital Due Diligence Process for Early-Stage Startups," *Bagchi Law*, May 5, 2015. Accessed April 14, 2018. http://bagchilaw.com/how-to-avoid-presenting-a-flat-tire-for-a-buyer-to-kick-a-guide-to-the-venture-capital-due-diligence-process-for-early-stage-startups/.

Huang, Laura, Andy Wu, Min Ju Lee, Jiayi Bao, and Elaine Bolle, *The American Angel*. Philadelphia, PA: Wharton Entrepreneurship and Angel Capital Association, November 2017.

Hudson, Marianne, "How Much Due Diligence Does an Angel Really Need to Do?" *Forbes*, January 15, 2015. Accessed April 3, 2018. https://www.forbes.com/sites/mariannehudson/2015/01/15/how-much-due-diligence-does-an-angel-really-need-to-do/#64d4ccaa4e0e.

Ilgaz, Zeynep, "The 5 Best Pitch Tactics I Heard as an Angel Investor." *Entrepreneur*, March 27, 2015. Accessed April 1, 2018. https://www.entrepreneur.com/article/244115.

Iskold, Alex, "8 Things You Need to Know About Raising Venture Capital." *Entrepreneur*, July 15, 2015. Accessed April 3, 2018. https://www.entrepreneur.com/article/248377.

Jacobsohn, Sean, "Here's a Look Inside a Typical VC's Pipeline (a Must-Read for Entrepreneurs)." *VentureBeat*, April 19, 2014. Accessed September 4, 2017. https://venturebeat.com/2014/04/19/heres-a-look-inside-a-typical-vcs-pipeline-a-must-read-for-entrepreneurs/.

Kawasaki, Guy, "The Only 10 Slides You Need in Your Pitch." *Guykawasaki.com*, March 5, 2015. Accessed April 5, 2018. https://guykawasaki.com/the-only-10-slides-you-need-in-your-pitch/.

Kelley, Donna, Stavica Singer, and Mike Herrington, *Global Entrepreneurship Monitor 2015/16 Global Report*. Babson Park, MA: Global Enterprise Research Association, 2016.

Kellner, Aaron, "What You Need to Know about Liquidation Preferences." *Seed Invest Blog on Startup Investing*, August 30, 2017. Accessed May 1, 2018. https://www.seedinvest.com/blog/startup-investing/liquidation-preferences.

Knight, Shawn, "Tesla Now Has 455,000 Reservations for Its Mainstream Model 3 Sedan." *Techspot*, August 3, 2017. Accessed May 3, 2018. https://www.techspot.com/news/70426-tesla-now-has-455000-reservations-mainstream-model-3.html.

Lesonsky, Rieva, "A Business Plan Doubles Your Chances for Success, Says a New Survey." *Small Business Trends*, January 20, 2016. Accessed May 27, 2018. https://smallbiztrends.com/2010/06/business-plan-success-twice-as-likely.html.

Lettich, Tony, "14 Types of Information Investors May Request as Part of their Due Diligence Checklist for Your Startup." *Funding Sage*, June 14, 2017. Accessed April 3, 2018. https://fundingsage.com/14-types-of-information-investors-may-request-as-part-of-their-due-diligence-checklist-for-your-startup/.

Levensohn, Pascal, and Andrew Krowne, "Why SAFE Notes Are Not Safe for Entrepreneurs." *Tech Crunch*, July 8, 2017. Accessed May 1, 2018. https://techcrunch.com/2017/07/08/why-safe-notes-are-not-safe-for-entrepreneurs/.

Livesay, John, "TSP019: Sam Horn—Intrigue Expert Teaches How To Get Investors' Attention," *The Successful Pitch*, August 5, 2015, podcast, audio, 42:55. Accessed April 1, 2018. https://www.youtube.com/watch?v=-dDThPGGVgo.

Matveeva, Sophia, "What Makes Great Startup Teams, and How to Find It." *Forbes*, April 30, 2018. Accessed May 2, 2018. https://www.forbes.com/sites/sophiamatveeva/2018/04/30/what-makes-great-startup-teams-and-how-to-find-it/#ef77c316f6cc.

McDermott, John, "75 percent of Venture-backed Startups Fail." *Inc.*, 09-20-2012. Accessed September 4, 2017. https://www.inc.com/john-mcdermott/report-3-out-of-4-venture-backed-startups-fail.html.

McGinn, Daniel, "What VCs Really Care About." *Inc.*, October 30, 2012. Accessed April 30, 2018. http://www.inc.com/magazine/201211/daniel-mcginn/what-vcs-really-care-about.html.

Medal, Andrew, "5 Questions Investors Ask Themselves Before Putting Their Chips into Your Startup." *Entrepreneur*, April 25, 2017. Accessed April 28, 2018. https://www.entrepreneur.com/article/293155.

"Microsoft to Acquire LinkedIn," *Microsoft News Center*, June 13, 2016. Accessed May 8, 2018. https://news.microsoft.com/2016/06/13/microsoft-to-acquire-linkedin/.

Mitra, Sramana, "1Mby1M Virtual Accelerator Investor Forum: With Heidi Roizen of DFJ (Part 1)." *One Million by One Million* (blog), April 30, 2018. Accessed May 10, 2018. https://www.sramanamitra.com/2018/04/30/1mby1m-virtual-accelerator-investor-forum-with-heidi-roizen-of-dfj-part-1/.

Mitteness, Cheryl R., Richard Sudek, and Melissa Baucus, "Entrepreneurs as Authentic Transformational Leaders: Critical Behaviors for Gaining Angel Capital." *Frontiers of Entrepreneurship Research* 30:5 (June 12, 2010): 3, 5. Accessed March 8, 2018. http://digitalknowledge.babson.edu/fer/vol30/iss5/3.

Moon, Brad, "10 Worst Tech Products of 2017 Include a 'Smart' Hairbrush." *InvestorPlace*, September 26, 2017. Accessed May 2, 2018. https://investorplace.com/2017/09/worst-tech-products-2017-juicero/.

Owens, Jeremy C., "Tesla Stock Falls on Report of Gigafactory Issues with Model 3 Batteries." *MarketWatch*, January 25, 2018. Accessed May 2, 2018. https://www.marketwatch.com/story/tesla-stock-falls-on-report-of-gigafactory-issues-with-model-3-batteries-2018-01-25.

Paley, Eric, "Running Out of Money Isn't a Milestone." *Tech Crunch*, June 24, 2015. Accessed May 1, 2018. https://techcrunch.com/2015/06/24/running-out-of-money-isnt-a-milestone/.

Patel, Neil, "13 Tips on How to Deliver a Pitch Investors Simply Can't Turn Down." *Entrepreneur*, October 21, 2015. Accessed April 20, 2018. https://www.entrepreneur.com/article/251311.

Payne, Bill, "Scorecard Valuation Methodology: Establishing the Valuation of Pre-revenue, Startup Companies." *Bill Payne* (blog), January 2011. Accessed April 1, 2018. http://billpayne.com/wp-content/uploads/2011/01/Scorecard-Valuation-Methodology-Jan111.pdf.

Payne, Bill, "Valuations 101: The Venture Capital Method," *Gust* (blog), November 1, 2011. Accessed April 1, 2018. http://blog.gust.com/startup-valuations-101-the-venture-capital-method/.

Pearson, Noah, "An Easier Business Model Canvas Template: The Lean Plan Template." *LivePlan* (blog), February 23, 2017. Accessed April 5, 2018. https://www.liveplan.com/blog/2017/02/an-easier-business-model-canvas-template-the-lean-plan-template/.

Pearson, Noah, "Business Planning Makes You More Successful, and We've Got the Science to Prove It." *Bplans.com*, no date. Accessed April 5, 2018. https://articles.bplans.com/business-planning-makes-you-more-successful-and-weve-got-the-science-to-prove-it/.

Preston, Susan L. *Angel Investment Groups, Networks, and Funds: A Guidebook to Developing the Right Angel Organization for Your Community*. Kansas City, MO: Ewing Marion Kauffman Foundation, 2004.

Rachleff, Andy, "Demystifying Venture Capital Economics, Part 3." *Wealthfront* (blog), December 2, 2014. Accessed April 1, 2018. https://blog.wealthfront.com/demystifying-venture-capital-economics-part-3/.

Rajala, Liisa, "Angel Market Shrank in 2016." *NH Business Review*, June 6, 2017. Accessed September 4, 2017. http://www.nhbr.com/June-23-2017/Angel-market-restructures-in-2016-to-focus-to-seed-and-startup-funding/.

Ralston, Geoff, "A Guide to Seed Fundraising." *Y Combinator* (blog), January 7, 2016. Accessed May 10, 2018. https://blog.ycombinator.com/how-to-raise-a-seed-round/.

Rao, Leena, "Things to Consider Before Saying 'I Do' to Investors." *Tech Crunch*, April 8, 2012. Accessed April 10, 2018. https://techcrunch.com/2012/04/08/things-to-consider-before-saying-i-do-to-investors/.

Robinett, Judy, *How to Be a Power Connector: The 5+50+100 Rule for Turning Your Business Network into Profits*. New York: McGraw-Hill Education, 2014.

Rowley, Jason D., "Charting the Adoption of Direct Startup Investments by Family Offices." *Crunchbase.com*, March 26, 2017. Accessed June 2, 2018.

https://news.crunchbase.com/news/charting-adoption-direct-startup-investments-family-offices/.

Schnieders, Amanda, "4 Things Every Entrepreneur Should Do Before Meeting an Investor." *Entrepreneur*, May 20, 2014. Accessed April 14, 2018. https://www.entrepreneur.com/article/234060.

Schools, Dave, "The Holy Grail of Entrepreneurship: The Term Sheet, Pt. 2—Offering Terms." *Funding Sage*, May 21, 2018. Accessed May 30, 2018. https://fundingsage.com/holy-grail-entrepreneurship-term-sheet-pt-2-offering-terms/.

Scott, Emlyn, "7 Things that Angel Investors Look for in Startups." *Capital Pitch Blog*, January 25, 2017. Accessed June 4, 2018. http://www.blog.capitalpitch.com/7-things-that-angel-investors-look-for-in-startups.

Shane, Scott, "How Investors Choose Startups to Finance." *Entrepreneur*, October 17, 2016. Accessed September 4, 2017. https://www.entrepreneur.com/article/251624.

Shochat, Eden, "How to Make the Most of Your Investor Relationships." *Microsoft Startups* (blog), February 25, 2015. Accessed May 1, 2018. https://startups.microsoft.com/en-us/blog/how-to-make-the-most-of-your-investor-relationships/.

Shontell, Alyson, "Tinder, a $500 Million Dating App, Used This Pitch Deck When It Was Just a Tiny Startup." *Business Insider*, July 11, 2014. Accessed April 20, 2018. http://www.businessinsider.com/tinders-first-startup-pitch-deck-2014-7#just-like-tinder-today-match-box-showed-you-single-people-nearby-and-only-allowed-you-to-message-people-who-liked-your-profile-in-return-7.

Sjogren, Candace, "4 Ways to Predict the Result of Your Investment Pitch." *Entrepreneur*, July 17, 2017. Accessed May 1, 2018. https://www.entrepreneur.com/article/296713.

Small, Jonathan, "5 Ways to Win Your Pitch, According to 'Shark Tank's' Robert Herjavec." *Entrepreneur*, October 12, 2017. Accessed May 1, 2018. https://www.entrepreneur.com/article/301175.

"Small Businesses Start with $10,000 or Less," *Quickbook Study*, no date. Accessed September 4, 2017. https://quickbooks.intuit.com/r/trends-stats/know-small-businesses-start-10000-less/.

"Startup Funding: A Look at the Top Sources of Startup Funding" (infographic). *Fundable.com*, January 2015. Accessed September 4, 2017. http://www.fundable.com/learn/resources/infographics/startup-funding-infographic.

Suster, Mark, "I Met with an Investor, What Happens Next?" *Both Sides of the Table* (blog), September 20, 2009. Accessed May 1, 2018. https://bothsidesofthetable.com/i-met-with-an-investor-what-happens-next-63d443648f36.

Suster, Mark, "Some Advice Before You Hit the Fund Raising Trail." *Both Sides of the Table* (blog), May 6, 2018. Accessed April 21, 2018. https://bothsidesofthetable.com/some-advice-before-you-hit-the-fund-raising-trail-73dc646f077e.

Suster, Mark, "Understanding the Herd Mentality of VCs and How Not to Let It Psyche You Out." *Both Sides of the Table* (blog), May 10, 2018. Accessed May 22, 2018. https://bothsidesofthetable.com/understanding-the-herd-mentality-of-vcs-and-how-not-to-let-it-psyche-you-out-27c1071c446b.

Techli team, "10 Greatest Startup Failures of All Time." *Techli*, April 25, 2013. Accessed April 22, 2018. https://techli.com/2012/04/10-greatest-startup-failures/.

"The Top 20 Reasons Startups Fail," *CB Insights*, February 2, 2018. Accessed May 1, 2018. https://www.cbinsights.com/research/startup-failure-reasons-top/.

U.S. Small Business Association Office of Advocacy, "Frequently Asked Questions About Small Business Finance," *Figure 2: Top Sources of Startup Capital (Percent)*, July 2016. Accessed September 4, 2017. https://www.sba.gov/sites/default/files/Finance-FAQ-2016_WEB.pdf.

Urevig, Andrew, "5 Successful Startups That Failed & What You Can Learn from Them." *Foundr*, February 27, 2018. Accessed May 1, 2018. https://foundr.com/how-5-successful-startups-that-failed-but-got-back-up/.

Uzzi, Brian, and Shannon Dunlap, "How to Build Your Network." *Harvard Business Review*, December 2005. Accessed May 5, 2018. https://hbr.org/2005/12/how-to-build-your-network.

Varshneya, Rahul, "How the Top VCs Want to Be Pitched." *Entrepreneur*, July 31, 2015. Accessed April 15, 2018. https://www.entrepreneur.com/article/248053.

Vozza, Stephanie, "The Only 6 People You Need on Your Founding Startup Team." *Fast Company*, July 2, 2014. Accessed March 8, 2018. https://www.fastcompany.com/3032548/the-only-6-people-you-need-on-your-founding-startup-team.

Warren, Liz, "How Do You Stand Out from 1000 Pitches? 4 VCs Tell All." *Builtinnyc.com*, January 26, 2018. Accessed April 4, 2018. https://www.builtinnyc.com/2018/01/26/vcs-best-pitches.

Wasserman, Noam, "How an Entrepreneur's Passion Can Destroy a Startup." *The Wall Street Journal*, August 25, 2014. Accessed April 1, 2018. https://www.wsj.com/articles/how-an-entrepreneur-s-passion-can-destroy-a-startup-1408912044.

Watson, A. J., "One Factor that Improves Angel Investment Returns by 7x." *Fundify*, August 11, 2015. Accessed April 1, 2018. https://medium.com/a-startup-blog/one-factor-that-improves-angel-investment-returns-by-7x-e2367240f1f6.

"What Investors Look for in Startups & Founders," *Product Hunt* (blog), February 9, 2016. Accessed May 5, 2018. https://blog.producthunt.com/what-investors-look-for-in-startups-founders-e782380c2b55.

"What Investors Look for When Buying into a Startup," *Economic Times*, December 28, 2014. Accessed April 30, 2018. https://economictimes.indiatimes.com/small-biz/startups/what-investors-look-for-when-buying-into-a-startup/articleshow/45661616.cms.

Willis, Janine, and Alexander Todorov, "First Impressions: Making Up Your Mind After a 100-Ms Exposure to a Face." *Psychological Science*, Volume: 17 issue: 7, page(s): 592-598. Accessed June 10, 2018. https://doi.org/10.1111/j.1467-9280.2006.01750.x.

Xavier, Siri Roland, Donna Kelley, Jacqui Kew, Mike Herrington, and Arne Vorderwülbecke, *Global Enterprise Monitor 2012 Global Report*. Babson Park, MA: Global Enterprise Research Association, 2012.

Young Entrepreneur Council, "12 Essential Traits of Successful Startup Leaders." *Inc.*, January 18, 2013. Accessed May 2, 2018. https://www.inc.com/young-entrepreneur-council/12-traits-of-successful-startup-leaders.html.

Ziegler, Tania, E. J. Reedy, Annie Le, Bryan Zhang, Randall S. Krosner, and Kieran Garvey, *The 2017 Americas Alternative Finance Industry Report: Hitting Stride*. Chicago: Cambridge Centre for Alternative Finance, Polsky Center for Entrepreneurship and Innovation, and The University of Chicago Booth School of Business, 2017.

ENDNOTES

PART I

1. Chance Barnett, "The All-in-One Startup Funding Guide," *Startup Grind*, last modified September 7, 2016, accessed May 24, 2018. https://medium.com/startup-grind/the-startup-funding-guide-pitch-deck-term-sheets-investors-equity-crowdfunding-a212ba9cdab7.

Chapter 1

1. Donna Kelley, Stavica Singer, Mike Herrington, *Global Entrepreneurship Monitor 2015/16 Global Report* (Babson Park, MA: Global Enterprise Research Association, 2016).
2. Robert W. Fairlie, Anobio Morelix, Inara Tareque, *The Kauffman Index Startup Activity: National Trends 2017* (Kansas City, MO: Ewing Marion Kauffman Foundation, 2017), p. 4.
3. "Small Businesses Start with $10,000 or Less," *Quickbook Study*, accessed September 4, 2017. https://quickbooks.intuit.com/r/trends-stats/know-small-businesses-start-10000-less/.
4. U.S. Small Business Association Office of Advocacy, "Frequently Asked Questions About Small Business Finance," Figure 2: Top Sources of Startup Capital (Percent), July 2016, accessed September 4, 2017. https://www.sba.gov/sites/default/files/Finance-FAQ-2016_WEB.pdf, p. 1; Siri Roland Xavier, Donna Kelley, Jacqui Kew, Mike Herrington, Arne Vorderwülbecke, *Global Enterprise Monitor 2012 Global Report* (Babson Park, MA: Global Enterprise Research Association, 2012).
5. "17 Statistics Every Business Owner Needs to Be Well Aware Of," *Fundera* (blog), accessed September 4, 2017, https://www.fundera.com/blog/small-business-statistics.
6. "17 Statistics Every Business Owner Needs to Be Well Aware Of."
7. U.S. Small Business Association Office of Advocacy, "Frequently Asked Questions About Small Business Finance," p. 1.
8. U.S. Small Business Association Office of Advocacy, "Frequently Asked Questions About Small Business Finance."
9. Liisa Rajala, "Angel Market Shrank in 2016," *NH Business Review*, June 6, 2017, accessed September 4, 2017. http://www.nhbr.com/June-23-2017/Angel-market-restructures-in-2016-to-focus-to-seed-and-startup-funding/.
10. *4Q 2017 PitchBook-NVCA Venture Monitor* (Seattle, WA: Pitchbook Data, Inc., 2018), pp. 3, 4.
11. Jason D. Rowley, "Charting the Adoption of Direct Startup Investments by Family Offices," *Crunchbase.com*, 26 March 2017, accessed June 2, 2018. https://news.crunchbase.com/news/charting-adoption-direct-startup-investments-family-offices/.

12. Tania Ziegler, E. J. Reedy, Annie Le, Bryan Zhang, Randall S. Krosner, Kieran Garvey, *The 2017 Americas Alternative Finance Industry Report: Hitting Stride* (Chicago: Cambridge Centre for Alternative Finance, Polsky Center for Entrepreneurship and Innovation, and The University of Chicago Booth School of Business, 2017), p. 15.

13. Ziegler et al., *The 2017 Americas Alternative Finance Industry Report*, p. 16.

14. Fabric Ventures and Token Data, *The State of the Token Market 2017: A Year in Review & an Outlook for 2018*, white paper, downloaded June 4, 2018. https://static1. squarespace.com/static/5a19eca6c027d8615635f801/t/5a73697bc8302551711523ca/1517513088503/The+State+of+the+Token+Market+Final2.pdf.

15. "Startup Funding: A Look at the Top Sources of Startup Funding," infographic, *Fundable.com*, January 2014, accessed September 4, 2017, http://www.fundable.com/learn/resources/infographics/startup-funding-infographic.

16. Email communication from Cindy Padnos to Judy Robinett, June 14, 2018.

17. Ziegler et al., *The 2017 Americas Alternative Finance Industry Report*, p. 37.

18. Ziegler et al., *The 2017 Americas Alternative Finance Industry Report*, p. 41.

19. Scott Shane, "How Investors Choose Startups to Finance," *Entrepreneur*, October 17, 2016, accessed September 4, 2017. https://www.entrepreneur.com/article/251624.

20. Jean Hagen, "Top 12 Reasons Why Businesses Fail." In Eric Koester (ed.), *What Every Engineer Should Know About Starting a High-Tech Business Venture* (Boca Raton, FL: Taylor & Francis Group, 2009), p. 44.

21. Punit Arora, "5 Questions Every Startup Should Ask before Choosing a Incubator," *Entrepreneur*, November 13, 2013, accessed September 4, 2017. https://www.entrepreneur.com/article/229856.

22. Elias G. Carayannis, Maximillian von Zedtwitz, "Architecting gloCal (Global–Local), Real-Virtual Incubator Networks (G-RVINs) as Catalysts and Accelerators of Entrepreneurship in Transitioning and Developing Economies: Lessons Learned and Best Practices from Current Development and Business Incubation Practices," *Technovation*, February 2005, 25:2, 95–110, abstract accessed September 4, 2017. http://www.sciencedirect.com/science/article/pii/S0166497203000725.

23. Email communication from Ramphis Castro to Judy Robinett, August 5, 2018.

24. John McDermott, "75 percent of Venture-backed Startups Fail," *Inc.*, September 20, 2012, accessed September 4, 2017. https://www.inc.com/john-mcdermott/report-3-out-of-4-venture-backed-startups-fail.html.

25. Sean Jacobsohn, "Here's a Look Inside a Typical VC's Pipeline (a Must-Read for Entrepreneurs)," *VentureBeat*, April 19, 2014, accessed September 4, 2017. https://venturebeat.com/2014/04/19/heres-a-look-inside-a-typical-vcs-pipeline-a-must-read-for-entrepreneurs/.

Chapter 2

1. David Hornik, "Startup Advice: How Entrepreneurs Gain Credibility," *Venture Blog*, January 21, 2011, accessed May 2, 2018. http://www.ventureblog.com/2011/01/startup-advice-how-entrepeneurs-gain-credibility.html.

2. Paul A. Gompers, Anna Kovner, Josh Lerner, David S. Scharfstein, *Performance Persistence in Entrepreneurship*, Working Paper 09-028, (Cambridge, MA: Harvard Business School, 2008), pp. 8–9.

3. Laura Huang, Andy Wu, Min Ju Lee, Jiayi Bao, Elaine Bolle, *The American Angel* (Philadelphia, PA: Wharton Entrepreneurship and Angel Capital Association, November 2017), p. 12.

4. Mark Suster, "Some Advice Before You Hit the Fund Raising Trail," *Both Sides of the Table* (blog), May 6, 2018, accessed April 21, 2018. https://bothsidesofthetable.com/some-advice-before-you-hit-the-fund-raising-trail-73dc646f077e.

5. Judy Robinett, *How to Be a Power Connector: The 5+50+100 Rule for Turning Your Business Network into Profits* (New York: McGraw-Hill Education, 2014), p. 39.

6. Emlyn Scott, "7 Things that Angel Investors Look for in Startups," *Capital Pitch Blog*, January 25, 2017, accessed June 4, 2018, http://www.blog.capitalpitch.com/7-things-that-angel-investors-look-for-in-startups.

7. Suster, "Some Advice Before You Hit the Fund Raising Trail."

8. David Amis and H. H. Stevenson, *Winning Angels: The Seven Fundamentals of Early-stage Investing* (London: Pearson Education, 2001).

9. Amis and Stevenson, *Winning Angels*, p. 3.

10. Hornik, "Startup Advice: How Entrepreneurs Gain Credibility."

11. Janine Willis, Alexander Todorov, "First Impressions: Making Up Your Mind After a 100-Ms Exposure to a Face," *Psychological Science* 17:7, pp. 592–598. Accessed June 10, 2018. https://doi.org/10.1111/j.1467-9280.2006.01750.x.

12. Lakshmi Balachandra, Harry Sapienza, Dennie Kim, "How Critical Cues Influence Angels' Investment Preferences," *Frontiers of Entrepreneurship Research* 34:1 (2014), p. 9. https://digitalknowledge.babson.edu/fer/vol34/iss1/1.

13. Balachandra et al., "How Critical Cues Influence Angels' Investment Preferences," pp. 2, 4.

14. Telephone interview with Sean Sheppard and Andrew Goldner, May 10, 2018.

15. Telephone interview with Sean Sheppard and Andrew Goldner.

16. Cheryl R. Mitteness, Richard Sudek, and Melissa S. Baucus, "Entrepreneurs as Authentic Transformational Leaders: Critical Behaviors for Gaining Angel Capital," *Frontiers of Entrepreneurship Research* 30:5 (2010), accessed March 8, 2018. http://digitalknowledge.babson.edu/fer/vol30/iss5/3, 10.

17. Based on research done by Marc Gruber, Vice-President for Innovation, Ecole Polytechnique Federale de Lausanne. Reported in Alain Herzog, "Where to Play: A Practical Guide for Running Your Tech Business," press release, September 26, 2017, accessed June 1, 2018. https://actu.epfl.ch/news/where-to-play-a-practical-guide-for-running-your-t/.

18. Email communication from Marcia Nelson to Judy Robinett, April 30, 2018.

19. Emlyn Scott, "7 Things that Angel Investors Look for in Startups."

PART II

1. Murray Newlands, "10 Ways to Find Investors for Your Startup," *Huffington Post*, September 11, 2015, accessed May 9, 2018. https://www.huffingtonpost.com/murray-newlands/10-ways-to-find-investors_b_8118236.html.

Chapter 3

1. Jason Wiens and Jordan Bell-Masterson, "How Entrepreneurs Access Capital and Get Funded," Ewing Marion Kauffman Foundation, June 2, 1025, accessed April 22, 2018. https://www.kauffman.org/what-we-do/resources/entrepreneurship-policy-digest/how-entrepreneurs-access-capital-and-get-funded.
2. U.S. Small Business Administration Office of Advocacy, "Frequently Asked Questions about Small Business Finance," July 2016, accessed April 15, 2018. https://www.sba.gov/sites/default/files/Finance-FAQ-2016_WEB.pdf.
3. Geoff Ralston, "A Guide to Seed Fundraising," *Y Combinator* (blog), January 7, 2016, accessed May 10, 2018. https://blog.ycombinator.com/how-to-raise-a-seed-round/.
4. Hans Swildens and Eric Yee, "The Venture Capital Risk and Return Matrix," *Industry Ventures* (blog), February 7, 2017, accessed April 22, 2018. http://www.industryventures.com/2017/02/07/the-venture-capital-risk-and-return-matrix/.
5. Dana Anspach, "20 Years of Stock Market Returns, by Calendar Year," *The Balance Retirement Decisions—Investing*, June 23, 2018, accessed July 4, 2018. https://www.thebalance.com/stock-market-returns-by-year-2388543.
6. Jamie Pennington, "The Best Way to Ask Friends and Family for Seed Capital," *Entrepreneur*, May 15, 2014. https://www.entrepreneur.com/article/233926.
7. Pennington, "The Best Way to Ask Friends and Family for Seed Capital."
8. Ewing Marion Kauffman Foundation, "State of the Field: Debt," June 14, 2016, accessed May 15, 2018. https://www.kauffman.org/microsites/state-of-the-field/topics/finance/debt.
9. U.S. Small Business Association, "Investment Capital," SBA.gov, accessed May 14, 2018. https://www.sba.gov/funding-programs/investment-capital. On the website you'll also find an alphabetical list of SBICs.
10. Ben Rashkovich, "Want Free Money? Check Out This List of 106 Small Business Grants," *Fundera.com* blog, June 18, 2018, accessed July 20, 2018. https://www.fundera.com/blog/small-business-grants.
11. Martin Zwilling, "Every Startup Gains from an Incubator or Accelerator," *Entrepreneur*, May 25, 2016, accessed May 10, 2018. https://www.entrepreneur.com/article/276269.
12. Hubert Zajicek, "Accelerator vs. Incubator: Which Is Right for You?" *Entrepreneur*, May 26, 2017, accessed May 10, 2018. https://www.entrepreneur.com/article/294798.
13. Zwilling, "Every Startup Gains from an Incubator or Accelerator."
14. Punit Arora, "5 Questions Every Startup Should Ask Before Choosing an Incubator," *Entrepreneur*, November 13, 2013, accessed May 9, 2018. https://www.entrepreneur.com/article/229856.

15. "Who's Got Your Back? We Do," Springboard Enterprises, no date, accessed August 3, 2018. https://sb.co/about/.
16. Email communication from Kay Koplovitz to Judy Robinett, August 6, 2018.
17. Martin Zwilling, "Super Angels Answer the Prayers of Startups Starved for Funding," *Entrepreneur*, December 19, 2014, accessed May 20, 2018. https://www.entrepreneur.com/article/240972.
18. Laura Huang et al., *The American Angel.*
19. Telephone Interview with Dave Berkus, May 11, 2018.
20. Email communication from Paul Grossinger to Judy Robinett, May 2, 2018.
21. Ewing Marion Kauffman Foundation, "State of the Field: Equity Investments," page last edited June 15, 2016, accessed May 2, 2018. https://www.kauffman.org/microsites/state-of-the-field/topics/finance/equity.
22. Interview with Sean Sheppard and Andrew Goldner, May 10, 2018.
23. Marion Ewing Kauffman Foundation, "State of the Field: Corporate Venture Capital (CVC)," September 19, 2016, accessed May 15, 2018. https://www.kauffman.org/microsites/state-of-the-field/topics/finance/equity/corporate-venture-capital.
24. Paul Karger and Wes Karger, "Family Money: An Emerging Funding Source for Startups," *VentureBeat/Entrepreneur*, March 25, 2017, accessed May 10, 2018. https://venturebeat.com/2017/03/25/family-money-an-emerging-funding-source-for-startups/.
25. Nicholas Moody, "Avoiding the 'Michael Fish Moment': Behavioural Finance and the Family Office," *Campdenfb.com*, April 5, 2018, accessed May 10, 2018. http://www.campdenfb.com/article/avoiding-michael-fish-moment-behavioural-finance-and-family-office#.Wubkwu7rP3Q.twitter.
26. Email from Nelson to Robinett.
27. Sherwood Neiss, "Regulation Crowdfunding Surpasses $100,000,000 in Capital Commitments—Signaling an Industry that Is Here to Stay and Reaching $1 Billion in the Next 5 Years," email to Judy Robinett, January 25, 2018, accessed April 1, 2018.
28. Dvorah Rut, "2017 Peer-to-Peer Lending: The Year in Pictures," *Peerform* (blog), December 28, 2017, accessed June 30, 2018. http://blog.peerform.com/2017-peer-to-peer-lending/.
29. Telephone interview with Matthew Sullivan, May 10, 2018.
30. *The State of the Token Market 2017: A Year in Review & an Outlook for 2018* (London, U.K: Fabric Ventures + TokenData, January 2018), accessed May 1, 2018. https://static1.squarespace.com/static/5a19eca6c027d8615635f801/t/5a73697bc8302551711523ca/1517513088503/The+State+of+the+Token+Market+Final2.pdf.
31. Sullivan telephone interview.
32. Email from Paul Martens to Judy Robinett, August 2, 2018.
33. Email from Alex Migitko and Sergey Sholom to Judy Robinett, May 30, 2018.

Chapter 4

1. Carlos Eduardo Espinal, *Fundraising Field Guide* (London, UK: Reedsy Ltd. 2015), Kindle Locations 167–169.
2. Mark Suster, "Some Advice Before You Hit the Fund Raising Trail," *Both Sides of the Table* (blog), May 6, 2018, accessed May 15, 2018. https://bothsidesofthetable .com/some-advice-before-you-hit-the-fund-raising-trail-73dc646f077e.
3. Espinal, *Fundraising Field Guide*, Kindle Locations 425–427.
4. Asheesh Advani, "How to Value Your Startup" (originally published as "What's Your Biz Worth?") *Entrepreneur.com*, December 21, 2004, accessed May 15, 2018. https://www.entrepreneur.com/article/72384.
5. Amanda Schnieders, "4 Things Every Entrepreneur Should Do Before Meeting an Investor," *Entrepreneur*, May 20, 2014, accessed April 14, 2018. https://www. entrepreneur.com/article/234060.
6. Paul Graham, "How to Raise Money," *Paul Graham* (blog), September 2013, accessed May 10, 2018. http://www.paulgraham.com/fr.html.
7. Mike Belsito, *Start Up Seed Funding for the Rest of Us: How to Raise $1 Million for Your Startup—Even Outside of Silicon Valley* (Seattle, WA: Amazon Digital Services, LLC, 2015), p. 60.
8. Dave Berkus, "Take Only 'Smart Money' Investments," *Berkonomics* (blog), February 13, 2018, accessed May 1, 2018. https://berkonomics.com/?p=3293.
9. Telephone interview with Sean Sheppard and Andrew Goldner.
10. Laura Huang et al., *The American Angel*, p. 13.
11. Sean Jacobsohn, "Here's a Look Inside a Typical VC's Pipeline (A Must-Read for Entrepreneurs)."

Chapter 5

1. Ashton Kutcher, quoted in "What Investors Look for in Startups & Founders," *Product Hunt* (blog), February 9, 2016, accessed May 5, 2018. https://blog. producthunt.com/what-investors-look-for-in-startups-founders-e782380c2b55.
2. See Malcolm Gladwell, "The Law of the Few," *The Tipping Point: How Little Things Can Make a Big Difference* (New York: Little, Brown and Company, 2000), pp. 30–88. Also Brian Uzzi and Shannon Dunlap, "How to Build Your Network," *Harvard Business Review*, December 2005, accessed May 5, 2018. https://hbr.org/ 2005/12/how-to-build-your-network.
3. Jeff Bussgang, "Getting Introductions to Investors—The Ranking Algorithm," *Seeing Both Sides* (blog), June 12, 2014, accessed May 4, 2018. http://bostonvcblog. typepad.com/vc/2014/06/getting-introductions-to-investors-the-ranking-algorithm.html?utm_source=feedburner&utm_medium=feed&utm_campaign=- Feed percent3A+typepad percent2FnqcX+ percent28Seeing+Both+Sides percent29 &utm_content=FeedBurner.
4. Daniel McGinn, "What VCs Really Care About," *Inc.*, October 30, 2012, accessed April 30, 2018. http://www.inc.com/magazine/201211/daniel-mcginn/what-vcs-really-care-about.html.

5. David Hornik, "Startup Advice: How Entrepreneurs Gain Credibility," *VentureBlog*, January 21, 2011, accessed May 2, 2018. http://www.ventureblog. com/2011/01/startup-advice-how-entrepeneurs-gain-credibility.html.

6. Uzzi and Dunlap, "How to Build Your Network."

7. Hornik, "Startup Advice: How Entrepreneurs Gain Credibility."

8. Bernardo J. Carducci, Quentin L. Stubbins, and Michael R. Bryant, "Still Shy After All These (30) Years," Poster presentation at the American Psychological Association 115th National Conference, Boston, MA, August 17, 2008, accessed May 1, 2018. http://psibeta.org/site/wp-content/uploads/APA2008-Carducci-Stubbins-Bryant-2008.pdf.

9. Paul Graham, "How to Raise Money," Paul Graham's blog, September 2013, accessed May 10, 2018. http://paulgraham.com/fr.html.

10. "What Investors Look for in Startups & Founders."

11. Mark Suster, "I Met with an Investor, What Happens Next?" *Both Sides of the Table Blog*, September 20, 2009, accessed May 5, 2018. https://bothsidesofthetable. com/i-met-with-an-investor-what-happens-next-63d443648f36.

12. Eden Shochat, "How to Make the Most of Your Investor Relationships," *Microsoft Startups*, February 25, 2015, accessed May 1, 2018. https://startups.microsoft.com/ en-us/blog/how-to-make-the-most-of-your-investor-relationships/.

PART III

1. "What Investors Look for When Buying into a Startup," *Economic Times*, December 28, 2014, accessed April 30, 2018. https://economictimes.indiatimes. com/small-biz/startups/what-investors-look-for-when-buying-into-a-startup/ articleshow/45661616.cms.

Chapter 6

1. Quoted by Stephanie Vozza, "The Only 6 People You Need on Your Founding Startup Team," *Fast Company*, July 2, 2014, accessed March 8, 2018. https://www. fastcompany.com/3032548/the-only-6-people-you-need-on-your-founding-start-up-team.

2. Shai Bernstein, Arthur Korteweg, and Kevin Laws, "Attracting Early Stage Investors: Evidence from a Randomized Field Experiment," *The Journal of Finance* 72:2 (April 2017), pp. 509–538, accessed June 11, 2018. https://doi.org/10.1111/ jofi.12470.

3. Kate Clark, "Airbnb, Instacart and 8 More Companies that Sprinted to $1B Valuations," *Pitchbook*, April 27, 2018, accessed May 8, 2018. https://pitchbook. com/news/articles/airbnb-instacart-and-8-more-companies-that-sprinted-to-1b-valuations.

4. "The Top 20 Reasons Startups Fail," *CB Insights*, February 2, 2018, accessed May 1, 2018. https://www.cbinsights.com/research/startup-failure-reasons-top/. The top two reasons for startup failure were no market need (42 percent) and not enough cash (29 percent).

5. Telephone interview with Sean Shepperd and Andrew Goldner, May 10, 2018.
6. Vozza, "The Only 6 People You Need on Your Founding Startup Team."
7. Noam Wasserman, "How an Entrepreneur's Passion Can Destroy a Startup," *The Wall Street Journal*, August 25, 2014, accessed April 1, 2018. https://www.wsj.com/articles/how-an-entrepreneur-s-passion-can-destroy-a-startup-1408912044.
8. Martin Hoffman, "Is Your Startup Worth the Risk? 5 Questions You Need to Answer," *Entrepreneur*, March 9, 2018, accessed May 1, 2018. https://www.entrepreneur.com/article/309893.
9. Young Entrepreneur Council, "12 Essential Traits of Successful Startup Leaders," *Inc.*, January 18, 2013, accessed May 2, 2018. https://www.inc.com/young-entrepreneur-council/12-traits-of-successful-startup-leaders.html.
10. Steve Hawk, "How to Build a Better Startup Team," *Insights by Stanford Business*, December 14, 2016, accessed April 30, 2018. https://www.gsb.stanford.edu/insights/how-build-better-startup-team.
11. Sophia Matveeva, "What Makes Great Startup Teams, and How to Find It," *Forbes*, April 30, 2018, accessed May 2, 2018. https://www.forbes.com/sites/sophiamatveeva/2018/04/30/what-makes-great-startup-teams-and-how-to-find-it/#ef77c316f6cc.
12. Matveeva, "What Makes Great Startup Teams, and How to Find It."
13. Emmie Martin, "How This Graffiti Artist Made $200 Million Overnight," *CNBC Make It*, September 7, 2017, accessed September 28, 2018. https://www.cnbc.com/2017/09/07/how-facebook-graffiti-artist-david-choe-earned-200-million.html.
14. Steve Hawk, "How to Build a Better Startup Team."

Chapter 7

1. Quoted in Mark Henricks, "Do You Really Need a Business Plan?" *Entrepreneur*, December 2008, accessed May 1, 2018. https://www.entrepreneur.com/article/198618.
2. Andrew Burke, Stuart Fraser, and Francis Greene, "The Multiple Effects of Business Planning on New Venture Performance," *Journal of Management Studies* 47:3 (2010), pp. 391–415, accessed May 2, 2018. https://doi.org/10.1111/j.1467-6486.2009.00857.x
3. Reported by Rieva Lesonsky, "A Business Plan Doubles Your Chances for Success, Says a New Survey," *Small Business Trends*, January 20, 2016, accessed May 27, 2018. https://smallbiztrends.com/2010/06/business-plan-success-twice-as-likely.html. Statistics are as follows:

Total Survey Respondents:	2,877	
Number completing a plan:	Yes: 996	No: 1,556
Secured a loan:	297 (36 percent)	222 (18 percent)
Secured investment capital:	280 (36 percent)	219 (18 percent)
Grew their business:	499 (64 percent)	501 (43 percent)

4. Brad Feld and Jason Mendelson, *Venture Deals: Be Smarter Than Your Lawyer and Venture Capitalist*, 3rd edition (New York: Wiley, 2016), p. 25.

5. Xiao-Ping Chen, Xin Yao, and Suresh Kotha, "Entrepreneur Passion and Preparedness in Business Plan Presentations: A Persuasion Analysis of Venture Capitalists' Funding Decisions," *Academy of Management Journal* 52:1 (2009), pp. 199–214, accessed May 7, 2018. https://doi.org/10.5465/amj.2009.36462018.

6. Email from Nelson to Robinett.

7. Noah Pearson, "Business Planning Makes You More Successful, and We've Got the Science to Prove It," *Bplans.com*, no date, accessed April 5, 2018. https://articles.bplans.com/business-planning-makes-you-more-successful-and-weve-got-the-science-to-prove-it/.

8. Noah Parsons, "An Easier Business Model Canvas Template: The Lean Plan Template," *LivePlan* (blog), February 23, 2017, accessed April 5, 2018. https://www.liveplan.com/blog/2017/02/an-easier-business-model-canvas-template-the-lean-plan-template/.

9. Brian Hamilton, "Your Startup Doesn't Need a Business Plan," *Inc.*, March 12, 2015, accessed April 8, 2018. https://www.inc.com/brian-hamilton/why-your-startup-doesn-t-need-a-business-plan.html.

Chapter 8

1. Zeynep Ilgaz, "The 5 Best Pitch Tactics I Heard as an Angel Investor," *Entrepreneur*, March 27, 2015, accessed April 1, 2018. https://www.entrepreneur.com/article/244115.

2. Quoted in Liz Warren, "How Do You Stand Out from 1000 Pitches? 4 VCs Tell All," *Builtinnyc.com*, January 26, 2018, accessed April 4, 2018. https://www.builtinnyc.com/2018/01/26/vcs-best-pitches.

3. Guy Kawasaki, "The Only 10 Slides You Need in Your Pitch," Guykawasaki.com, March 5, 2015, accessed April 5, 2018. https://guykawasaki.com/the-only-10-slides-you-need-in-your-pitch/.

4. Alyson Shontell, "Tinder, A $500 Million Dating App, Used This Pitch Deck When It Was Just a Tiny Startup," *Business Insider*, July 11, 2014, accessed April 20, 2018. http://www.businessinsider.com/tinders-first-startup-pitch-deck-2014-7#just-like-tinder-today-match-box-showed-you-single-people-nearby-and-only-allowed-you-to-message-people-who-liked-your-profile-in-return-7.

5. Thanks to Sam Horn, the Intrigue Expert, for this formula. You can hear John's interview with Sam on his podcast, "TSP019: Sam Horn—Intrigue Expert Teaches How To Get Investors' Attention," *The Successful Pitch*, August 5, 2015, podcast, audio, 42:55, accessed April 1, 2018. https://www.youtube.com/watch?v=-dDThPGGVgo.

6. Neil Patel, "13 Tips on How to Deliver a Pitch Investors Simply Can't Turn Down," *Entrepreneur*, October 21, 2015, accessed April 20, 2018. https://www.entrepreneur.com/article/251311.

7. Cheryl R. Mitteness, Richard Sudek, and Melissa Baucus, "Entrepreneurs as Authentic Transformational Leaders: Critical Behaviors for Gaining Angel Capital," *Frontiers of Entrepreneurship Research* 30:5:3 (June 12, 2010), p. 5, accessed March 8, 2018. http://digitalknowledge.babson.edu/fer/vol30/iss5/3.

8. Quote by Arthur Ashe accessed April 15, 2018. https://www.cmgww.com/sports/ashe/quotes/.

9. Amy J. Cuddy, S. Jack Schultz, and Nathan E. Fosse, "*P*-Curving a More Comprehensive Body of Research on Postural Feedback Reveals Clear Evidential Value for Power-Posing Effects: Reply to Simmons and Simonsohn (2017)," *Psychological Science* 29:4 (April 1, 2018), pp. 656–666, accessed April 15, 2018. https://doi.org/10.1177/0956797617746749.

10. Email communication from Mallory Dyer to John Livesay, May 25, 2016.

11. Rahul Varshneya, "How the Top VCs Want to Be Pitched," *Entrepreneur*, July 31, 2015, accessed April 15, 2018. https://www.entrepreneur.com/article/248053.

Chapter 9

1. Martin Hoffman, "Is Your Startup Worth the Risk? 5 Questions You Need to Answer," *Entrepreneur*, March 9, 2018, accessed April 2, 2018. https://www.entrepreneur.com/article/309893.

2. "253 Startup Failure Post-Mortems," *CB Insights Research Briefs*, April 17, 2018, accessed May 1, 2018. https://www.cbinsights.com/research/startup-failure-post-mortem/.

3. Shawn Knight, "Tesla Now Has 455,000 Reservations for Its Mainstream Model 3 Sedan," *Techspot.com*, August 3, 2017, accessed May 3, 2018. https://www.techspot.com/news/70426-tesla-now-has-455000-reservations-mainstream-model-3.html.

4. Eric C. Evarts, "Study Shows 23 Percent Cancellations on Tesla Model 3 Deposits," *Green Car Reports*, June 4, 2018, accessed May 2, 2018. https://www.greencarreports.com/news/1117043_study-shows-23-percent-cancelations-on-tesla-model-3-deposits.

5. Robert Ferris, "Tesla Battery Production Is the Real Bottleneck, Not Model 3 Production, Analyst Says," *CNBC.com*, April 18, 2018, accessed May 2, 2018. https://www.cnbc.com/2018/04/18/tesla-battery-production-is-the-real-bottleneck-not-model-3-production.html.

6. Jeremy C. Owens, "Tesla Stock Falls on Report of Gigafactory Issues with Model 3 Batteries," *MarketWatch*, January 25, 2018, accessed May 2, 2018. https://www.marketwatch.com/story/tesla-stock-falls-on-report-of-gigafactory-issues-with-model-3-batteries-2018-01-25.

7. "253 Startup Failure Post-Mortems."

8. Techli team, "10 Greatest Startup Failures of All Time," *Techli*, April 25, 2013, accessed April 22, 2018. https://techli.com/2012/04/10-greatest-startup-failures/.

9. Marc Hedlund, "Why Wesabe Lost to Mint," *Marc Hedlund's Blog*, October 1, 2010, accessed April 22, 2018. http://blog.precipice.org/why-wesabe-lost-to-mint/.

10. Tyler Gaffney, "Pricing Lessons from Working with 30+ Seed and Series A B2B Startups," *First Round Review*, May 3, 2018, accessed May 22, 2018. http://firstround.com/review/pricing-lessons-from-working-with-30-seed-and-series-a-b2b-startups/?utm_campaign=new_article&utm_medium=email&utm_source=newsletter.

11. "253 Startup Failure Post-Mortems."

12. Brad Moon, "10 Worst Tech Products of 2017 Include a 'Smart' Hairbrush," *InvestorPlace.com*, September 26, 2017, accessed May 2, 2018. https://investorplace.com/2017/09/worst-tech-products-2017-juicero/.

13. Pascal-Emmanuel Gobry, "10 Brilliant Startups That Failed Because They Were Ahead of Their Time," *Business Insider*, May 4, 2011, accessed May 1, 2018. http://www.businessinsider.com/startup-failures-2011-5. Benjamin Horowitz and Patricia R. Olsen, "The Boss: Making Peace with Risk," *New York Times*, July 15, 2007, accessed May 1, 2018. https://www.nytimes.com/2007/07/15/business/yourmoney/15boss.html; Saul Hansell, "Marc Andreessen's LoudCloud Finally Rains Money," *New York Times "Bits"* (blog), July 23, 2007, accessed May 1, 2018. https://bits.blogs.nytimes.com/2007/07/23/marc-andreessens-loudcloud-finally-rains-money/.

14. Andrew Urevig, "5 Successful Startups That Failed & What You Can Learn from Them," *Foundr*, February 27, 2018, accessed May 1, 2018. https://foundr.com/how-5-successful-startups-that-failed-but-got-back-up/.

15. Keen Home, accessed May 1, 2018. https://www.crunchbase.com/organization/keen-home#section-funding-rounds.

16. Daniel Bukszpan, "10 Key Elements of a Perfect Investor Pitch," *Entrepreneur*, January 13, 2014, accessed April 8, 2018. https://www.entrepreneur.com/slideshow/230715.

17. Email from Nelson to Robinett.

18. "What Investors Look for in Startups & Founders," *Product Hunt* (blog), February 9, 2016, accessed April 8, 2018. https://blog.producthunt.com/what-investors-look-for-in-startups-founders-e782380c2b55.

19. "253 Startup Failure Post-Mortems."

20. Eric Paley, "Running Out of Money Isn't a Milestone," *Tech Crunch*, June 24, 2015, accessed April 1, 2018. https://techcrunch.com/2015/06/24/running-out-of-money-isnt-a-milestone/.

21. Andy Rachleff, "Demystifying Venture Capital Economics, Part 3," *Wealthfront.com* blog, December 2, 2014, accessed April 1, 2018. https://blog.wealthfront.com/demystifying-venture-capital-economics-part-3/.

22. "Microsoft to Acquire LinkedIn," *Microsoft News Center*, June 13, 2016, accessed May 8, 2018. https://news.microsoft.com/2016/06/13/microsoft-to-acquire-linkedin/.

23. Quoted in Jonathan Small, "5 Ways to Win Your Pitch, According to 'Shark Tank's' Robert Herjavec," *Entrepreneur*, October 12, 2017, accessed May 1, 2018. https://www.entrepreneur.com/article/301175.

24. Andrew Medal, "5 Questions Investors Ask Themselves Before Putting Their Chips into Your Startup," *Entrepreneur*, April 25, 2017, accessed April 28, 2018. https://www.entrepreneur.com/article/293155.

25. Candace Sjogren, "4 Ways to Predict the Result of Your Investment Pitch," *Entrepreneur*, July 17, 2017, accessed May 1, 2018. https://www.entrepreneur.com/article/296713.

26. Mark Suster, "Understanding the Herd Mentality of VCs and How Not to Let It Psyche You Out," *Both Sides of the Table* (blog), May 10, 2018, accessed May 22, 2018. https://bothsidesofthetable.com/understanding-the-herd-mentality-of-vcs-and-how-not-to-let-it-psyche-you-out-27c1071c446b.

PART IV

1. Ryan Caldbeck, "How to Close Your Funding Round," *Forbes*, July 7, 2016, accessed May 2, 2018. https://www.forbes.com/sites/ryancaldbeck/2016/07/07/how-to-close-your-funding-round/.

Chapter 10

1. Brad Feld and Jason Mendelson, *Venture Deals: Be Smarter Than Your Lawyer and Venture Capitalist*, 3rd edition (New York: Wiley, 2016), p. 37.
2. Leena Rao, "Things to Consider Before Saying 'I Do' to Investors," *Tech Crunch*, April 8, 2012, accessed April 10, 2018. https://techcrunch.com/2012/04/08/things-to-consider-before-saying-i-do-to-investors/.
3. See Pascal Levensohn and Andrew Krowne, "Why SAFE Notes Are Not Safe for Entrepreneurs," *Tech Crunch*, July 8, 2017, accessed May 1, 2018. https://techcrunch.com/2017/07/08/why-safe-notes-are-not-safe-for-entrepreneurs/.
4. Dave Schools, "The Holy Grail of Entrepreneurship: The Term Sheet, Pt. 2—Offering Terms," *Funding Sage*, May 21, 2018, accessed May 30, 2018. https://fundingsage.com/holy-grail-entrepreneurship-term-sheet-pt-2-offering-terms/.
5. Matthew Bartus, "Negotiating Term Sheets: Focus on What's Important," *CooleyGo.com*, no date, accessed May 1, 2018. https://www.cooleygo.com/negotiating-term-sheets/.
6. Sramana Mitra, "1Mby1M Virtual Accelerator Investor Forum: With Heidi Roizen of DFJ (Part 1)," *One Million by One Million* (blog), April 30, 2018, accessed May 10, 2018. https://www.sramanamitra.com/2018/04/30/1mby1m-virtual-accelerator-investor-forum-with-heidi-roizen-of-dfj-part-1/.
7. Dave Berkus, "After 20 Years Updating the Berkus Method of Valuation," *Berkonomics* (blog), November 4, 2016, accessed April 28, 2018. https://berkonomics.com/?p=2752.
8. Bill Payne, "Scorecard Valuation Methodology: Establishing the Valuation of Pre-revenue, Startup Companies," *Bill Payne & Associates*, January 2011, accessed April 1, 2018. http://billpayne.com/wp-content/uploads/2011/01/Scorecard-Valuation-Methodology-Jan111.pdf.
9. Bill Payne, "Valuations 101: The Venture Capital Method," *Gust* (blog), November 1, 2011, accessed April 1, 2018. http://blog.gust.com/startup-valuations-101-the-venture-capital-method/.
10. Alexander J. Davie, "Venture Capital Term Sheet Negotiation—Part 2: Valuation, Capitalization Tables, and Price per Share," *Strictly Business Law* (blog), October 14, 2013, accessed May 8, 2018. https://www.strictlybusinesslawblog.com/2013/10/14/venture-capital-term-sheet-negotiation-part-2-valuation-capitalization-tables-price-per-share/.
11. For an excellent discussion of liquidation preferences, see Aaron Kellner, "What You Need to Know about Liquidation Preferences," *Seed Invest Blog on Startup Investing*, August 30, 2017, accessed May 1, 2018. https://www.seedinvest.com/blog/startup-investing/liquidation-preferences.
12. Sramana Mitra, "1Mby1M Virtual Accelerator Investor Forum."

13. Mike Belsito, *Start Up Seed Funding for the Rest of Us*, p. 106.
14. Geoff Ralston, "A Guide to Seed Fundraising," *Y Combinator* (blog), January 7, 2016, accessed May 10, 2018. https://blog.ycombinator.com/how-to-raise-a-seed-round/.

Chapter 11

1. Tony Lettich, "14 Types of Information Investors May Request as Part of Their Due Diligence Checklist for Your Startup," *Funding Sage*, June 14, 2017, accessed April 3, 2018. https://fundingsage.com/14-types-of-information-investors-may-request-as-part-of-their-due-diligence-checklist-for-your-startup/.
2. A. J. Watson, "One Factor that Improves Angel Investment Returns by 7x," *Fundify*, August 11, 2015, accessed April 1, 2018. https://medium.com/a-startup-blog/one-factor-that-improves-angel-investment-returns-by-7x-e2367240f1f6.
3. Watson, "One Factor that Improves Angel Investment Returns by 7x."
4. "How to Avoid Presenting a Flat Tire for a Buyer to Kick: A Guide to the Venture Capital Due Diligence Process for Early-Stage Startups," *Bagchi Law*, May 5, 2015, accessed April 14, 2018. http://bagchilaw.com/how-to-avoid-presenting-a-flat-tire-for-a-buyer-to-kick-a-guide-to-the-venture-capital-due-diligence-process-for-early-stage-startups/.
5. "How to Avoid Presenting a Flat Tire for a Buyer to Kick."
6. "Appendix 8: Issues to Consider in Due Diligence," *Angel Capital Association*, no date, accessed April 1, 2018. https://www.angelcapitalassociation.org/data/Documents/Resources/AngelCapitalEducation/Angel_Guidebook_-_Due_Diligence_Questions.pdf?rev=C7C4.
7. Katherine Homuth, "Ask an Investor: How Do I Prepare for Due Diligence on My Startup?" *Canadian Startup News*, February 3, 2017, accessed April 3, 2018. https://betakit.com/ask-an-investor-how-do-i-prepare-for-due-diligence-on-my-startup/.
8. Email from Nelson to Robinett.
9. Alex Iskold, "8 Things You Need to Know About Raising Venture Capital," *Entrepreneur*, July 15, 2015, accessed April 3, 2018. https://www.entrepreneur.com/article/248377.
10. Rick Vaughn quoted in Marianne Hudson, "How Much Due Diligence Does an Angel Really Need to Do?" *Forbes*, January 15, 2015, accessed April 3, 2018. https://www.forbes.com/sites/mariannehudson/2015/01/15/how-much-due-diligence-does-an-angel-really-need-to-do/#64d4ccaa4e0e.
11. Dave Clark, "Dilution: The Real Meaning of Funding Success," *Funding Sage*, April 16, 2018, accessed May 9, 2018. https://fundingsage.com/dilution-real-meaning-funding-success/.
12. Bob Ackerman, "You've Got the Money—Now What?" *Venture Beat*, May 1, 2013, accessed April 10, 2018. https://venturebeat.com/2013/05/01/youve-got-the-money-now-what/.
13. Ackerman, "You've Got the Money—Now What?"

INDEX

At a certain set of the tide Cap'n Charlie often went with the children to swim and play in the water, but he did not want them to go alone, even though they were all excellent swimmers.

This careful father also took the children into the thick forest. They climbed trees of all sizes. Cap'n Charlie taught them to "size up" trees, to know which were brittle and which of the cedars could be cut to get good ship knees. Cap'n Charlie liked cedars best of all the trees for this use. Knees are like the ribs of a ship with only ten necessary to make a large boat. Metal long ago replaced wood in ship building.

In all the years the Swans lived on the island, no serious accidents occurred and no bones were broken. Much of this

Forest—Bald Head Island